Information Security

Protecting the Global Enterprise

ISBN 0-13-017323-1

9 780130 173232

90000

Hewlett-Packard® Professional Books

Information Security

Protecting the Global Enterprise

Donald L. Pipkin

Hewlett-Packard Company

www.hp.com/go/retailbooks

Prentice Hall PTR
Upper Saddle River, New Jersey 07458
www.phptr.com

Editorial/production supervision: *Joanne Anzalone*
Cover design director: *Jerry Votta*
Cover design: *Talar Agasyan*
Manufacturing manager: *Maura Goldstaub*
Acquisitions editor: *Jill Pisoni*
Editorial assistant: *Justin Somma*
Marketing manager: *Bryan Gambrel*

Manager, Hewlett-Packard Retail Book Publishing: *Patricia Pekary*
Editor, Hewlett-Packard Professional Books: *Susan Wright*

© 2000 by Hewlett-Packard Company

Published by Prentice Hall PTR
Prentice-Hall, Inc.
Upper Saddle River, New Jersey 07458

Prentice Hall books are widely used by corporations and government agencies for training, marketing, and resale.
The publisher offers discounts on this book when ordered in bulk quantities. For more information, contact Corporate Sales Department, Phone: 800-382-3419; FAX: 201-236-7141;
E-mail: corpsales@prenhall.com
Or write: Prentice Hall PTR, Corporate Sales Dept., One Lake Street, Upper Saddle River, NJ 07458.

HP and HP-UX are registered trademarks of Hewlett-Packard Company. IBM, IBM Power2 Architecture, RS/6000, System/360, System/370, and System/390 are trademarks or registered trademarks of International Business Machines Corporation. Intel is a registered trademark of Intel Corporation. MIPS is a registered trademark of MIPS Technologies, Inc. Other product or company names mentioned herein are the trademarks or registered trademarks of their respective owners.

Printed in the United States of America
10 9 8 7 6 5 4

ISBN 0-13-017323-1

Prentice-Hall International (UK) Limited, *London*
Prentice-Hall of Australia Pty. Limited, *Sydney*
Prentice-Hall Canada Inc., *Toronto*
Prentice-Hall Hispanoamericana, S.A., *Mexico*
Prentice-Hall of India Private Limited, *New Delhi*
Prentice-Hall of Japan, Inc., *Tokyo*
Pearson Education Asia Pte. Ltd.
Editora Prentice-Hall do Brasil, Ltda., *Rio de Janeiro*

In memory of my parents

Contents

Foreword

The greatest source of confusion in the business world today is information security. Executives read articles about the latest theft of credit cards or the billions of dollars in losses to hackers, and expect that a quick solution can be found. The burden typically falls upon computer professionals who are otherwise brilliant at what they do, but have little knowledge about security issues.

This situation leads to real Information Warfare. This information war is not one that is fought by governments, terrorists, or militias, but by system administrators and those computer professionals who have been given security responsibilities. Basically the war is about whether the would-be hackers, criminals, etc., have better information than the people protecting the information and computers. If the hackers have better information, than your information and computers are lost. If the computer professionals have the information, then the hackers lose.

Unfortunately, the underground communities are much better at sharing information than computer professionals. This means that the underground usually wins the real Information War. This does not have to be the case. There is no reason why computer professionals cannot be more effective at sharing basic security information.

This book can be the first step for computer professionals to come out ahead of the underground. Pipkin discusses the fundamental principles of Information Security. These principles are laid out in such a way that computer professionals not only learn about security tasks, they learn them in a logical order that provides a framework for performing those tasks. Computer professionals who are interested in learning security principles, as well as gaining a foundation for implementing a security program, will find this book an extremely valuable reference.

— Ira Winkler
Founder and President
Internet Security Advisors Group

Preface

Information security is more than computer data security. It is the process of protecting the intellectual property of an organization. This intellectual property is paramount to the organization's survival. Businesses are built on their information – their company secrets. These secrets may be secret ingredients, manufacturing methods, pricing agreements with suppliers, or customer lists. All of these business secrets contribute to the profitability of the company. They all must be protected.

Everyone is involved in, and in some part responsible for, the safekeeping of information. One leak can sink the entire organization. Information must be continuously protected from all sides. This requires that everyone must understand and utilize the security that protects information.

There are no simple answers to the issues of security. Unfortunately, people are all too often convinced that all they need to do to secure their information systems is to install a firewall, improve their authentication method, or write a security policy. True, each of these can help improve security, but none of them is a complete solution.

Dependence on computerized information systems is integral to all aspects of an organization. Information-related problems must be understood and managed, the same as any other business resource. Management must recognize the importance of setting policies, standards, and procedures for the protection of information and allocation of resources to achieve it. This book details the relationship between security policies and procedures and clarifies how they can reduce the chance of losses on information systems. It is a must for anyone who is responsible for information assets or a complete overview of information security.

This book is designed to unveil the breadth of issues that encompasses information security. It is an introduction to information security addressing both the business issues and the fundamental aspects of securing information. It is not going to give you directions to close any specific security problem. However, it will open your eyes to security issues that are often overlooked. It delves into the issues involved with understanding the value of information assets, their potential cost to the organization if they are lost or disclosed, and how to determine the appropriate level of protection and response to a security incident; the technical process involved with building an information security design that is consistent, reasonable, and which utilizes appropriate intrusion detection and reporting systems; and the legal issues which require adequate protection and an appropriate response, so that not only is the information protected but also the corporate officers who are responsible for the safekeeping of the organization's information assets. It describes essential components of an information resource protection process. This process can be applied to information in any location from a personal computer to a large data processing facility. It is necessary in companies of any size – from 50 employees to 50,000 or more.

This book is derived from numerous presentations to CEOs and CIOs about information security. It addresses the issues from a business perspective, detailing the entire process of information security inside and outside the computer center. It addresses the business concerns of management as they pertain to information security.

In the security evaluations that I have performed for companies both large and small, it has been my experience that organizations have a security "hot button," one aspect of security they have addressed very well, and have overlooked other areas.

This book takes you through the steps of designing an information security program – from evaluating current processes to reviewing incident response procedures. Each section of the book, as follows, addresses one of these major steps which are required for a complete, cohesive information security program:

- **Inspection** is the process of determining the current status and evaluating the appropriate level of security. It is this phase that creates a level of understanding of the issues and the organization's ability to address them.

- **Protection** is the proactive process of creating an environment that is as secure as possible. This phase examines the ten fundamental aspects of information security and the issues involved.

- **Detection** is the reactive process of determining inappropriate activities and alerting responsible individuals. Detection is required for those things that cannot be protected or predicted.

- **Reaction** is the process of responding to a security incident. This phase focuses on resolving a security incident to minimize the impact.

- **Reflection** is the follow-up processes necessary to evaluate the quality of the security implementation. These post-incident procedures are necessary for the organization to learn from the incident and share that experience.

This book will also explore the fundamental aspects of information security. These basic building blocks are categorized as follows:

- **Awareness** is assuring that everyone understands the importance of security.
- **Access** defines the medium used to contact the resource.
- **Identification** is what is used to identify a user.
- **Authentication** is how the user's identity is validated.
- **Authorization** is what a user is allowed to do.
- **Availability** is the ability to utilize the resource whenever it is needed.
- **Accuracy** is the assurance that the information is correct.
- **Confidentiality** is keeping the resource from being disclosed.
- **Accountability** is assigning responsibility for actions taken on and by the resource.
- **Administration** is the ability to manage the security attributes of the information.

Each of these aspects must be addressed to adequately protect your information.

After reading this book, you will have the knowledge to analyze your information systems' security needs, to best allocate your security resources, and to put into place the proper policies and procedures in order to secure your information.

About the Author

Donald L. Pipkin is an expert and noted speaker in information security. He is versed in all aspects of security including policy and procedures and has hands-on experience with computer intrusions. He has made presentations on security at various conferences from a regional to an international level. With his expertise, he helps businesses look at the bigger security picture, beyond the computer center.

As a Security Systems Architect for the Internet Security Division of Hewlett-Packard and in his fifteen plus years in the industry, Don has seen corporate computer use grow – with greater numbers of users in ever-more-widespread geographical areas – moving from a centralized to a distributed computing environment, which causes the issues of securely conducting business across the enterprise to become increasingly complex. His years of experience have allowed him to bring his understanding of security issues and his experiences with computer crime to bear when consulting with Fortune 500 companies on issues of policies and procedures as addressing specific security issues.

He is the author of *Halting the Hacker: A Practical Guide to Computer Security*. That book presents a hacker's view of information systems and explains how they attack systems and how you can protect your information assets.

In addition to this book, he was a contributing author of *Unix Security*, and has written security articles for computer publications such as *SysAdmin* magazine.

Acknowledgments

To my family: I appreciate your understanding when my time was needed for the book and your patience during the chaos of meeting deadlines.

There are a number of organizations within Hewlett-Packard that have been of great assistance. I would like to thank all of those individuals in the Internet Security Division and the Open Systems Core Security Team who reviewed my manuscript and gave input into the process. I wish to thank Write in Style for reviewing the manuscript and researching some of the news items. I want to thank Rob Dempsey for his assistance with reviewing this book, and my earlier book, and reminding me that information security is a global issue. I'd like to thank Pat Pekary and Susan Wright, with Hewlett-Packard Technical Press, for their support.

Finally, I would like to specifically thank Jeff Moss, Winn Schwartau, Marcus Ranum, Gene Spafford, and Gene Schultz for allowing me to use their words.

– Don Pipkin

The Future of Business

We are standing on the precipice of a new world economy based on information – where it's not knowledge that is power; but rather, the access to information. Many of us were taught that the basics for an economy are men and material, land and labor, and that these were the raw materials needed to build wealth. Today, however, the top of the Fortune 500 list is full of corporations who do not build with sweat and steel, but instead have made their fortunes by the application of information. Even with those companies who produce goods, there has been a dramatic shift in the relative value of information. More information is kept, such as who buys the goods and when and where they are bought, or information that is used in the production, marketing, forecasting, and designing of the next new and improved model. Information is a company's most valuable asset, whether it is the secret recipe, a better manufacturing process, or a customer list. These are the things that give a company a competitive advantage. The effective use of information by a corporation is what makes the difference between success and failure; it has become the key ingredient in corporate success.

The Business Environment is Changing

The relationships between business organizations, the workforce, the IT environment, and the business environment are changing. To address this new complexity existing information security must evolve to meet current and future business needs.

The Global Economy

A global economy, falling profits, and many other business factors have caused countless businesses to make dramatic changes to their business organization. Many of these have resulted in personnel being relocated, demoted, or let go. The uncertainty of business reorganization leads to disgruntled employees who lose trust in and loyalty to their employer.

The new economics that face businesses today has led some companies to be less ethical in the methods they use to gather competitive information. Governments are involved in gathering national economic assets. Corporate and economic espionage is on the rise. Political changes have made industrial secrets more valuable than political secrets.

The global economy has put dramatic economic pressures on business — to produce products less expensively, to bring products to market more quickly, and to address foreign markets. Businesses are compelled to move into foreign markets, either to find new markets in which to sell their products or to locate more cost effective manufacturing environments. In short, global business growth has accelerated.

Reducing the costs of manufacturing on a mature process often requires moving the process to areas with a lower cost of labor. This may mean moving production outside the country. However, along with the manufacturing process, information and infrastructure must also be exported. Often the information needed to support the manufacturing process is proprietary. Other countries have different laws and attitudes about the value, confidentiality, and privacy of information and electronic data.

Many countries do not allow completely foreign-owned businesses to operate within their borders. To do business there some type of relationship must be established with a local business. In some instances this relationship has been used to gather information and technology. The variation of laws from country to country can make the same activity legal in one locality, but deemed industrial espionage somewhere else.

Time to Market

There is a phenomenon, called Internet Time, which is described as the accelerated speed at which things occur on the Internet. Corporate decisions which would have taken months are now decided in a matter of weeks. This phenomenon is used to explain how a company with little assets can appear on the Internet and become an overnight success. It has also led to the belief that to delay decisions for a moment can spell the difference between success and failure.

Increasing the speed in which a product can be brought to market may force a company to accept new technologies more rapidly than it is prepared to. This can move a company from the leading edge to the bleeding edge. It can also create employees difficulties as they have new technologies thrust upon them at a rate that may be faster than they can absorb them, causing frustration and confusion. Employees may not know how to use the available security, or may put security aside as just "one more thing" that seems unimportant when they don't feel comfortable using the technology in the first place.

Changes in Technology

New technologies require that employees be retrained on the use and administration of these technologies. Employees who do not know how to use a technology, or how to properly secure it, can accidentally cause security risks by their inexperience. Most security incidents are in part because of improper or inadequate administration.

Historically, most companies would wait until a technology was proven before implementing it — this could be six months for a new version of software or years for a new operating system. However, this shortened life cycle of technology has made it become obsolete more quickly, forcing companies to adopt new technologies more rapidly. Today these same companies are running their critical business systems on unproven and unsecure technology.

Companies may need to be on the leading edge of technology to remain competitive, but early adopters will pay a price, often in security. It seems to be a fact of life that software has bugs that can be exploited. The longer a piece of software has been used, the more likely that the bugs will be noticed and repaired. Every new version of software will bring new bugs.

Business Relationships are Changing

Today, business relationships are entered into more rapidly and are of shorter duration. The use of outsourcing and business partnerships has increased. Cooperative business ventures have become a popular business tactic to reduce the risk of entering unfamiliar territory. These ventures generally require sharing a significant amount of confidential information. So even though the financial risk of the venture is reduced, the increased access to company information may increase the security risk.

Ventures into areas of new technologies often mean creating close relationships with start-up companies that may have very little history. It may be difficult to get good background information about the company and the quality of workers they employ. When you enter into a partnership with another company you might inherit any certain hostilities that individuals may have toward the other company.

Large, established companies are not immune to problems either. Larger companies may have other business activities that may make them tempting targets, particularly when working with foreign companies where you do not know all the political aspects.

Companies will often find themselves needing to partner with a company in one area, while that same company is a competitor in another area. This requires granting access to some while denying access to others in the same company. These complicated business relationships often blur the usual lines of trust and make security issues more complex.

Any of these relationships require intercompany communication, which often increases the complexity of data and communications networks. Extending the corporate network to interconnect with the associated companies' information infrastructure opens new doors to security risks. These extended networks allow corporate partners access to internal information through connections that are generally not protected by the company's normal firewall systems, which protects the company's information from the Internet. These connections need a more flexible solution that allows communication in both directions but still protects both companies from unauthorized activities.

Cooperative ventures are often short lived and change quickly. They have a tendency to confuse partners who do not know what information can be shared with what partners. Who actually works for whom? Employees may not understand which information is appropriately shared and which is not. Accidental disclosure of sensitive information can occur and has been used against the unwary partner.

Complicated business relationships – contractors, consultants, joint ventures – redefine the level of trust in individuals that have to have access to proprietary information. The same organization may be a partner in one business area and a competitor in another. Contractors and consultants may be working for your competitors as well as for you. These relationships call for a more restrictive environment and better controls on your information assets.

Employees

The reporting structures of organizations are no longer simple trees. Employees report to multiple managers and have multiple duties. Organizational boundaries are dissolving as more workers are reporting to multiple business units. Authority is being pushed lower in the organization. Departments are being forced to become more responsible for their own profitability and are being given more independence – purchasing their own information systems and taking charge of these systems independently of corporate IT – without the experience of managing a secure IS environment.

Businesses are looking for ways to accelerate the productivity of their employees. This has led to an explosive growth in hiring temporary contract employees or alternate (outsourced) workers – workers who have access to a company's confidential information, from the mailroom to the reception desk to higher levels. These people are subjected to the same stresses that may lead permanent employees astray, but may not feel the same obligation to your company that permanent employees have. Often security guards, the very people we expect to protect our businesses, work for an independent contracting company and may have less loyalty to the business at which they physically work. The background checks and screenings performed by the temp service or outsourcing company may not be as stringent as those your company performs.

To rapidly gain access to specialized knowledge, many businesses are hiring consultants at very critical positions within the company where they have access to crucial information. These same consultants may also be working for your competitor where information may be disclosed accidentally. They may be unaware of the proprietary nature or the business-critical nature of the information. Independent consultants may be tempted by monetary gains. Temps and contract employees are often targeted by industrial spies.

Employee policies do not apply to contract employees. Issues of security, nondisclosure, and appropriate behavior must be spelled out in the contract with them. These contracts are often with a contracting company, not specifically with the contract employee and the individual's understanding of your company's security policies may be lacking.

Business Information is Changing

Businesses create and collect a tremendous amount of information – information that is critical to the success of the business, information that is proprietary to the company. For some companies this is the secret ingredient, while other companies' proprietary information is in their manufacturing process.

After making huge investments in back-office automation, businesses are capitalizing on the collected data by creating data warehouses – great volumes of data from many diverse sources with a variety of security requirements. Needless to say, this creates a monumental security challenge.

As information becomes one of a company's primary assets, it demands security. Information cannot be confined within the walls of a company. It continuously leaves the safety of the data center. This requires a new method of securing information in all its locations.

Business relationships are being built at an ever-increasing rate based on the information that is brought into the relationship. Companies are bought not for their distribution channel, but rather for the consumer information that the distribution channel collects.

Customer Information

In many environments customer information is a prized asset. However, in many consumer markets, consumer information is more valuable as a commodity to be sold than as a prized asset to be protected. There is also a legal responsibility to protect the confidentiality of the information that is held about others. This requirement varies from one locality to another.

- **Leveraging Information** – Companies that have taken control of their consumer information have discovered the power that it has. Focusing on profitable customers with target marketing, specific to or associated with products purchased, yields greater returns.

  Understanding sales trends allows for better inventory control, such as having enough product in stock when it is needed and not stocking it when there is no demand. In some cases, retailers have taken control of the supply chain process, ordering what they know they need, not what the supplier thinks they need.

  Customer information is often enticed from the customer by giving discounts, basically paying for the information. However, a growing segment of consumers are unwilling to sell information due to concerns about its use. In most of these "preferred customer" programs there are no contracts stating the purpose of the information that is being gathered or any assurances on how the information will be used or with whom it will be shared. The consumer is expected to trust that the business will be responsible with the information about the consumer.

- **Selling Information** – A number of companies have discovered that profits can be made by selling consumer information. Purchasing profiles can be rapidly developed by capturing the products purchased, a common task for modern cash registers, and associating it to an individual through the use of a common identifier, such as the checking account number or the credit card number used to purchase the items. Some stores offer incentives to customers to assist in making a more complete profile through the use of "frequent shopper" cards. The store then gives discounts on products and collects more accurate shopping information.

    This is not restricted to businesses. Government agencies such as the U.S. Postal Service and state Departments of Motor Vehicles are selling personal information about the public to anyone willing to pay their price.

    Target marketing is built on the ability to create complete and accurate customer profiles. These profiles are used to determine if one is likely to purchase a specific product and to focus the marketing effort of that product.

Online Information

Clearly, doing business on the Internet has moved beyond a static Web site to conducting core business transactions with employees, customers, and suppliers. This typical evolution goes from building an initial marketing presence on the Internet, to internal publication, messaging and collaboration applications, and now to customer-facing business applications.

Online businesses have always been plagued with issues of security and privacy. Whether it has been the capturing of e-mail addresses of visitors or using "cookies" to track their activities, online consumers have been leery of having their online activities watched. Online businesses have also been the target of hackers, who have attacked their sites to steal credit card numbers. Many of these online merchants are new to open networks and unfamiliar with the level of security required to protect sensitive information.

Nowhere is information security more visible than in online commerce.

- **E-Commerce** – E-commerce, the online sales to customers, has been made possible through the phenomenal growth of home computers and the Internet. These trends have made e-commerce more than just a novelty for techies. It has become a significant distribution channel. It has created opportunities for new companies to enter previously impenetrable markets by using the new distribution channel and has allowed existing companies to create a new lower cost distribution channel.

    - **Physical products** are made available into locations that have not been served due to barriers to entry, such as market size. Small companies can offer products without the costs of stores and warehousing. The products are shipped directly to the customer when they are ordered.

- **Digital delivery** it is used to distribute products that can be sent electronically. This makes them immediately available and eliminates normal delivery charges. The type of products that are being delivered digitally is growing to include software, music, videos, and even books.

To date, the greatest inhibitor to the growth of e-commerce is the public's lack of trust in the security of the Internet. The public is not yet totally comfortable with transmitting personal financial information, like credit card numbers, online.

- **E-Business** – E-business is online interaction within a business or between businesses. It is built on both the corporate intranet, for the automation of business processes, and the Internet, for business to business interaction. E-business is not really a new endeavor – electronic data interchange, or EDI, has been around for a long time.

Many of the same attributes that make e-commerce a reality have made e-business successful. The automation of employees by widespread distribution of PCs and company networks have allowed companies to make many employee services available on-line – finally taking steps toward the paperless office.

- **Between businesses** it is used to streamline the supply chain through the automation of purchasing. Historically, its use generally has been limited to large companies due to the effort required to implement it. The use of the Internet, however, has reduced the cost of the communication channel to the point that Internet-based EDI has become much more widespread.

- **Within a business** it is used to streamline internal processes – to reduce paperwork, save time, and reduce the number of employees that are involved in support of other employees, such as help desks and administrative assistants. These processes are generally not part of the commercial side of the business. More often they are auxiliary processes, such as expense reporting and tracking, employee benefits and labor reporting.

- **E-Services** – E-services are a process of adding more value to existing e-commerce and e-business applications. The goal of e-services is to increase customer satisfaction with the web service being provided. With the diversity and reach of the Web, the consumer has access to a tremendous amount of information at their fingertips and many purchasing choices, which gives them unprecedented power in product selection. In the new digital economy, the balance of power is rapidly shifting from vendor to consumer.

In this environment, the importance of strengthening customer retention programs and enhancing customer support has never been higher. E-services enhance the consumer's experience by performing some of the work for him. E-services add value through one of the following methods:

- **Consolidation** of services into a single location, called a porthole, simplifies service scheduling by offering one-stop shopping. The common example is that of a business travel porthole where the customer indicates where and when he needs to travel and the porthole responds with reservations for airline tickets, a rental car, and a hotel room.

- **Brokering** is the locating of an e-service provider who best meets the wants and needs of the consumer. These types of e-services do the legwork of finding all of the e-service providers who provide comparable services and evaluate them based on a set of requirements, giving the consumer the "best" service for his situation.

- **Integration** is the interconnecting of e-services into corporate systems so that they can be utilized without user intervention. For example, if the office supply inventory system indicated that an item needed to be reordered, an integration e-service will automatically reorder the items. This e-service might utilize a brokering e-service to provide the best price and quickest delivery. The transaction will take place within defined business parameters without human interaction.

Ubiquitous Information

Many have envisioned a not-so-distant future where information appliances will be inter-connected everywhere and all the time. The computers and networks needed to support this environment will become unnoticed. They will disappear into the walls, like electricity, and become part of everyday items. They will only be noticed when they aren't working.

Soon everything will be integrated – from in the home, where our refrigerators will monitor their contents and reorder items automatically from the local grocery delivery service when they are needed, to on the road, where our automobiles will be monitoring themselves and schedule repairs when they are needed in advance of when something actually breaks (in accordance with your time management organizer), to work, where all of your business interactions will be handled between computers. This integration of systems requires extensive data sharing between systems without human intervention.

Information Technology is Changing

As companies migrate from a centralized to a distributed computing environment and networks continue to grow – with greater numbers of users in ever-more-widespread geographical areas – the need to organize and conduct business securely across the enterprise network becomes increasingly critical and complex. While distributed processing, global networking, and open architectures make computer systems easier to use than ever before and give computers access to a wider population, they dramatically complicate the challenge of securing an organization's information resources. To remain competitive in today's increasingly distributed network environment, companies need to extend their view of the enterprise to include customers, business partners, and suppliers. Yet as opportunities for electronic commerce and information exchange become more prevalent in the extended enterprise, security becomes a critical factor.

Today, your organization's critical information assets travel around the world on networks and in portable computers creating new challenges to the security of your information. Differences in laws and cultural views of the value and privacy of information increase the challenge of creating a cohesive, globally secure environment.

Information Networks

Some companies are attempting to address globalization issues through the use of the Internet. For some time, corporate networks have been the backbone for conducting business. Internally, corporations have automated systems to minimize paperwork and expedite processes. E-mail has become a critical business process, as it is being used to submit spreadsheets of sales forecasts, expense reports, marketing information, and many other critical flows of information.

Companies want to extend these increases in productivity and savings in time and money to their business partners and customers. Businesses are sharing more functions to eliminate duplication and provide economies and efficiencies of scale. This requires distributed information channels, which thereby creates greater demands for online information to flow outside the organization, forcing greater use of the Internet.

Internet

The world is being revolutionized by the Internet. This revolution will include challenges, both technical and cultural. It gives rapid access to information about customers, suppliers, competitors, and new market opportunities. However, there are no guarantees on the Internet. The Internet is not accountable; there is no assurance that information sent over the Internet will get to its destination. The Internet is impersonal, so with no verification of identity no one can be sure with whom they are conducting business. The Internet is not private; there is no guarantee that the information sent over the Internet will not be overheard or intercepted. Even with all of these issues, companies are rushing to the Internet because it is a very inexpensive communications medium; it is ubiquitous, reaching every corner of the globe and into most homes. Yet many companies have rushed to the Internet ill-prepared for what awaits them.

Mobile Employees

Mobile computing allows employees to work while they are traveling, creating virtual offices whereever they are – at home, hotel rooms, hotels, business partners' offices, and customer sites. This gives them the power to access time-critical information everywhere and never be out of touch. However, it also allows megabytes of company information to walk out the door every day. Confidential information leaves the security of a company's building in portable computers, generally unsecured.

Mobile computing has made working while on the road commonplace. Businessmen are working at the airport while waiting for a flight, on the airplane, and in other public places where they have no idea who is sitting next to them. Open laptop computers draw curious glances, but some may be more than curious – they may be intentional.

Airplanes are a common place for information to be "gathered." Conversations are often struck up with strangers and can be overheard by people sitting nearby. One individual said that he was able to close a half-million dollar sale due to information which he overheard on a flight, while another individual reported reading an entire IPO on a laptop being used by the person adjacent to him.

Hotels are ripe targets for corporate espionage. Portable computer thefts are on the rise. Many reports indicate that laptop thefts are often targeted for the information that they contain and the ability to leverage the theft of the laptop into compromising the organization. There have been numerous reports of portable computers stolen from hotels, and many security organizations have issued security warnings about leaving computer equipment unattended in hotel rooms, especially in hotels outside the United States.

Many companies have moved employees out of the office and into their homes. With so many employees traveling, and salespeople who should be at customer sites not in the office, it makes sense for companies not to be paying for unused office space. However, having business information going to an individual's home adds a variety of information security issues.

Proprietary information will be available in the employee's home, where generally the security is not as tight as at the office. Home offices generally employ a variety of technologies: portable computers, cellular phones, and fax machines, with all of their security problems. In addition, homes often do not have someone available for postal and package pickup and delivery during regular business hours. Packages may sit on the porch or mail may sit in a mailbox for hours or even days.

Home offices often require remote access to corporate resources, requiring that the company extend its network to include access from its work-at-home employees. This increases the number of access points in the security perimeter, thus increasing the complexity of securing the perimeter. Even if the company provides the computer to the work-at-home employees, they have little ability to control the security of and the access to that computer, thereby limiting the security it can apply to corporate resources.

Home computer systems are utilized not only by the employee, but also by family members and friends. Sensitive information and access must be restricted so that it cannot be compromised by family members and become part of domestic problems.

Information Security Must Change

Information is the key difference between companies. A company's proprietary information about products, processes, customers, and suppliers is what makes the company unique. Safeguarding this information must be a founding business principle.

Information takes many forms. It can be stored on computers, transmitted across networks, printed or written on paper, and spoken in conversations. Information and Information Technology systems are assets of vital importance to the daily operation and survival of an organization. Information requires consistent security, regardless of the form that it takes.

Information security is broader than the data center. Data is only one manifestation of information. Since most of the organization's intellectual property is contained in the minds of the organization's employees, they must be educated how to handle this valuable resource.

Organizations need to establish effective security measures to ensure the safety of information held by the organization, the continued availability of systems to support critical activities, and the implementation of appropriate controls to protect information from intentional or accidental disclosure, manipulation, modification, erasure, or copying.

Corporate security must effectively manage risk, maintain employee accountability for the protection of information assets; establish a basis for a stable process environment, assure compliance with applicable laws and regulations, and preserve management options in the event of asset misuse, loss, or unauthorized disclosure.

A company must do everything that is reasonable and prudent to ensure the confidentiality of its information in order to avoid being held liable. Information security cannot be viewed as an optional cost – something to be worried about later. It is a business enabler, without which adequate security business processes cannot be confidently undertaken.

Unfortunately, most people are not educated in the issues of information security. Even among those that are, this last decade has brought such wide-ranging changes to the world of business that the old rules no longer apply.

Information Security

Information systems security is an oxymoron.
– Anonymous Hacker

Even though many computer systems were designed to make sharing information as easy as possible, this does not mean that they cannot be made reasonably secure. The basic principles of identifying users, isolating resources, and monitoring activities are universal to the issue of protection.

The security of information systems is just one piece of information security. Information exists both inside and outside the computer and has to be protected wherever it travels. Information security has to be evaluated like any business process to determine how much security is needed to protect the information asset.

Information is a Business Asset

Information is the one unique asset owned by an organization. Whether that information is the relationship with buyers and sellers, a singular way of doing business, or the secret recipe to the organization's product, it is the use of information which primarily distinguishes one organization from another, which makes it unique, which will determine its success or failure, and which must be protected so that the organization will survive.

Information technology has enabled organizations to leverage their information assets. Businesses are collecting more information than ever before – customer information, sales detail information, product testing information. Basically, almost any information that is available is stored and kept in the hopes that it will be useful at some future time. The size and speed of today's computer systems allow for this information to be rapidly correlated to create consumer profiles to improve marketing and product availability. Sales and production information is used by marketing to design pricing structures and by procurement to negotiate better pricing.

Huge warehouses of information are being created for the process of evaluating "what if" scenarios. These warehouses make information (which comes from a wide variety of sources) available to a vast number of users. These information reserves are so valuable that many companies have succumbed to the temptation to sell information, while others collect information for the sole purpose of selling it.

The following unique attributes of information must be protected to safeguard its value as an asset:

- **Confidentiality** – The ability to allow the information to be shared among other individuals or organizations that need to be able to utilize the information while not allowing access to individuals or organizations that do not have a need to know. The confidentiality of the information must be maintained during its collection, storage, processing, and dissemination even when the information is co-mingled with other information or is processed in a manner where the original information is reproducible. Different types of information have different confidentiality requirements with different audiences. Some information requires confidentiality because it is proprietary information that is created and owned by the company, while other information is only in the custody of the organization. This is usually personal information about customers or employees and must be kept confidential due to legal concerns. Confidentiality is driven by the financial impact on the operation of the business that the public release of the information would have.

- **Accuracy** – In information security, accuracy encompasses two issues. First is the issue of starting with reliable, verifiable information from a known good source. The quality of information will not improve over time, so it is imperative that the information start out as correct as possible. Second is the issue of integrity. Integrity is the assurance that information has not been corrupted, degraded, or undergone unauthorized modification. Accurate information is required to make good business decisions. A security architecture must provide indisputable evidence of the identity of the person or process that created or modified the data. Integrity also refers to the state of computer resources and electronic processes. The quality of the processing will directly affect the quality of the resulting information.

- **Availability** - The usable presence, for business purposes, of information and information resources. Business information must be available to those who need it and kept from those who don't. Conducting business depends on the availability of business information and processing. This concept is important because the threat of denial of service could make data or resources unavailable to users.

Security is a Business Process

Security is the process of reducing risk or the likelihood of harm. Security tends to be a *weak link* problem, where the total security is no better than the weakest point in the organization. Security therefore must be evaluated broadly across the entire organization to understand where these weak links may be.

Security is a series of trade-offs: the greater the level of security required, the more administration and controls that are required, and the greater the tendency to reduce ease of use. These trade-offs must be evaluated in the same way as any business asset and process – with a clear understanding of the issues and an appropriate financial picture. An understanding of the costs of implementing security measures must be weighed against the value of information resources being protected and the price of having a security incident because the security measures were not implemented.

- **Access** - The method of getting to the information. This is the path that the data takes. Today, access is usually focused on data networks, but information access can also include telephone, faxes, or the postal service. Security demands that the access methods are understood and adequately protected.

- **Identification** – The ability to uniquely distinguish an entity. An entity is anyone or anything that wishes to utilize an information resource or that is to be used by an information resource. A truly secure system must be able to identify the individual requesting the information, the hardware and software that is going to process it, and the networks over which it will travel. Identification is a fundamental process of security upon which all other aspects of security are built.

- **Authentication** – The ability to prove positively that the entity is what it claims to be. Authentication is usually associated with individuals, but any entity must be authenticated before it can utilize or be utilized by an information resource. Authentication is the basis of trust. Everything that contributes to the information must be trusted in order to trust the information. Any single untrusted point allows the information to be corrupted at that point.

- **Authorization** – The ability to determine what information any given entity has the ability to utilize. Authorizations control the use of information. Limiting an entity's authorizations restricts that entity's access. Defining narrow scopes to specific authorizations can give very fine grain controls on what can be done with that authorization. This can dramatically improve accountability.

Information Security is a Business Requirement

Businesses must have security to protect their investment in their information assets. Not only is it good business sense, it is a legal necessity. Companies must adequately protect their business assets or be subject to stockholder suits, and they must protect information about individuals in their custody to avoid personal privacy suits.

The following three additional aspects of information security are necessary to provide adequate protection:

- **Accountability** – The ability to associate activities with those who performed them. Accountability must be assigned at the appropriate level and processes must be monitored to assure accountability. This accounting identifies the entity so that repudiation – the ability to claim that the entity did not perform the task – is not possible. Accountability also implies auditability, the ability to evaluate the activities of any entity after the fact by outside organizations. Often a legal requirement of some industries, it is always a good business practice.

- **Awareness** – The level of understanding among the user community of the security processes and how to use them. These are the people who use the information on a daily basis and have to use the security to keep the information secure. They are also among the first people who are most likely to know that there is a problem with the information.

- **Administration** – The process of managing the security of the system and its impact on the standard administration of the information systems. Implementing better security requires utilizing efficiencies in the security implementation by integrating security management into systems and network management and using physical security measures that protect employees to also protect information.

Building an Information Security Plan

A complete security program must address the business information and the security process. A security plan must be reasonable and prudent for the organization. What is a reasonable and prudent level of security depends on many things, including the type of information being protected, the type of business being conducted, and with whom the business is being conducted. Industry and governmental regulations will also define some of the security measures that are required as a minimum.

An information security plan is a large and wide-ranging undertaking. It encompasses risk analysis, business impact analysis, disaster planning, and business continuity plans. It addresses the core business processes throughout the organization and requires the support of all the business units.

The information security plan is composed of four main components. The business impact analysis defines the scope of the information security plan and those information assets that have the greatest impact on the business processes. The risk analysis defines the probability of harm and the extent of the possible damage. Disaster planning evaluates the best method to minimize the effects of harm. It identifies the functions needing quickest recovery, and establishes the recovery strategies. The business continuity plan is concerned with not only what to do when there is a disaster, but how to continue to conduct business at all times, disaster or not.

An information security plan brings together all of these issues. It identifies critical business processes (those processes required for an organization's survival), determines the necessary resources to perform each process, and evaluates the impact of an interruption to the process. It determines the costs of assuring a minimum quality of service, develops into a plan to meet this level of service, and puts into place the processes needed to deploy the plan.

Organizations can no longer regard security as an option, only needed for government contracts. Today's business environment makes security a requirement without which the company will most certainly suffer damaging losses. The information security plan must be integrated into the core business planning and review process. This keeps information security visible to senior management during all phases of the planning process. It also simplifies the process of having senior management review and endorse the plan, since they have been involved during the planning process.

The five main phases of an information security plan are as follows;

- **Inspection** – The most important tasks in developing an Information Security Plan are identifying the key corporate functions, the capabilities they need, when they need those capabilities, and how they interact with other functions. The inspection phase evaluates the security needs of the organization, as well as its current level of preparation.

- **Protection** – Proactive risk reduction includes any process that is in place to prevent a business interruption, such as identifying and qualifying second sources, purchasing spare equipment, expanding product pipeline duration, backing up critical documentation, and outsourcing operations if necessary. In this phase, decisions are made as to what needs protection, what level of protection is required, and how to best implement this level of protection. This is accomplished by creating a comprehensive security design.

- **Detection** – Reactive risk reduction includes any process that is in place to minimize the losses from an incident that could cause an interruption of business processes. This phase explores the process of detecting misuses by examining the attacker, the methods of attack, and the technologies that are used to detect them.

- **Reaction** – The emergency response plan determines how to respond when there is a security incident. It must define the process of responding to probable scenarios. The response must be identified, documented, and tested before there is an incident so that everyone knows what to do during the crisis. The incident response plan is a critical part of the business continuity plan. Preparation is key to a successful response.

- **Reflection** – When the security incident is over and the smoke clears, the organization must perform follow-up steps to be able to put the incident behind and move forward.. The processes that need improvement will undoubtedly be processes that are defined in the business continuity plan. As these improvements are evaluated, a big picture view is needed to see if there are other areas of the business continuity plan to which these changes would be beneficial, or if the changes would impact other areas of the plan.

Every organization needs to review its information security plans. During this process many will discover their business plans do not address the issue of information security. Global security direction must be created for the organization so that specific policies can be built in a consistent manner.

This book will guide you through the five phases of a security plan, highlighting the key points, emphasizing those areas that are critical to an organization's success, and relating stories to illustrate the possible consequences.

Inspection

If systems were built with care and good software engineering practice, we would have a greatly reduced problem with information security.[1]

– Eugene H. Spafford

Τhe inspection phase of information security delves into the financial aspects of assets and resources and the harm that can be caused if they are lost, altered, or disclosed. The type and size of the threat must be evaluated, as well as the availability and effectiveness of security precautions and countermeasures. Once the whole picture is understood, then informed decisions can be made.

Security reduces risk. To determine the level of security required, one must understand the probability of a security incident and the scope of the damage that the incident could cause. This is the basis of the risk analysis.

A risk analysis is required to understand the potential impact on operations and to justify the expenditures on security. This analysis should include a thorough information resource inventory and threat assessment. We must understand what is of value to the organization, how it can suffer losses, and how much protection is appropriate.

An enterprise-wide risk analysis is required to collect all of this information. This is by no means a small task. Since everyone in the organization handles information, it requires significant support from management and involvement from individuals throughout the organization.

The organization's policies which are already in place will need to be examined to determine how they can be applied to information security or how to draft new policies that follow

---

[1]   "Reexamining Intrusion Detection," Presented at the University of Virginia, January 1999.
Gene Spafford is a Professor of Computer Sciences at Purdue University and the director of the Purdue CERIAS (Center for Education and Research in Information Assurance and Security), and was the founder and director of the (now superseded) COAST Laboratory. He is also the interim Information Systems Security Officer for Purdue University. Related to this, he is the founder and de facto director of the PCERT (Purdue Computer Emergency Response Team).

them. Often an organization's employee personnel policies and physical security policies can directly apply or be broadened to encompass information security.

A risk analysis is a basic business process that should be performed on all major projects and new technologies before they are implemented to assure the feasibility of these projects. It is performed to understand the potential losses associated with the implementation of the project, and the likelihood of these losses. Since information systems technology is continuously changing, the risk analysis should be reviewed periodically, and when there is a major change in the project.

During the risk analysis phase you need to understand the value of the assets, the potential loss if the assets are compromised, the type and size of threats, where vulnerabilities exist, and what safeguards are appropriate and most effective in your situation.

Although risks can be minimized, they cannot be eliminated. When reliance upon a computer facility or application is substantial, some type of contingency plan should be devised to allow critical systems to be recovered following a major disaster, such as a fire. There are a number of alternative approaches that should be evaluated to most cost-effectively meet the agency's need for continuity of service.

An organization that is not analyzing the risk of a project is not doing all that is prudent to ensure the success of that project.

Defining Resources

An organization's resources are those things that add value to the organization or whose loss would remove value from the organization. Information resources are those resources that either store information, transport information, create information, use information, or are information.

One must adequately identify the organization's resources that are to be protected to appropriately evaluate risks and apply proper security measures. This process should include some indication of the size and type of investment that the asset represents, the impact on the organization that the loss of the asset would represent, and the ease with which the asset may be replaced. Unauthorized access to information may represent the loss of an asset, even though the information is still available to the organization. Security requirements should vary depending upon the importance of the particular resource. Security cannot make it impossible to suffer a loss. What it can do is reduce the likelihood and make the cost of a malicious attack prohibitive for the information gained.

An organization's resources take a variety of forms: both tangible and intangible assets, as well as resources that are not the organization's property but are required for the organization to operate. Resources can be grouped into the following categories:

- **People** make the organization work, they supply information, maintain systems, etc. They are the creators, consumers, and caretakers of the organization's information.

They include employees and contractors; everyone who adds value to the organization's bottom line.

- **Property** denotes the physical assets of the organization. These assets usually have the greatest value on the books.

- **Information** relates to those proprietary items that differentiate one organization from any other.

- **Infrastructure** refers to the basic services that are required for the operation of the organization, such as electricity, communication, transportation, etc.

- **Reputation** is the value of a good name. The monetary value of an organization's reputation may be hard to define. However, the cost to a organization when its reputation is damaged can be devastating.

Some resources, such as property and information, are in the organization's direct control. The organization can determine where they go, who has access, and how quickly they can be repaired or replaced.

Other resources, such as people and infrastructure, are not in the direct control of the organization. The organization can only make requests of those in control to take action. The organization can educate people to appropriate security procedures and behaviors and can sign quality of service contracts with infrastructure suppliers. However, these are indirect processes. The organization cannot dictate the priorities of other organizations.

Assessing Threats

A threat assessment is a critical part of risk analysis. Threats are always present. They are outside the direct control of the organization. The threats themselves cannot be eliminated, only anticipated, but safeguards can be put in place to minimize their impact.

The size and type of threats are based in part on the type of business the organization conducts and the level of technology embraced.

Information systems face a variety of threats including computer-based fraud, espionage, vandalism, accident, natural disaster, computer viruses, and computer hackers. As the world's dependence on information continues to increase, threats become more widespread, more ambitious, and increasingly sophisticated. Threats come in a variety of forms, including:

- **Human Errors** are accidents caused by undue care and attention or lack of knowledge. They can include user error, an accidental power disconnect, operator error, or inadequate procedures – in other words, any time a mistake causes losses.

- **System Failures** include both hardware and software problems affecting not only the systems that failed, but any system that depends on the failed system.

- **Natural Disasters** such as an earthquake, hurricane, flood, fire, or tornado, cause widespread physical damage and outages of critical infrastructure, such as electricity, transportation, and communications. Due to the scope of natural disasters, recovery is often a slow process.

- **Malicious Acts** can be either human or automated attacks of systems or theft of equipment and resources. Internal attacks come from disgruntled employees—the organization's greatest threat, while external attacks can be corporate espionage, malicious attacks, or hackers.

The explosive expansion of the Internet and its demands for connectivity require the addition of new external connections which in turn has led to the creation of a large number of remote users. These users include employees who need remote access, direct network connections to remote offices, and connections with outside parties, over whose network environment you have no control. As a result, most companies are much more vulnerable than they were a few years ago.

As technology and computer systems become more complex, they are more prone to have security holes. At the same time, computer hackers are becoming more knowledgeable and sophisticated. Amateur hackers and sophisticated industrial espionage will continue to proliferate. Knowledge of security holes and hacking techniques is being spread widely and quickly by highly available communication channels and networks.

Networks also enable quicker spreading of problems such as computer viruses and undesirable messages, whether they are intentional or not. These problems may cause certain mission-critical resources to be unavailable.

The threats to assets should be assessed (denial of service, destruction, disclosure of information, theft, and unauthorized access). The examination of threats must include a discussion of both the probable and maximum possible impact of the realization of the threat, including both direct impact and flow-on consequences.

To fully understand the threats, not only do the sources of the threats need to be examined; one must also examine the organization as a prospective target. The malicious threat to an organization is often based on the organization's image or perceived image, or the organization's business activities and associations. Good employee and public relations can be the greatest tool to minimize malicious threats. In this area perception is truth. That is, the truth is not as important as the perception, since it is this perception that the attacker is responding to, whether it is a disgruntled employee or an external attacker. These threats need to be recognized and understood so that appropriate security measures can be implemented to minimize the potential losses.

Evaluating Potential Losses

The severity of loss to a specific resource depends on the importance of the resource to the organization and the timing of the loss. Information can be valuable because of what it is worth to the organization. The timing of the loss can have a dramatic impact on the cost of the loss –

such as information disclosure just before important decisions are to be made, or the inability to access information systems when the information is needed. The following types of losses are commonplace:

- **Denial of service** is the *loss of availability* and is the most visible of all losses. The loss of availability is immediately apparent to any entity that needs access and is unable to get access. Availability is often considered the most important attribute in service-oriented businesses that depend on information (e.g., airline schedules and online inventory systems).

- **Disclosure** is the *loss of confidentiality* and indicates that the resource has the potential to release information to unauthorized entities. For some types of information, confidentiality is a very important attribute. Examples include research data, medical and insurance records, new product specifications, and corporate investment strategies. In some locations, there may be a legal obligation to protect the privacy of individuals. This is particularly true for banks and loan companies; debt collectors; businesses that extend credit to their customers or issue credit cards; hospitals, doctors' offices, and medical testing laboratories; individuals or agencies that offer services such as psychological counseling or drug treatment; and agencies that collect taxes. Information disclosure is generally the area of greatest concern to an organization.

- **Destruction or Corruption** is the *loss of integrity* and indicates that unauthorized changes have been made to information, whether by human error or intentional tampering. Integrity is particularly important for critical safety and financial data used in activities such as electronic funds transfers, air traffic control, and financial accounting. If the quality of the resource is in question, then all the decisions that utilize that resource must also be in question. Information corruption may be the most devastating type of loss to an organization.

To completely understand the impact that a loss will have on a business, a business impact analysis should be performed to understand all the implications of the incident. Often there are significant downstream effects that may not be initially apparent. This information is not maintained in a vacuum. It is used for business decisions that affect the organization and its employees, partners, creditors, and competitors. Poor business decisions can have significant, far-reaching implications. There are also issues of collateral damage: the impact on things that were thought to be unrelated but, due to location or other circumstances, are affected by the incident or the response to the incident.

Identifying Vulnerabilities

Vulnerabilities are compromised by a threat that causes a loss. They are also one of the most difficult areas to define before there is a security incident, but always identified as the cause of a security incident. Vulnerabilities exist in hardware and software, in policies and procedures, and in people. Anything that can be exploited to an advantage is a vulnerability. Common sources of vulnerabilities include the following:

- **Security Design Flaw** is a vulnerability that exists because of the nature of the design, such as sending passwords over a network in clear text. These flaws may exist because security was not part of the design, because this specific security issue was not foreseen, or because the system is now being used in a manner that is outside the original design scope.

- **Incorrect Implementation** is the case of not installing or administering the system correctly. Often the default settings are not the most secure settings. Administrators will bypass security settings to make the system easier to operate with less administration or to quickly solve an operational issue.

- **Innovative Misuses** come about when the system is used in a fashion that was not anticipated by its designers. It may have never been considered that a feature that was designed to do a specific function, such as testing or diagnostics, could be used to disable the system, thus allowing a denial of service attack.

- **Social Engineering** is the process of convincing people to divulge information that they should not. Often built on false pretenses and misidentification, social engineering is extremely effective. Only appropriate training can reduce this vulnerability.

Vulnerabilities which are already known are the most common source for intrusions. Hackers write tools to exploit these vulnerabilities. Administrators must keep up to date by researching known vulnerabilities for all the systems in use to avoid losses. This one step can significantly reduce loss.

Assigning Safeguards

A company must do everything that is reasonable and prudent to safeguard its resources. Once there is an understanding of what resources need to be protected, their value, the size of the threat, and the likelihood of vulnerabilities, then appropriate safeguards can be assigned. These previous processes will help define the appropriate size of the safeguard and how to best protect the resource.

Safeguards must be fashioned to protect the vulnerability based on the knowledge of the vulnerability, the threats that are likely to exploit the vulnerability, the potential loss that could occur, and the likelihood of its occurrence. Safeguards can be implemented with hardware or software or with policies or procedures. Each situation must be evaluated for the best solution. Often a combination of safeguards is the best strategy.

Safeguards can be proactive, that is, they can serve to protect the information before it is compromised. Or they can be reactive – they can detect that the information is being compromised and take appropriate measures to minimize the damage. Proactive safeguards are preferred; better to stop the incident before it occurs. However, they may not always be possible. Reactive safeguards are always needed, since not all vulnerabilities can be predicted and incident detection is crucial to loss minimization.

Security practices and procedures should be appropriate to the value of the resource and the degree of company reliance on the resource. These measures should be proportionate in direct and indirect costs to the severity, probability, and extent of potential harm. The safeguards also need to be all-inclusive and comprehensive.

Evaluate Current Status

Most organizations have some basic security, even if they are only informal activities. The current status of the security procedures must be evaluated, not only for their effectiveness but also for their applicability to the areas that the risk analysis has determined to be important. It needs to be determined if they appropriately address the areas of security that are most important to the organization. Evaluation of the effectiveness of current processes requires analysis of the procedures and testing of the practices.

- **Assess** the policies and procedures by reading them. Determine if they cover all the necessary topics and give enough detail in response to the defining and handling of infractions. Compare them to the policies and procedures of other similar organizations.

- **Test** the quality of the implementation. This should focus on evaluating the level of compliance to the policies and the completeness of the implementation. Security practices must be practiced throughout the organization.

The evaluation will determine the effectiveness of the current security environment and may highlight areas that were not previously considered.

The inspection process covers a tremendous range of issues, and like most projects, the more analysis that is done upfront the more successful the project will be. Good planning will reduce the impact of security on the efficient running of the system.

CHAPTER 1

Resource Inventory

Forty-three percent of companies surveyed don't take the basic step of classifying their data into security categories.[2]

A resource is something that has value to the organization, which if lost or damaged, would cause a loss to the organization as a whole. Resources are more than just assets; they include employees, infrastructure, relationships with customers or partners, and corporate reputation.

All of these resources have security requirements that vary depending upon the importance of the particular resource. However, before proper security measures can be applied, the company's resources must be identified and their value and cost to the company should they be disclosed or destroyed, must be assigned. A complete inventory of company resources is required to know what the company needs to protect. All major information resources must be accounted for and have a designated owner and security classification.

A comprehensive documentation of resources is required to appropriately evaluate the level of security necessary to protect the organization.

Identifying Resources

The first step is to identify the organization's information resources. This will determine the scope of the security evaluation. In theory, all of the organization's information resources would be considered. However, constraints of time, money, and area of responsibility often limit the evaluation.

The various assets and security processes associated with each individual system should be identified and clearly defined. The responsible individual for each information asset and for each specific security process should be agreed upon and the responsibility documented; authorization or approval levels for any changes should also be defined and documented.

---

[2]   PricewaterhouseCooper, " Global Security Survey," *Information Week*, 1998.

Every asset should be clearly defined. These include information and processes as well as physical assets. Often these assets can be put into logical groupings of closely associated information and processes. These asset groups can then be managed as a single asset.

Information

Defining information resources at the appropriate level is a task that requires experience with the information. Data items that are always used together as a unit of information can be considered a single information resource. It is safest to evaluate the information at the data element level. After the information is evaluated, it can be aggregated together to simplify administration. These aggregates must be clearly defined and equivalent to the sum of their parts.

Algorithms

Many organizations have proprietary processes and information contained in the algorithms and software which they have created that need to be adequately protected. In many of the process industries, it is the process more than the data that is unique and has value to the company. They first need to be identified and inventoried.

Software

Purchased software is a significant investment for most organizations. It needs to be accounted for so that if it is stolen an appropriate value can be determined. Adequate software inventories are also necessary to demonstrate that the organization is following its contractual requirements as described in the license agreement for each software package.

Equipment

Physical assets are usually already inventoried and the value and owner for them defined. Be sure to utilize this existing information when it is available. However, information system equipment needs to be evaluated for costs associated with unavailability to be able to create appropriate risk reduction plans.

Assigning Ownership

Ownership assigns accountability. Accountability helps ensure that adequate security protection is maintained. Owners of major assets should be identified and assigned responsibility for maintenance of appropriate security measures. The implementation of the security measures may be delegated, but the owner of an asset will remain ultimately accountable for its protection.

The information owner should be the individual or position in the organization who has fiduciary responsibility for the information. This person should understand the responsibility of maintaining the security of the information. This individual should be able to help define the value of the information. The owner of a resource will need to evaluate it to be assured that the resource receives the appropriate level of security.

The asset owner is responsible for determining the value of the information asset as well as assigning a security classification to the information. The owner will be expected to have significant input to the handling procedures for the information.

Creator

The creator of the information usually has a good understanding of the value of the information and often controls the utilization of the information. He often feels a personal ownership of the information.

Maintainer

The person who is responsible for maintaining the information, controlling its use, and ensuring its integrity is often selected to be its owner, since the maintainer has the greatest control over the information. Assigning fiduciary responsibility can help ensure proper management.

User

The manager of the user community for the information has a vested interest in the information, since it is his people who rely on it for their work. This person would be the first choice to be the information owner. However, the user community does not always have a single manager who is responsible for their work.

Determining who should be the owner of an information item can be as easy as evaluating who would have the greatest impact on its business function if it suffers a loss.

Determining Value

Determining the value of information assets is pivotal to determining the appropriate level of security. Assets may have an obvious tangible value, such as their purchase price, or an intangible value assigned to them by their owner or creator. The asset owner defines how the value of the asset is to be determined. Identifying the value of an asset is required to understand the possible loss and the appropriate level of security required.

This value is composed of the cost of creating or acquiring the information and the business impact if the information is lost or compromised. The business impact is an estimate of the degree of harm from both short-term and long-term consequences. Long-term consequences are usually more financially significant than short-term. They can include loss of business, violations of privacy, injury, and death.

It is important to evaluate the cost of creating the information, the cost of re-creating the information, and the loss to the company if the information is disclosed to determine the value of the information.

Cost of Re-creation

What was the cost in time – man and machine hours – to collect, enter, and correlate the information? This is often the cost basis for information that is collected from real-time data collection systems. The data collected from nuclear tests or space probes is extremely expensive to create and may be impossible to re-create.

Information with a high cost of re-creation needs adequate protection to avoid the destruction of the information, usually by using redundant storage of information. The cost of recovering the information may be reduced though appropriate backup and recovery procedures. However, the value of the information does not change because of good backup and recovery practices. If it took millions of dollars to create the information archive, the information is not worth less because the cost of recovering the information from backups is less. This is different from the physical world, where the value of an asset is often based on the cost to repair or restore the asset and not necessarily the cost to re-create the item.

Cost of Unavailability

Many businesses, such as financial trading organizations, depend on rapid access to their information resources. The inability to access information to make decisions rapidly can have enormous financial effects on the organization. It can even be life threatening to individuals, as in the case of medical monitoring systems.

Unavailability is a slippery subject, since the cost of the information being unavailable is very dependent on timing, duration, and situation. For example, the information needed to shut down a nuclear power plant and avoid a nuclear meltdown may not be needed for years. However, if it is unavailable at the moment that the reactor needs to be shut down, the cost of unavailability is enormous.

Security often focuses on worst case scenarios. Typical scenarios must also be considered. The frequency, and the duration of critical needs, must be evaluated for business decisions. The "one in a million" scenario must be considered; however, the financial picture may require implementation for only the typical scenario.

Systems for which availability is of prime importance require a high level of redundancy to eliminate points of failure — not to protect the information, but rather to protect the access to the information.

Cost of Disclosure

The level of information detail will affect the cost of disclosure. The more detailed the information, the more costly a disclosure will be.

Information whose public disclosure would have drastic consequences will have a high security classification, which will in itself help define what precautions are necessary. However, there are two issues with the cost of disclosure. The first is with proprietary information, where the disclosure of this information will cause the business to lose sales, market position, or some advantage. Disclosure of proprietary information has a direct effect on the business' ability to continue to conduct business in a profitable manner. It goes straight to the bottom line of the organization. The second issue is private information about individuals with which the company is entrusted. These individuals may be employees, customers, patients or partners. Disclosure of private information has an impact on both the individual, who the information is about, and the company, who is its caretaker. The organization can suffer indirect damages through a loss of confidence and through legal actions taken by those individuals who suffered because of the disclosure.

When it comes to the level of secrecy or cost of disclosure, most information often has a life cycle. In the area of planning, whether it is marketing plans or military plans, the longer in the future the information relates to, the higher the cost of disclosure. Plans that will become public tomorrow may not cause the same level of damage as plans that cover the next three to five years. The security classification of information needs to be periodically reviewed and reevaluated. Information security reclassification is a regular part of maintaining appropriate information security.

Security Classification

All resources do not have the same potential to cause an organization monetary loss and therefore all resources do not require the same expenditure for their protection. Resource owners must consistently convey the relative importance of loss through modification, destruction, disclosure, or unauthorized use of their resources to the company. Classifications are organized around the attributes of confidentiality, integrity, and availability as they relate to the organization's resources.

Assigning classification is only the first step into a classified environment. It is the continual, day-to-day use of the security classifications that is difficult. The information's classification determines how it is handled, transmitted and stored, who has access, and where the information is allowed to go. Classified information must be labeled appropriately, and this label must follow the information wherever it goes, in whatever form it takes, including printed information and screen displays.

Security classifications allow for a logical grouping of resources to assign general security levels so that information of a given classification always receives a defined minimum level of security. Most companies do this to some degree — papers are marked "Not for Publication" or "Company Confidential." In general, however, this security is only loosely used and minimally enforced.

Classification is conceptually very easy. Determine the value and risks and assign an appropriate classification. However, information has varying degrees of importance and sensitivity, and a classification system must be used to ensure that the information receives an appropriate level of protection. Classifications may be used to indicate the need and priorities for security protection.

The following factors should be considered when assigning a resource's security classifications:

- **Sensitivity of the information** is the leading factor when setting the level of security classification for the information.

- **Consequences of disclosure** define the financial impact of a loss to the information. This helps set the value of the information and thereby sets the appropriate costs of the safeguards to protect it.

- **Legal and contractual obligations and penalties** will define the minimum level of security required for the information to which the law or contract applies. Besides specific laws that place security requirements on information, such as the Privacy Act of 1974, there are laws, court cases, legal opinions, and other similar legal materials that may affect the security classification directly or indirectly.

- **Standards and guidelines** that are defined by government, industry, locality, or the organization itself will help determine the security classification for the information. They will likely define features, assurances, and operational practices for specific types of information. Many organizations specify baseline requirements for systems that have specific functions.

- **Information lifecycle** affects the security classification of the information, since the importance of the information changes over time. Generally, the closer the information is to being officially made public, the lower its security classification will be.

An information resource's overall security classification is the combination of a resource's individual availability, integrity, and confidentiality classifications.

Confidentiality

The confidentiality classification describes the impact from disclosure. It could be in the form of business losses from disclosed proprietary information or the personal damage caused by disclosed private information. Confidentiality classifications are what is generally thought of when the term "security classification" is used.

Availability

The availability classification indicates the urgency of the information and the systems that utilize it. The measure for availability is often based on the lost revenue or productivity that would result from an outage.

Integrity

The integrity classification reflects the severity of the damage that would be caused if the information was altered and then utilized. The damages derive from inappropriate decisions or behaviors based on faulty information. Compromised integrity can be responsible for everything from financial damage to loss of life.

Classification, and the periodic review of classifications in conjunction with risk assessment, will lead to appropriate expenditure in its protection, rather than unnecessary expense. Information classification requirements change over time so it is necessary to review these needs and reclassify information that has had a change in its requirements.

It is best to avoid using military classifications; they have very rigid definitions that may not fit a nonmilitary environment. Their use will create preconceived expectations of the information or its handling.

Checklist

— Make formal inventory of all your information assets.

— Identify all information resources (information, systems, networks, programs, etc.).

— Assign ownership based on business relationships (fiduciary responsibility).

— Determine the value of the resource to the organization.

— Create security classifications for availability, integrity, confidentiality.

This example spreadsheet illustrates the type of information required for the inventory.

			Value		Security Classification		
Identifier	Description	Owner	Dollars	Determination	Availability	Integrity	Confidentiality

Description of fields:

Identifier – the unique identifier of the information resource
Description – describes the information resource
Owner – the assigned owner of the information resource
Value
   Dollars – the monetary value of the information resource
   Determination – describes the process that was used to determine the value of the information resource. It should indicate if the value was based on the cost of creation, re-creation, unavailability, or disclosure
Security Classification
   Availability – the classification based on the availability requirements of the information resource (*Chapter 12*)
   Integrity – the classification for the integrity requirements of the information resource (*Chapter 13*)
   Confidentiality – the classification based on the confidentiality requirements of the information resource (*Chapter 14*)

CHAPTER 2

Threat Assessment

Sixty-five percent of respondents reported computer security breaches in 1998 – a dramatic increase of 16% over 1997 and a 22% increase over 1995.[3]

Threats cause potential loss. You have no direct control over threats and little can be done about threats themselves other than trying to understand them. You can only implement safeguards to protect yourself from the threat. The size of the threat faced by an organization can be based on the location of the business, the morale of its employees, the organization's image or perceived image, and the organization's business, associations and public relations. There are two categories of threats to computer security: deliberate threats and non-deliberate ones. Deliberate threats involve acts intentionally taken to breach computer security. Non-deliberate threats involve situations when computer security is threatened by non-human forces, or by human actions that are not intended to breach security but have that effect. Threats can be internal or external. Internal threats are from entities that have legitimate access, while external threats come from entities that have unauthorized access.

The goal of a threat assessment is to understand the type of threat and the likelihood that the threat will cause a loss.

- **Threat identification** is the process of identifying a user or event with the potential to cause harm. Typical threats are errors, fraud, disgruntled employees, fires, hackers, and viruses. It is most important to be able to identify the threats that are most likely to be able to cause harm. To do this you must identify what your system has that would be of interest to attackers. Company information might be of interest to your competitors. Personal information such as credit card numbers, medical information, etc., may be of interest for a number of reasons. Access to the system itself may be of value if the system is particularly powerful or has other unique aspects.

---

[3] "1998 CSI/FBI Computer Crime and Security Survey," *Computer Security Issues & Trends*, Spring 1998.

- **Likelihood assessment** is the process of estimating the chance that a threat will cause a loss. A likelihood assessment considers the presence, tenacity, and strengths of threats as well as the effectiveness of safeguards and presence of vulnerabilities. Threats can be categorized by the likelihood of their occurrence, which can be used as a multiplier of the likely damage that the threat could cause. Common categories include: frequent, probable, occasional, remote, and improbable. In general, statistical information about physical threats for specific areas is available. However, reliable information about the likelihood of human threats is weak at best. Therefore, experience in this area is important to evaluating the likelihood of losses.

Human Error

Error is by far the most common threat against an organization's resources. Human error involves authorized users making mistakes that cause losses. Mistakes cost a company time and money. Every user, developer, and administrator is subject to making mistakes. User friendliness increases ease-of-use, but it also makes it easier to make mistakes. Dragging and dropping information into the wrong spot can be catastrophic. What appears to be simple actions may create a great amount of work to repair.

Simple data entry errors or inappropriate procedures can cause catastrophic failures, as the story below indicates.

> The British destroyer, HMS Sheffield, was sunk during the war in the Falklands by a French-made Exocet missile fired from an Argentinian ship. Original reports indicated that the French-made missile had not been registered as an enemy weapon in the ship's defense database and was detected as friendly fire. This cause was officially denied, and later reports indicated that electronic anti-missile defenses were jammed by a telephone call from the captain to naval headquarters.[4]

Human error is caused by individuals who have access and are authorized to use the system. These are internal users so internal processes are required to minimize these losses. Human error can be reduced by educating users and by improving the safety of the users' environment through the process of reducing the user's authorizations.

A limited environment for users not only makes systems easier to use and individuals more productive, but it must also make it difficult for the user to make mistakes that cause losses. The impact of a mistake can be reduced by limiting the user's authorizations. The practice of

[4]   *New Scientist*, Vol. 97, page 502, 24 February 1983.

least privileges is a paradigm where a user is given only the minimum privileges necessary to perform the required task and only for the minimum time necessary to perform the task. Not having these privileges limits the scope of damage caused by any mistake.

Educating your employees is the most cost-effective security program available. When users know how to use the systems that they are expected to use, they are less likely to make mistakes and are more productive. When users understand the importance of security, how to use it, and where to report suspected violations, they can do a great deal to reduce the risk to the organization.

Education needs to be comprehensive. All users need to know how to protect the information for which they are responsible. Education is an ongoing process – new users need training and trained users need reminding, especially when new technologies or processes are introduced. Education needs to be personal – each user must understand how he fits in the process and why security is important to him. Education needs to be a priority – it should be made part of every employee's review process.

Natural Disasters

All businesses are subject to natural disasters even though the exact type of disaster (earthquake, fire, flood, hurricane, tornado, etc.) varies by location. Historically, disaster plans focused extensively on preparing for, and reacting to, natural disasters. Natural disasters are often quite devastating because of the magnitude of the impact. They will often kill or injure people and destroy property and disrupt infrastructure (roads, electricity, communications, etc.), all of which leads to information being unavailable for a long period of time.

Offsite storage of information is a basic tenet of disaster survival. All the information, systems, and infrastructure necessary to rebuild the information system should be kept offsite in case of physical disaster. Since a physical disaster destroys physical assets, it is necessary to be able to conduct your business from an alternate location; this includes keeping critical information, such as the configuration of systems and disaster recovery procedures, in an alternate location. Much of this information will need to be in a human readable form; since your systems have just been destroyed, electronic forms of the information may not be accessible.

Physical separation between the primary site and the recovery site, whether that is just the storage of backups or a standby system, is critical to the quality of the disaster recovery plan. The distance required is dependent on the type of natural disaster that it is being protected against. There must be enough separation so that both sites will not be affected by the same disaster and that the likelihood of multiple disasters affecting both sites is minimal.

Normal disaster plans will address the possibility of having a backup site in a different location so that the natural disaster will not disrupt both sites. However, this may not be enough.

> A Houston-based company arranged to have its Dallas data center be the disaster recovery site for its Houston data center. Their major natural disaster concern was hurricanes.
>
> A tropical storm came ashore in Galveston and tracked directly to the Houston area. Damage to the company and loss of communication in the area made the company enact its disaster recovery plan, which went very smoothly. The company was back up and running out of its Dallas offices almost immediately. However, the storm continued inland dumping record levels of rain – up to 43 inches in 24 hours in some areas. In Dallas, the excessive rain caused flooding and the company's Dallas data center was closed due to flash flooding.[5]

All scenarios need to be evaluated and tested. An organization's survival depends on the quality of the disaster plan and its ability to be executed in the event of a disaster.

An organization that does not have a written, tested, and practiced disaster plan is betting that the unthinkable will not happen. Of course, it inevitably will. Disaster plans should be tested under a variety of scenarios with different types of disasters, multiple disasters, and with a variety of unexpected complications.

The human factor must be taken into account when a disaster plan is developed. Redundancy is needed in people as well as systems. There must be multiple individuals who can perform each of the necessary functions of the plan. Natural disasters will impact these individuals as well as the organization. They may be unwilling or unable to participate, especially if it requires travel across the country to the backup site when their home and families have just suffered the same disaster. Natural disasters rarely happen when the weather is good, so travel may not be an option; you may be required to have personnel at the backup site who can perform the necessary functions in the case of a disaster or be prepared to rely on untrained local personnel.

The reason for a disaster plan is to rapidly recover from the disaster. This will almost always entail restoring systems and information from previously stored backups.

The first rule in disaster planning is you can never lose more information than that which has changed since your last backup. Backing up your information is critical to system recovery. How often a backup is taken, the scope of the backup, and the storage process of the backup is determined by the value of the information, generally the cost of re-creating the information. Backups are fundamental to the installation of new systems after the destruction of your existing system and to the updating of your hot-site systems.

---

[5]   "Claudette Hits Houston, Drowns Dallas," *Houston Chronicle*, 20 July 1979.

System Failures

Information systems are composed of hardware, software, and infrastructure. All of these have the potential of failure. Hardware systems can experience mechanical difficulties, software can fail due to unexpected input and infrastructure is dependent on mechanical systems. Some, like power and communications, also face the issues of having to transport their services over long distances where they are physically vulnerable to a wide variety of threats.

However, hardware system failures are generally one of the most solvable areas of concern.

> A major network bandwidth supplier thought they were prepared for disaster when the communications satellite, Galaxy IV, malfunctioned. Although they were crippled, since most of its international communications utilized this satellite, they had a sophisticated monitoring system that would page service technicians in the case of communications failure. Unfortunately, the paging service also used the same satellite, so the technicians were not notified of the outage in a timely fashion.[6]

Hardware

Today's hardware systems are more reliable than ever before. The widespread use of computers has increased the production volume and increased component reliability. Systems require fewer moving parts and less routine maintenance. Falling hardware prices make redundancy more affordable. There are a variety of ways to add redundancy and increase reliability.

Hardware redundancy employs the use of multiple hardware elements so that any single failure will not cause a system failure. This is called single point redundancy. Often, only the elements that are most likely to fail, those with moving parts, or those critical to the system are replicated. Disk drives are usually the first element to be replicated.

Disk mirroring is the process of having multiple copies of the data on different disk drives so that a mechanical failure of the disk will not cause the loss of data or even down time. Power supplies are another often-duplicated element. They are susceptible to power fluctuations and are critical to the entire system.

Some systems may employ dual point redundancy—no two failures will cause the system to fail. This type of redundancy increases the cost of a system and the complexity of the monitoring system.

---

[6]   "Pager messages lost in space," *CNN Online*, 20 May 1998.

Failover systems are two or more systems that monitor the health of the other systems and take control of the resources of a system that fails. Each of these systems is usually not a highly-available, redundant system by itself, but in concert they work to make a highly available cluster of computers.

Self-healing systems are starting to appear. These systems detect when a component is starting to fail then automatically disable the component, reroute as necessary to keep the faulty component from causing the entire system from failing, and contact the support organization to report the failure. Today, this technology is being used with memory and CPUs as well as in the area of networking. Technologies are being developed in the labs that will allow a computer to repair itself by rewriting its own circuits.

Information redundancy is the process of having more than one copy of your information so that if a hardware failure damages the media containing your information, the information is still recoverable. To ensure continuous availability to information during a media failure, a more extensive process of redundancy, such as mirroring, must be employed.

Software

The issues of software quality have long been a concern in the information systems industry. There are many books dedicated to the issue of software quality and there have been a number of methodologies created to help address these issues.

The computer industry's near-panic over the year 2000 is a problem of years of bad coding – shortsighted programmers who used only two digits to represent the year, causing the comparison of two years to be incorrect when one of the years is from the 1900s and the other from the 2000s.

- **Software complexity** is the largest contributing factor to the reliability of software. Most useful information systems require that the software processes be large and rather complex. Software complexity comes from a variety of sources – just the size of the tasks that computers are expected to perform leads to large complicated software systems. The basic functions of a computer system, its operating system, are immensely more complicated today than just a few years ago. The operating system must handle a wide variety of media, disks, and tapes, with divergent data storage methods, networks, and a plethora of input devices including audio and video and produce output that is more complicated than ASCII text.

  These systems are expected to interface with a large number of other systems, both hardware and software systems, which all may have unique requirements for these interfaces. This is especially true when there is no good standard for the interface or where there are multiple competing standards.

  Compatibility with previous systems often requires that previous poor designs be reimplemented in the new system. Often security is sacrificed due to the compatibility requirements of the system design.

- **Software evolution** is the process of how software changes over time through the addition of new features and application of fixes. Even though it is the goal to improve software every time it is changed, this is not always the case. Software can have a surprisingly long life, so it is not likely that the people who originally designed and implemented the software are the same people who continue to maintain, patch, and enhance the software. These maintenance programmers have different design styles that do not always mesh with the design of the original software. This can lead to flaws that can be exploited.

- **Software testing** and quality have become key issues with many companies who understand that the cost of doing it right is less than doing it over. Quality software testing is the hallmark of a good software development process. However, software quality is usually focused on the correctness of the application, not the ability of the application to be subverted or used to compromise another part of the information systems. Software must be tested for both accuracy and security.
Security testing is quite different from typical software testing. Normal software testing checks for the accuracy of output from given input and tests for the reporting of specific errors. However, security testing deals with how the system responds to the unexpected. It is the unexpected input that will cause a software system to fail and often give a hacker the opportunity to exploit the software to compromise the resources that the software has access to. Security testing requires an understanding of how systems are subverted through processes like buffer overruns and a level of creativity to be able to use software in new and inventive ways.

- **Change management** is the process of monitoring and managing the changes that are made to a software product. Implementing change management procedures can curtail many software failures. If systems are not managed so that the specifics of changes to software are not tracked, then the identification of when and where the introduction of problems occur is much more difficult. Often the implementation of a new revision of software will in itself cause failures. Every time that software is changed it should be improved. Over the life span of a software system, the software will change due to external influences. Good code management can improve the reuse of software modules and decrease the overall complexity of the system.

Infrastructure

Infrastructure outages can be just as devastating to an organization as a system outage. Whether the information consumer is unable to access the information because the communications network is down, or the power is unavailable to the information systems, or the building climate control is not working, he or she is still unable to do his job. The larger problem is that the infrastructure is under the control of outside organizations. You cannot control the level of security or redundancy that your electric supplier implements.

Your only option is to address these issues through your contract with your infrastructure supplier in the form of service levels that define required levels of availability.

There is also the option of building redundancy into your infrastructure by multisourcing your infrastructure so that there are multiple suppliers; if one of them is unable to supply the service, the other will be able to. It is necessary to determine if there is a common link between the suppliers that could potentially make both of the suppliers out of service.

Infrastructure dependence is increasing in business. Geographically dispersed organizations require more infrastructures to maintain communications. Businesses that move to providing services over the Internet become dependent on the infrastructure for customer access. Electronic data interchange, or EDI, with partners increases the dependency on infrastructure.

System failures occur for any number of reasons. Most of the time they are products of mistakes which are made in the normal operation of the systems. However, there is a growing concern about malicious acts. The number of attacks against information systems is increasing.

Malicious Acts

Malicious attacks are those attacks from individuals or groups who specifically target systems. Attacks are often aimed at acquiring something you have. If your system contains financial information, then your system will be a target of a very wide variety of hackers. If your system contains only company information that would be damaging only to the company or of benefit to its competitors, then its attackers will be much more likely be disgruntled employees or corporate spies.

> Vandals hacked the New York City Police Department's voice-mail system and replaced the usual polite announcements with "You have reached the New York City Police Department. For any real emergencies, dial 119. Anyone else — we're a little busy right now eating some donuts and having coffee." It continued "You can just hold the line. We'll get back to you. We're a little slow, if you know what I mean. Thank you." The bogus messages continued for 12 hours before they were corrected by officials.[7]

The size of the threat depends on the type of business and how that fits in with the hacker's motives. Hackers have a wide variety of motives. The more criminal or personal the hacker's motives, the more dangerous he will be. If the system is being attacked because it contains

---

[7]   *New York Post*, 19 April 1996.

information the hacker wants, or the hacker has specific reason to attack your system, then he won't go away until he is successful or he is repelled.

Some hackers are anarchists wanting to perform random acts of violence or wanting to become famous; others have a personal score to settle with someone or some company, while others plan to get rich from stealing information on the electronic frontier and hack only for the financial rewards. Still others are classic hackers who just want to learn how systems work and hack for the thrill and excitement. Even though external threats are quite numerous and get the most publicity and attention when they are successful, they are not generally as damaging as the internal threat. The external threat can be either a random or specific attack.

A site might be attacked for the resources it has access to, or as a strategic location to attack another site. Many sites that do not consider that the information that they have has enough value to be a target may have information that can be used by an attacker in other ways to leverage a position against another organization or individual.

Evaluate Yourself as a Target

You may feel that since you have nothing to steal, you have nothing to worry about. Every company has information that is desired by their competitors, otherwise there would not be a competitive intelligence industry. This information may be customer lists, product plans, or marketing strategies. This information in the hands of your competitors would give them a decisive advantage.

There are resources, in addition to information, that may make you a target. Computer resources, such as supercomputers or computers with specialized systems, will draw attention to those who want to have access to these resources. Network bandwidth is valuable to those who would set up a beachhead on one of your systems to utilize your high-speed network to probe other sites. (However, the availability of high-speed networks has reduced this threat.) Dial-out modems are still a valuable resource for those who wish to launder connections by dialing out to another system to make tracing the connections more difficult.

Electronic funds have created another area of motives for attackers – the possibility of being able to steal money electronically. This is a very powerful motive to some. Companies that are involved in electronic commerce have yet another reason to be targeted.

Who you are is still the prime contributor to being a target. Visibility attracts both customers and critics. The more visible or better known the organization is, the more likely someone will have a reason to attack the organization. The reason may only be known to the attacker. Famous people and famous organizations are often targets just because of their fame. Any organization that has information about a person or organization that is likely to be a target will themselves become a target to get that information.

> RSA Security, a major player in the security industry whose slogan is "The Most Trusted Name in E-security," seemed very unlikely to fall victim to an attack that would penetrate their own network security. But according to the reports, an attacker, who calls himself "Coolio," defaced their home page. Anyone attempting to access the web site would see the attacker's handiwork.
>
> In fact, the attacker never came close to RSA's network or web site. Instead, it was a case of DNS spoofing, where an upstream DNS server, owned and managed by someone else, was convinced to report the wrong address for the site. Preliminary investigation showed that the defaced page was being served up from a host computer in Colombia, where a university-owned machine was itself likely compromised.[8]

Some companies are at a greater risk just because of the industry that they are in. Energy companies are targets for protestors who object to the practices of the energy industry. Government organizations are targets because of individuals who dislike the government.

More importantly, how the business conducts itself will have a greater impact on its becoming a target. Cyberactivism is on the rise and there are thousands of causes that may focus on an organization because of what they perceive it is doing and how it impacts their cause.

Even where a business is located and where it does business does, to some degree, affect the likelihood of it becoming a target. There are very diverse social views on intellectual property and hacking. In some countries hacking is legal and intellectual property may have very few rights. Theft of information may not even be considered theft.

Public relations and employee satisfaction are the two biggest steps that can be taken to reduce the chances of becoming a target. Satisfied customers and employees will eliminate many of the motives that lead to attacks. Using public relations to communicate your position on causes that relate to the organization's business in a positive light will reduce cyberactivism.

Malicious acts are motivated by need, greed, and revenge.

Malicious Software

Malicious software is software that creates or exploits a vulnerability. Software algorithms are not inherently either bad or good; they are only tools that can be used either constructively or destructively. However, there are some types of programs that are often utilized maliciously.

---

[8]   Bonisteel, Steve, "Crackers Cripple RSA Server," *Newsbytes,* 15 February 2000.

Buffer Overflow

A buffer overflow occurs when a program attempts to put more data in a storage location than it will hold – the extra data overflows the buffer. The problem is where the data goes that does not fit into the buffer. Some systems may trap this as an error and terminate the program, other times it overwrites other data or, even worse, it may overwrite executable code.

Buffer overflows are very common. This is in some part because of system libraries that do not do adequate range checking. The most well known, and possibly the most widely spread, is a number of utilities that are part of the C language library, known as libc. These are a series of utilities that manipulate character data.

> Ever since the early days of web sites, thousands of web sites have been maliciously defaced – the information they contained altered, quite often to include pornographic pictures. Many of these attacks were the result of exploiting vulnerabilities in the applications that are hosted on the web site. This includes both production software and the example software that was distributed with nearly every web server. The software has problems of buffer overflows that allow a carefully constructed URL to give an attacker the ability to execute commands on the web server, which could in turn give the attacker access to the machine. The attacker could then change the contents of the web site.[9]

Logic Bomb

A logic bomb is a program that lies dormant until it is activated. It can be activated by anything that the computer system can detect. Often it is time-based (a time bomb), or based on the absence or existence of some data, such as when a programmer's name is no longer in the payroll file. This trigger can be almost anything. Once activated, the logic bomb will "deliver its payload." This payload is any type of destructive software, commonly the deleting of files. The destruction can be widespread or focused at specific individuals. With computers now in control of so many physical systems, the attack could actually become a physical attack.

---

[9] "Sanitizing User-Supplied Data in CGI Scripts," *CERT® Summary CA-97.06,* December, 1997.

> An employee of defense contractor General Dynamics, who was key to the development of the database of parts and suppliers for the weapon system that was under development for the U.S. government, discovered that the database was not being properly backed up. He decided to plant a logic bomb that would destroy the database after he had quit the company. His plan was to come back as a "highly paid consultant" to rebuild the system.
>
> After he quit, but before the bomb went off, another technician was investigating an unrelated performance problem and by accident came across the bomb and defused it. The administrator said that if this attempt had been successful, they would never have been able to trace the origin of the logic bomb.[10]

Logic bombs are often utilized with viruses. The virus is used to distribute the logic bomb, which waits on the target system until the preprogrammed time arrives for it to unleash its payload. These viruses are often named after the date that the payload is programmed to be delivered (e.g., Columbus Day, April Fool's Day).

Parasite

A parasite is a piece of code that is added to an existing program and draws information from the original program. It is used to gather information for which the hacker may not have privileges. By its definition it is a covert, nondestructive program. It may use a virus to spread around a system.

> A parasite was planted in a printer script, the program that formats the printed output, at a military site. The parasite was programmed to send a copy of everything that was printed to the individual who planted it. This gave him copies of files for which he did not have access, since the printer script ran with the permissions of the user who was printing the file. The perpetrator was soon so overwhelmed with the volume of output from the parasite that he rewrote it so that it only sent him "classified" files.[11]

---

[10]   "Programmer Accused of Plotting to Sabotage Missile Project," *The Risks Digest*, Volume 11, Issue 95, 28 June 1991.

[11]   "Hackers Invade Milnet," *Newsday*, 30 September 1987.

Sniffer

A sniffer is a program that watches data travel through the system looking for a particular type of information. The sniffer may be attached to a network interface to watch all the network traffic or to a disk interface to watch all the data flowing to or from the disk. Sniffers can also be parasites, inserted inside a system, like the print spooler or login system, secretly gathering information.

> In what officials called the biggest scam of its kind, two people are accused of using a scanner to steal more than 80,000 cellular phone numbers from motorists driving past on a busy Brooklyn highway. The black box scanner, or digital data interceptor, was still picking up numbers from unsuspecting cellular phone users when police arrived. Thieves could get anywhere from $500 for a number to $1000 for a cloned phone. The cellular phone industry estimates revenue losses to phone fraud at $1.5 million a day, according to Bell Atlantic-NYNEX.[12]

Spoof

A spoof is a person or a program who assumes the identity of another person or program. This false identity is used to either convince the victim to grant services or permissions that she should not have, or to implicate someone other than the attacker. Spoofs are not limited to computer systems. Any systems or process that does not verify identity could become the victim of a spoof.

> A major electronics vendor had a policy of accepting faxed orders from customers who had purchase agreements. These orders would be filled and shipped without verification. Two ex-employees configured their fax machine to report the actual customer's name and fax number and faxed orders on the customer's letterhead to their previous employer.
>
> The orders were filled and shipped to the supplied address which was an abandoned warehouse. The attacker would visit the warehouse later and pick up the equipment.[13]

[12]   Power, Richard, *Current and Future Danger*, 1998.
[13]   Computer Security Institute, "Introduction to Network Security," 1992.

Spoofing is a common attack against computer systems that have trust relationships. A trust relationship is when a computer will trust an individual or program that comes from another specific computer. The assumption is that the other computer has authenticated the user and, since the computer is trusted, its authentication can also be trusted. However, if the system is spoofed into believing that another system is actually the trusted system then the trusting system will then trust the spoofing system.

E-mail spoofing, or forging a false address, is one of the oldest and simplest of all spoofs. E-mail exchange takes place using the simple mail transport protocol (SMTP), which is a simple protocol consisting of text commands. These commands can be easily entered by hand. The receiving host trusts that the sending host is who it says it is. This method of e-mail forgery has been around since the early eighties, and does not require improperly obtained passwords or privileges. Today, an additional identity protocol is available to help identify e-mail forgeries, yet there are still numerous e-mail forgeries daily.

Trojan Horse

A Trojan horse is a useful or apparently useful program containing hidden code that, when invoked, performs some unwanted function. Trojan horses can be used to accomplish functions indirectly that an unauthorized user could not accomplish directly.

AT&T's Fraud Control Group and the fraud investigation unit of the US Federal Trade Commission have brought suit against three people from Long Island, NY. The group has implemented a highly sophisticated multimillion dollar scam which used a Trojan-horse attack to hijack users' modems that in turn initiated phone fraud resulting in expensive long-distance phone calls to the Republic of Moldova. Visitors to several sex-related Web sites were asked to download a viewer for free "adult" pictures. The viewer included a Trojan-horse program which would take over the user's computer. First the program turned off the computer's speakers, to prevent hearing the modem sounds. Then it hung up the line to which the modem was connected and dialed a Moldovan phone number. Moreover, the Trojan horse program wouldn't allow the modem to hang up even when the customer signed off the Internet. Through the Internet, the group was somehow even able to penetrate network security systems of several phone companies and reroute international phone calls so that they were answered in Scarborough, Ontario.[14]

---

[14]   *The Atlantic Monthly*, Volume 280, No. 3; pages 19-22, September 1997.

Virus

A virus is a program that infects another program by replicating itself into the host program. Considered by itself, the virus has three phases: the infection phase, where the host is infected from a previously existing virus; the activation phase, where this new copy is triggered to find another host to infect; the replication phase, where the virus finds a suitable host and copies itself to the host. Most viruses are destructive, carrying a logic bomb with them, which is separately activated to deliver its payload. However, some viruses do not; they merely replicate consuming resources. These are referred to as bacteria, or rabbits.

Historically, viruses have been primarily targeted at PCs. But, as systems become more and more standard, they will become more prevalent on larger systems as well. Viruses are transported from one system to another by being in a file that is moved from one system to another.

> Dell Computer's plant in Cork, Ireland suffered five days of down-time after the company discovered that 500 of its computers had been infected with the FunLove virus. Staff had to track down the source of the infection and eradicate the virus from all its systems. The attack is regarded as one of the most damaging seen in Europe. In addition to the lost production time, the incident damaged customer relations, with some customers complaining about the delay in delivery of their systems.[15]

Viruses, even if they themselves are not destructive, have the largest global impact of any malicious software. The cost of detecting and removing them in man-hours and computational resources is enormous. Today, every computer should be running a virus scanner, which means that every time that a file is brought onto the system it must be analyzed to see if it has a virus. Virus software must be continuously updated, since new viruses are introduced daily. The resources lost to this problem are enormous.

Worm

A worm is a program that is used as a transport mechanism for other programs. It utilizes the network to spread programs from one system to another. It will utilize a flaw in a network transport, such as network mail or remote process execution, to get its package from one system to another. The worm has three basic processes. First, it will search for a receptive system. Second, it will establish a connection to that system. Finally, it will transport its program to the remote system and execute the program. This program may contain a worm itself so it can spread further, or it may be any other type of malicious code.

---

[15] Taylor, Paul, "Dell loses five days' production time to FunLove Virus," Reuters, November 1999.

> In 1988, Robert Morris, Jr., wrote a worm program that exploited a number of vulnerabilities and replicated itself across the Internet. However, flaws in this Internet worm failed to detect if the system was already infected with the worm, so a system would be overwhelmed with multiple copies of the worm and the network was overwhelmed with the worm being transferred to target systems repeatedly. The worm itself did not have a destructive payload; the disruption of services came from the process of the migration of the worm itself.[16]

Collateral Damage

Collateral damage is damage that is caused by the side effects of the actual incident. Sometimes referred to as downstream effects, they are usually seen in systems that are dependant on the systems that are involved in the incident. Collateral damage is a relatively new concern in the area of information security. There was little need with centralized data centers. However, today's distributed environments increase the risk of suffering damage from attacks that were not focused at the organization.

It does not take a bomb blast, such as the one at the federal building in Oklahoma City, which damaged buildings and took out communications for blocks around the site, for a company to become the victim of an attack on another group or organization. Not all collateral damage is from malicious attacks.

> In the early days of mainframe computers, when their prices were in the millions of dollars, a lightning storm threatened a midwest university's new mainframe. The storm hit on Friday afternoon of a holiday weekend after the system manager had left for the weekend. However, he did call in on the system's support modem after the storm passed to see if the system was still running and had survived the storm, which it had. The problem was that a lightning strike had disabled the air conditioning unit for the building. When the system manager returned after the weekend, he found the system still running, more or less, in a computer room that was well over a hundred degrees.[17]

---

[16]   Page, Bob, "A Report on the Internet Worm," Computer Science Department, University of Lowell, 7 November 1988.

[17]   "Will you be ready when disaster strikes?," *PC Week*, 6 February 1995.

The Proximity Problem

In both the physical world and in cyberspace there is the issue of proximity. If the company shares an office building with other companies that have a higher risk of physical attack, your company now shares some of that risk. These physical attacks can be anything from bomb threats to picketers, or any situation that impacts on your company's operations.

On the Internet, proximity means who shares your network provider or your web space provider. If any of them are at risk as being a target, it is likely that an attack against them will impact your services. Online attacks generally cripple an entire ISP or they may take down a web server that is serving many web sites. There have been cases where other businesses involved in illegal activities will have had their computer equipment confiscated even though this equipment was used by other companies.

Your risk is a sum of all shared risks from those other organizations in close proximity.

The hacker group called "Hacking for Girlies" set their sights on Carolyn P. Meinel, the author of "The Happy Hacker," by attacking her web site which was hosted on Rt66 Internet. On Easter day of 1998, the owner of the ISP discovered that his web site had been altered. He disconnected his Internet service for the 20 hours it took to repair the damage. The hacker group returned to Rt66 again in August. This time the ISP was off the network for over 60 hours while the system was rebuilt. Even with its rebuilt security Rt66 lost 15% of its 5,000 or so members in the next three months.

Meinel says that on a personal level the hackers "have hardly done any harm to me. They hurt bystanders. They harm the ISPs and their customers." Meinel also says the hackers can come after her all they want. "Sure helps me sell more books," she contends.[18]

Guilt by Association

In today's business world of partnerships and joint ventures, your partners may bring more to the table than just their expertise. They may be involved in other business ventures or with other partners who make them a target.

Attackers have discovered that they can increase the effectiveness of an attack by enlisting the wrath of the target's partners, thus making these partners indirect targets. By attacking the partners and making sure that the *cause* the attacker is supporting is known, and that the only reason the partners were attacked was because of their relationship with the target, then the attacker may be able to enlist displeasure with the targeted organizations from its partners.

---

[18]   Peneberg, Adam, "We were long gone when he pulled the plug" *Forbes Online*, 16 November 1998.

Attackers will also make indirect attacks appear to come from their target to increase the aggravation toward the target organization. They may also direct attacks in both directions to cause mutual distrust.

The potential threats to an organization come from a wide variety of sources and may not have clear intentions. The total threat is the sum of all threats. This makes the job of assessing the threats more difficult.

> Someone breached security on the Staples Web site and redirected browsers to the Web site of Office Depot, the victim's major competitor. Staples announced on that it filed a federal "John Doe" lawsuit against its assailant(s) claiming damages for lost business and for the recovery effort. Staples suggested, and Office Depot confirmed, that they doubted that Office Depot was in any way responsible for the attack.[19]

---

[19]   "Hacker links Staples to online rival Office Depot," *Security Wire,* November 1999.

Checklist

— Evaluate the organization's level of threats.

— Evaluate the organization's public image.

— What is the threat from natural disasters (hurricane, earthquake, tornado, flood, fire)?

— What groups would disapprove of your organization?

— Does your type of business/industry draw protestors?

— Do any of your partners draw protestors?

— Do any of the systems directly process money?

— Do any physical neighbors draw targets?

— Do any online neighbors draw targets?

For every identified information asset, list the threats that could cause damage to that asset and determine the likelihood of that threat.

The following columns are added to the information inventory spreadsheet.

Threat	
Description	Likelihood

Threat

    Description – A description of the threat.
    Likelihood – The likelihood that the threat will cause an incident within a period of time.

CHAPTER 3

Loss Analysis

Total losses of $123.7 million from information security breaches were reported by 163 organizations or about $759,000 per organization.[20]

A loss analysis helps define the impact of the loss. This loss is expressed in both financial and operational terms. By understanding these impacts, managers can define the parameters for their business continuity and risk management programs. Without this information business managers cannot correctly set disaster recovery budgets for their organization.

The business impact of any specific loss is dependent on the scope of the loss, the amount of time that the loss is for, and the type of business. Most organizations can survive outages if they are not at critical times. Understanding these critical times and applications is a key part of a business impact analysis. A business impact analysis quantifies business metrics like the hourly cost of downtime. It enables the evaluation of minimum acceptable recovery requirements and cost/benefits tradeoffs.

The impact on the organization is dependent on the use of the information and how that information affects the businesses, particularly how the disclosure, corruption, or deletion of that information could negatively affect the organization.

Losses can be classified into the following nine categories:

- **Denial of Service** is the loss of *availability* and is the most visible of all losses. The loss of availability is immediately apparent to any user that needs access and is unable to get access.

- **Theft of Resources** is the unauthorized use of information system resources. This includes computational resources, network resources, and the resources of computer controlled systems.

---

[20]   "1999 CSI/FBI Computer Crime and Security Survey," *Computer Security Issues & Trends*, Spring 1999.

- **Corruption of Information** is the loss of *integrity* and may be the most devastating blow to an organization. If the quality of the resource is in question, then all the decisions that utilize that resource must also be in question.

- **Destruction of Information** is the deletion of information.

- **Theft of Information** is taking information for personal financial gain.

- **Disclosure of Information** is the loss of *confidentiality* and indicates that the resource has the potential to release information to unauthorized entities. This is generally the area of greatest concern to an organization.

- **Theft of Software** (a.k.a. Software Piracy) is stealing software to use personally or to sell to someone else. The software may be either commercial software or in-house developed software.

- **Theft of Systems** is the physical theft of property. Notebook and laptop computers are easy targets.

- **Disruption of Controlled Systems** is the interruption of systems that are monitored and controlled by computer systems.

Companies today have all types of electronic information. Company secrets or proprietary information are always a concern to the company. This is information that is unique to each individual company. Company secrets must be protected to protect the company. However, most companies today also have a large amount of information about individuals. For some companies this is just customer purchase information which is not given the security that it deserves. Theft of customer lists is the most common corporate espionage. Access to your customer list may be of great value to your competitor, and if that information is compromised, it may cause damage to your company.

Other companies have a great amount of information about individuals which, if stolen, may be damaging to the individual whose profile is disclosed, even if it doesn't damage the business directly. Some industries, such as financial and medical, have regulated requirements on the privacy of their customer's records. Other organizations need to be able to evaluate the risk to their reputation or civil liability of not adequately protecting customer records.

Many companies rely heavily on computer controlled systems, from environment control to factory robotics and automated warehouses. The disruption of these systems can shut down an entire business or be life threatening in the area of robotics and medical systems. Critical processes like these must have a fail-safe environment.

The severity of loss to a specific resource depends on that resource and its importance, the timing of the outage, and the duration of the outage.

Denial of Services

Denial of services is the most common of all losses. It can affect an organization's resources, people, property, information, infrastructure, or reputation. Whenever an organization is unable to use any of these resources there is a denial of service. "Outages" are a common occurrence. These outages may have greatly differing consequences depending on the time of day or the time of month. Disruption of services during a critical processing time may be disastrous while the same outage at another time may be inconsequential.

Being unable to access a resource when it is needed is always immediately detectable, and usually rapidly reported. However, the causes of outages, especially temporary outages, often go undetected. When services are restored, particularly when no human intervention is required, the effort to determine the cause of the outage is often eliminated. So some periodic temporary outages may continue for a long period of time as long as the impact is minimal.

Denial of services is always an annoyance creating a loss of productivity. However, it can often be much more than that. In some cases the losses are more dramatic and tangible. Consider the situation where law enforcement personnel would be unable to call for reinforcements or unable to check on the identity and background of an individual – situations that could be life threatening. More often the losses are financial, like stock traders who are unable to make trades, or as in this report:

> A 35-year-old British computer operator caused more than a half million pounds of damage to his employer, Thorn UK, by secretly disconnecting cables from their AS/400 minicomputer because of a grudge against his supervisor. Defense counsel argued that, in addition, he had cracked under the strain of repeated back-to-back day and night shifts. The system went down repeatedly until an expensive specialist flown in from the U.S. discovered the sabotage. He was sentenced to a year in jail.[21]

As organizations become more geographically dispersed and more interconnected with partner companies, their dependency on infrastructure increases. Malicious denial of service attacks, especially on infrastructure systems, is becoming more common and more costly.

The general procedure to minimize this type of loss is to either provide redundancy, so that there are multiple methods to access the resource or multiple resources that provide the same service, or to minimize recovery time so that the resource will be unavailable for as short a time as possible.

[21]   *U.K. Press Association News*, 9 July 1996.

Theft of Resources

Theft of resources is the unauthorized use of computer resources, usually computing power, network bandwidth, or any system service. It is difficult to put a dollar amount on this type of theft, since nothing is physically stolen: information, programs, and data are not taken, only resources are utilized. Often, the utilization of resources does not create a denial of services, only poorer performance.

> A 28-year-old computer expert allegedly diverted 2,585 US West computers to assist him in his effort to solve a 350-year-old math problem – the search for a new prime number. Investigators estimate that during a very short period he used 10.63 years worth of computer processing time – lengthening lookup time for customers' telephone numbers from five seconds to five minutes and causing calls to be rerouted to other states. At one point, the delays threatened to shut down the Phoenix Service Delivery Center. The man, a contract computer consultant working for a vendor for US West, told investigators that he had been working on the math problem for a long time, and that all that computational power at US West was just too tempting.[22]

However, theft of resources is just the tip of the iceberg. Stealing computer resources slows response time, making legitimate users wait, which in time-critical applications such as stock trading, law enforcement, and medical systems can be very costly. With response times slowed, automated systems may not be able to respond quickly enough to keep pace with the real world system that they control, which could lead to devastating results. Sufficient theft of resources can lead to denial of services.

Historically, it has been a common defense since the resources were not being used, that the perpetrator did not in fact steal anything. This is like stealing a car for a joyride and returning it, claiming that no crime was committed since no one else was using it when it was stolen.

Deletion of Information

The destruction of information will put an organization into recovery mode. Little productivity will occur while data is being restored. All too often destroyed data is unrecoverable, either because the recovery procedures are untested (and fail), or the data had not yet been backed up. With data acquisition systems, the data collected from the monitoring of real world events may not be reproducible. Once gone – it's gone forever. Information cannot be lost if there is a usable backup copy that can be used for recovery. Not all losses of information are due to malicious activities.

[22]   *Edupage*, 17 September 1998.

A major system crash at London's North Middlesex Hospital lead to administrative chaos, due to the lack of appropriate backup facilities. Hundreds of hours were spent attempting to retrieve corrupted data. The fault arose due to the unrelated failure of two hard disk drives. Attempts to reload the records from backup tapes also failed. As a result of the crash, nurses were limited in their access to over a million patient files.[23]

Since a large loss of data is highly visible, it is not often a tactic often used by attackers. However, it is not uncommon for an attacker to delete logs and log entries to eliminate the evidence of his or her activities. In some cases attackers have deleted entire systems to cover their tracks.

Theft of Information

Theft of information is the taking of information for personal gain. Corporate espionage and blackmail are just a couple of methods of converting information into money. It does not necessitate denial of services or destruction of the information. More often, the information is left just as it was so that the theft is not quickly discovered.

If competitors get access to an organization's secrets, then they have an unfair advantage. They can use this information to adjust their strategies to best exploit the vulnerabilities or to move a competing product onto the market sooner.

Cyber-criminals rifled through confidential computer records of a major Japanese bank and stole information on customers' names, telephone numbers, addresses and even birthdays, the bank said. The computer system was used for such purposes as managing customers' time deposits. Sakura Bank Ltd. said data on up to 20,000 of its 15 million individual customers could have been stolen and that it had confirmed that files were then leaked to a mailing-list vendor in Tokyo. A Sakura Bank spokesman said the thieves did not gain access to customer accounts and no money was stolen. [24]

Today, there is a rapidly growing crime based on the theft of personal information – identity theft. The assailant gathers enough personal information about the victim, such as a Social Security number, date of birth, and mother's maiden name, to be able to impersonate him or her

---

[23]   *Computer Weekly*, 1993
[24]   "Japan reports cyber bank heist," *Reuters*, 5 January 1998

financially. The perpetrator will apply for credit cards, take out loans, and otherwise trade on the good financial history of the victim. Often the victim will be unaware of the crime until a credit check show these debts or a collection agency tries to collect.

Disclosure of Information

Disclosure of information makes public information that is of a private or proprietary nature. Information disclosure can be either malicious or accidental. Malicious disclosure may be done by someone, often a disgruntled employee, who wishes to exact revenge on the organization for a perceived wrong, or by someone who disagrees with the activities that the organization is involved in and wishes to expose these activities. Rarely is personal gain a motive for information disclosure.

Information can be disclosed through social interaction. Social engineering and other standard information gathering techniques are used by reporters, spies, and others who wish to get information from people. Information can also be disclosed accidentally through social interaction. It is common to discuss work with friends and acquaintances, especially if they are in the same industry. However, people in the same industry are more likely to use the information gathered for their personal or professional advantage.

There are also many ways that information systems may accidentally disclose information. There could be inadequate information handling procedures, such as improper disposal of output containing proprietary information or transmission of proprietary information over unsecured communications (listening to internal voice mail with a cellular telephone). Information also can be disclosed from applications (such as the referrer variable used in browsers, which tells the web server what previous web page the browser was on).

Disclosure of company information can damage a company's reputation. However, disclosure of personal information entrusted to the company, such as employee information or customer information, can be very costly to the company in the form of legal defense fees.

A computer error caused American telecommunications provider GTE to publish mistakenly the unlisted phone numbers of roughly 50,000 customers in a street directory leased to telemarketers.

The directories contained the names, demographics, addresses, and business and residential phone numbers of customers in Southern California. But they were not supposed to include the details of customers who had paid to be unlisted.

Telephone directories are leased by many telephone companies to marketing companies that call listed customers and try to sell products or services. Many people pay their telephone companies to have their details excluded from these directories to prevent unwanted marketing calls.

The company said it first found out about the error when a customer told it their details had been published. If found negligent for releasing the phone numbers, GTE could be fined up to $30,000 for each affected customer. But a company spokesman said GTE was confident that action would not be taken by the California Public Utilities Commission, the local government watchdog that monitors California's utility companies.

A GTE spokesman said the company has worked with the commission from the outset and followed what was agreed on as a prudent course of action. GTE has personally contacted all the affected customers and has replaced almost all the directories containing the unlisted numbers, the spokesman said.

The company said it plans to offer the affected customers a new phone number, free unlisted status for one year worth between $1 and $1.50 per month, and a refund of $25 for residential customers or $100 for business customers.[25]

Corruption of Information

Information is at the very core of most business today. Decisions are made, customers are billed, and employees are rewarded based on information that is expected to be correct and accurate. When the information is not correct, errors start to accumulate and problems start to manifest themselves which can spell disaster.

Information that is stolen is usually quickly discovered. However, corrupted information has the potential of being undiscovered for a very long time, continuing to cause damage until it is found.

An Internet security firm identified 11 shopping-cart applications that used online forms that intruders could exploit to change prices or discounts at e-commerce sites. These shopping-cart applications use hidden fields in forms to define product parameters such as quantity, name, and price. That hidden data could be modified on a user's machine, then loaded back into the browser and added to the shopping cart. The shopping cart application would then change the price on the site's database or e-mail invoice. Shopping-cart software shouldn't rely on the Web browser to set the price of an item.[26]

---

[25]   Clark, Venessa, "GTE Prints 50,000 Unlisted Phone Numbers," *Technology News*, 20 April 1998.
[26]   Harrison, Ann, "Shopping-cart glitch could let e-shoppers change product pricing," *Computer World*, 02 February 2000.

Corrupted information can have the most serious and the longest lasting damage. If corruption goes unnoticed, then this bad information may be used, and assumed correct, for an indeterminate amount of time. Business decisions can be made with faulty information.

Good software testing for reasonable information will spot many issues of data corruption. Limits and bounds testing will detect data that is not reasonable and will be able to detect some corrupted information. It is the malicious corruption of information that will not be easily detectable and will have the potential to cripple an organization.

Businesses also have a large amount of personal information about their employees and their customers. Corruption of this information can have very devastating effects at a personal level. Organizations that do not adequately protect personal information may find themselves involved in issues of libel or worse.

Theft of Software

Theft of software, or software piracy as it is called, is a major concern for companies who are in the business of producing commercial software. However, this is only one aspect of software theft; many organizations that do not produce software commercially still produce software for internal use. The production of this software is expensive and represents a large number of jobs. Often this software offers a competitive advantage to a company by being part of the organization's processes that make it more efficient, profitable, or unique. Other companies are hindered by the costs of producing comparable software.

Many organizations' secrets are not only in the information they have, but are also imbedded in the software that they have created internally. Theft of an organization's proprietary software can disclose some of the organization's most private secrets. This theft may also deprive the organization of the ability to use the software if the original copy is destroyed in the process of the theft, leading to an inability to continue to do business.

> A Chinese national who worked for Ellery Systems, which had done very sophisticated work for NASA and the European Space Agency, was alleged to have transferred more than 122 proprietary source code files to someone in the People's Republic of China. Ellery sustained serious financial losses as well as hundreds of jobs, but charges against the man were dropped because they had failed to get a signed non-disclosure agreement from him.[27]

Theft of software costs more than the cost of the software. It impacts the ability of the business to remain solvent and it affects jobs and people's lives. Ellery Systems is out of business today.

---

[27]   "Ex-employee Arrested in Computer-file Theft," *Denver Post*, p. 1C, Feb. 25, 1994.

Theft of Hardware

Theft of computer systems continues to be the largest area of loss to an organization. Computer systems continue to become smaller and more prevalent. Computer thefts are on the rise with thousands of computers being stolen every day. Stolen computer equipment can be easily sold on the used market or stripped and its components sold. The widespread use of personal computers has produced a market for used computers and has increased the general knowledge of what computer equipment can be easily sold.

There have been numerous reports of laptop computers stolen in airports, hotel rooms and other public areas. Reports indicate that many stolen laptops were not random theft, but were taken specifically for the information that they contained.

Greater potential damage than the actual cost of the stolen hardware is the loss of the information contained within the hardware. A theft of hardware causes a denial of service (you cannot use the machine if it has been stolen), a disclosure of information (the information on the systems is out of your control and available to anyone who gets access to the machine), and loss of information (if the information existed only on the machine it is gone – generally forever).

> An employee garnered a philanthropic reputation for treating his co-workers to pizza in the cafeteria on Friday afternoons. But while his colleagues munched on pepperoni, the employee's accomplice – the pizza man – stuffed his delivery bag with laptop computers and left the building without being challenged.[28]

Physical theft of equipment requires physical deterrents, such as cabling systems to furniture and applying physical labels or tattoos (electronic labels) to the computers. For information to be secured, the system that houses the information must be secured. The increased portability of these systems requires more data protection through the use of encryption.

The FBI reports that over 90% of stolen equipment is never recovered.[29]

Disruption of Computer Controlled Systems

All aspects of society are becoming increasingly controlled by computer, and so the costs of losses are not contained within the information technologies organization. There are often very large downstream costs – even life-threatening ones – when computer-controlled systems fail in places like hospitals or airtraffic control towers..

The more complicated a physical system is, the more likely that the system employs computerized controls. Which means the more difficult it is to manage a system manually, the more likely it is that it will be automated. So if the computer controlled systems are disrupted, it is

---

[28] "Stop Thief," *CFO Magazine*, October 1997.
[29] "Red Alert," *PC World*, April 1997

likely that the system will be difficult to operate manually, even at a reduced rate, if at all. This is why the more complicated and critical systems are most vulnerable to information security attacks.

All of the major systems, such as power, transportation, and communications, are extensively automated. We have seen where even limited outages can ripple through the system causing a large impact. Smaller systems (medical, security, environmental control), too, are becoming more automated, to the point that there are few areas where an outage to an automated system would not make an impact. Damaging these control systems can have huge ramifications – even deadly ones.

> A Massachusetts teen hacker pled guilty in return for two years probation, a fine, and community service after having disabled communications to the air traffic control tower at the Worcester, Massachusetts, airport. On March 10, 1997, the hacker broke into a Bell Atlantic computer system, causing a computer crash that disabled the phone system at the airport for six hours as well as phone service to 600 homes in the nearby town of Rutland.
>
> The computer crash knocked out phone service at the control tower, airport security, the airport fire department, the weather service, and carriers that use the airport. Also, the tower's main radio transmitter and another transmitter that activates runway lights were shut down, as well as a printer that controllers use to monitor flight progress. [30]

From time to time, software bugs will cause outages in computer controlled systems. (Look at the panic and speculation that the Y2K bug caused.) Bugs in software are usually easy to detect once they appear. However, if a system is attacked with the goal of disrupting a control system, the attacker will most likely attempt to cover his tracks so that the fault will not be detected. He may produce false readings so that the monitoring systems will not detect the failure in the controlled system.

The U.S. government has concerns about the national infrastructure's ability to be adequately protected. Power systems, transportation systems, and communication systems are all computer controlled and subject to computer attack. Since the companies that supply these critical infrastructure elements are private companies, the government does not have direct control over the level of security that these companies implement.

Disruption of communications and other basic services can cause panic and are at the heart of information warfare.

---

[30]   "Teen Hacker Faces Federal Charges," *CNN Interactive*, 18 March 1998

Checklist

— Quantify the losses based on the different types of losses.

For every information asset, evaluate both the monetary loss and the loss of productivity to the organization for each type of loss.

The following columns are added to the information inventory spreadsheet.

Denial of Service		Theft		Destruction		Corruption		Disclosure	
Time	Money	Time	Money	Time	Money	Time	Money	Time	Money

Denial of service – losses from the information asset being unavailable
Theft – losses from the information asset being stolen
Destruction – losses from the information asset being destroyed
Corruption – losses from the information asset being corrupted
Disclosure – losses from the information asset being made public

Identifying Vulnerabilities

In 1997, the CERT®/CC received 326 vulnerability reports and handled 2,134 computer security incidents affecting more than 146,484 sites.[31]

A vulnerability is a condition, weakness, or absence of security procedures, technical controls, physical controls, or other controls that could be exploited by a threat. Vulnerabilities are often analyzed in terms of missing safeguards. Vulnerabilities contribute to risk because they may "allow" a threat to harm the system.

Vulnerabilities are difficult to predict. However, when a vulnerability is discovered it is not uncommon for the same vulnerability to appear in a wide variety of similar applications. This is in some part due to the same software libraries being used by many applications, and in some part due to the fact that many applications have common roots in earlier applications. There are also the cases where software that had a vulnerability repaired will have the same vulnerability re-appear in later versions. This is generally caused by inadequate change management or source code controls. Version control is an involved process on large software systems. However, these types of recurring vulnerabilities allow for some proactive processes to predict and test for yet undiscovered vulnerabilities. Even though the security industry would like you to think otherwise, most vulnerabilities are not discovered until they are misused.

It is wise to benefit from the losses of others by repairing the vulnerabilities that have been discovered by those who have been compromised. This requires the monitoring of security advisories. These advisories describe, in general, a security flaw that has been detected and how to repair it. The repair may be a change in administration (changing permissions), upgrading to a newer version, applying a security patch, or disabling the service. Advisories are issued by hardware or software vendors, as well as security organizations (generally, emergency response teams) who have had to respond to an incident caused by the vulnerability.

---

[31]   CERT® Coordination Center 1997 Annual Report.

Location of Vulnerabilities

Vulnerabilities can be located in hardware, software, infrastructure, and in security procedures.

Hardware

Hardware is not just composed of unintelligent boards and wires. Today, most hardware systems include a base level of programming (firmware). Some of this firmware requires physical replacement to change the programming while others do not. Hardware is often harder and more expensive to fix, so vulnerabilities are less likely to be repaired and more likely to remain in service long after the vulnerability is identified. When replacement of hardware is required, the financial investment in or incompatibility of that hardware or incompatibility often makes it difficult or unrealistic to upgrade. Like all programs, there is also the possibility of bugs that can be exploited or features that can be abused.

Generally, the exploitation of hardware vulnerability leads to a denial of service. For example, there was a well-known vulnerability in a laser printer where a user could download a new communication configuration (line speed, stop bits, etc.) and then password-protect the new configuration so that it could not be revised without the new password.

Some hardware bugs can also cause physical damage. A number of early PC monitors and terminals could be damaged by switching the refresh rate repeatedly, and some disk drives could be physically damaged by seeking to locations that were outside appropriate operating range.

Since hardware flaws are at the lowest level of an information system, compromising a hardware flaw will usually compromise all the software and information that utilized that hardware. Vulnerabilities in hardware can be devastating, yet hardware flaws contribute to only a small portion of exploited vulnerabilities.

Software

Software includes both operating systems (software that controls the computer) and applications (that which does work for the user). Today both operating systems and applications are large software systems. Software vulnerabilities are the most prevalent type of vulnerability and the most exploited. Vulnerabilities in application software can span different hardware systems and operating systems.

Developing large software systems is a monumental task involving large numbers of programmers in diverse locations over an extended period of time. In these large systems the software designers are not directly involved with the actual development of the software. Often there is little communications between the design team and the developers.

Most of the code in a software project is rarely executed. It is involved in input and output and exception handling. These are the areas that are most often exploited, in some part because they are least tested. Many exploited software bugs rely on very specific events that are not likely to exist during normal operations, making the job of testing all possible scenarios extremely difficult.

Infrastructure

Infrastructure outages can be just as devastating to an organization as a system outage. When the information consumer is unable to do his job because the communications network is down, or the power is unavailable to the information systems, or the building climate control is not working, trouble is nearby. The larger problem is that the infrastructure is under the control of outside organizations. You cannot control the level of security or redundancy that your electric supplier implements.

Infrastructures are generally huge systems and networks (e.g., the U.S. power grid, global telecommunications) which are difficult to administer due to their size. Imagine patch maintenance on every phone switch on the globe. Upgrades are very expensive, so old systems stay in operation long after the security flaws are known. Trickle-down implementations redeploy the systems that were replaced by new systems, so that the old system is still in operation. New technologies are introduced slowly, only as old systems are discarded. The size of the systems creates many points of entry for attackers.

The components of infrastructure systems are very interdependent. Heating and cooling systems require power systems. The poles that carry the power lines to your location are often the same poles that carry the telephone and computer networks.

Processes

Security processes can be exploited to compromise information. Any flaw in a security process has the potential to be implemented and carried out in day-to-day practices. Usually, however, the problems are that security policies are misinterpreted or are not properly implemented and this is what causes the vulnerability. Policies have a tendency not to be updated very often, and if they do not adequately address new issues created by new technologies or new business processes, they, too, can become outdated and the source of security vulnerabilities.

Known Vulnerabilities

When identifying vulnerabilities you should start with what is already known. Known vulnerabilities account for the largest part of successful attacks. By the time a vulnerability becomes widely known, "hacker tools" (programs that exploit the vulnerability) will be available. These programs become very widely distributed and integrated into larger, easy-to-use "toolkits." So anyone, without concern for level of skill, has the ability to exploit all known vulnerabilities. Consequently all known vulnerabilities must be addressed.

Vendors have become amazingly quick in their ability to respond to new vulnerabilities with patches. Therefore, there is usually very little time between when a vulnerability becomes known and when there is a patch available for it. However, many sites do not consistently implement security patches. Nearly every known vulnerability has a fix or patch that repairs the vulnerability. Not implementing fixes to known vulnerabilities is being derelict in your duties to protect the organization's information assets. Your software vendor should be able to give you a listing of all security patches.

A variety of independent organizations track software vulnerabilities and fixes. These organizations have security advisory mailing lists that send out a message when a new vulnerability is detected. These mailings will indicate the appropriate precautions to protect the systems from the vulnerability.

> An unknown criminal hacker attacked the PANIX Internet Service Provider in New York City. Using the "SYN-flooding attack," in which a stream of fraudulent TCP/IP requests for connections to non-existent Internet addresses overwhelms a server, the hacker denied service to legitimate users. Within a week, TCP/IP specialists had patches to protect against this denial-of-service attack. Even though the incident was well-publicized and the fixes for the vulnerability were published, successful exploits utilizing this vulnerability continue.[32]

Security Design Flaws

Most security issues come from software with poorly designed security. Not that the software was poorly designed, more often security was never considered in the software design. Security design and testing is notably different than normal software design and testing. Software testing checks for accuracy of results and the rejection of expected exceptions. Security testing requires testing the unexpected. Software designers assume reasonable input so systems are built to only handle what is expected. These types of assumptions are often found in client-server applications where the assumption is that the information that is transmitted between the client and server could only come from the other, when in fact any program that connects to the port can communicate to the application. These are the types of errors that are often exploited by hackers to penetrate a system.

> 3Com issued a security advisory stating that customers should immediately change the SNMP Community string from the default to a proprietary and confidential identifier known only to authorized network management staff. This was due to the fact that the admin password was available through a specific proprietary MIB

[32]   Essick, Kristi, "Web Hosting Service Downed by Hacker," *PC World,* B1, 18 December 1996.

variable when accessed through the read/write SNMP community string.

The advisory was issued in response to the widespread distribution of special logins intended for service and recovery procedures issued only by 3Com's Customer Service Organization under conditions of extreme emergency, such as in the event of a customer losing passwords. Due to this disclosure, some 3Com switching products were vulnerable to security breaches caused by unauthorized access via special logins.

Customers were urged to log in to their switches and proceed to change the password via the appropriate password parameter to prevent unauthorized access for the accounts.[33]

Outlived Design

Many security design flaws come from the environment in which the original system was designed. Many software applications were written for desktop computers with DOS or early Windows environments that did not allow for multiple users or multiple copies of the same program to be running at the same time. The issues that were created from a multitasking environment were therefore not addressed. It was simply not necessary; the operating system did not allow for it. Today, however, those same programs are running on systems that allow multiple users or allow multiple copies of the software to run simultaneously and have opened the door to problems that are beyond the original design.

Older network protocols (e.g., telnet, ftp) were not designed with much concern about security. At that time the network that the systems were attached to were local area networks that generally did not leave the confines of a single laboratory, and certainly never left an administration domain.

Much of this early code has become "sacred code." It works, but no one understands it, so no one is willing to maintain it out of fear that they might break it and not be able to fix it. This code is often involved with interfacing with other programs, possibly programs from other organizations. The level of communication and coordination required to test changes to the code that controls these interfaces makes it unfeasible to update them. New software that is written to interact with these ancient protocols must therefore be written to be compatible with the old software, even to the point of reimplementing known vulnerabilities so that it is "bug level compatible."

It is nearly impossible to effectively add security to a system after it is designed. Scrapping the old system and building new ones that embrace new enterprise-wide security is the only effective solution.

[33]   "I-052: 3Com® CoreBuilder and SuperStack II LAN Vulnerabilities" *CIAC Advisory* , 20 May 1998.

Software Sources

Security is a matter of trust. You need to be able to trust your software suppliers. This is one of the reasons that some organizations will have a list of approved software suppliers and policies against using freeware and software from unknown sources. Free software may be quite good. However, it is difficult to monitor the quality, honesty, and reliability of software from a relatively anonymous author. Even in the cases where source code is made available to be inspected before it is implemented, it is difficult to verify software with only the source code.

Software from unauthorized sources can lead to many security issues. The security policy should clearly state the company's position on what are appropriate sources of software and what the process is to put the software onto the system. This should include both a reference to your "approved software list," which should contain details on the process to obtain software that is on the list and software that is not, and a reference detailing any corporate license agreements that the company may have.

If you are in an environment where the use of "freeware" is prevalent, or people regularly bring software onto your system, you are at greater risk of virus infection. You may wish to create a quarantine system. A quarantine system is a system on which any incoming software must live for a period of time so it can be checked for viruses and validated for proper software behavior. This system can also detect Trojan horses and spoofs. Virus detection is much the same as detecting parasites. You should petition your software suppliers to supply the size and checksum information with all of their software so you can be sure that you have a clean system.

Evaluating the security strength of purchased software is a difficult task. Evaluation of the security details is not possible without access to the source code. However, there are things that can be evaluated that will indicate the quality of the software.

With major software suppliers, one can evaluate their track record. How reliable and secure has their software been in the past? How quickly do they respond to a reported problem? What do their other customers think? Is there a user community? Does the software conform to appropriate security standards and integrate with security products? All of these things must be considered, with a special emphasis on security.

Common source trees for multiple applications increases productivity and common behavior, but bugs appear in all applications that share the buggy source. This also means that fixing one bug will repair many vulnerabilities. Standards-based software is often implemented from a reference implementation. Errors in that reference implementation will often be found in many of the implementations.

A huge amount of software, especially Internet software, has a common genesis. The origins of the Unix operating system, web browsers, and other software each have a core of software. Much of the software available today still contains a great deal of this common code. This is why when a vulnerability is found, it is a vulnerability to a wide selection of applications.

Software Development

Many organizations have a large and widely dispersed software development environment. Often different software development groups will interpret security statements differently, and thereby implement security differently. It is essential that all of these software development groups understand the importance of security and adhere to a globally accepted set of standards. If any one group does not adequately secure its software, that software may be able to be utilized to subvert the rest of the systems. The use of a central repository for security software by all development groups and the use of standard security programming interfaces can help facilitate a consistent security implementation.

Security technologies are rapidly evolving as new tools become available daily. Standard security APIs have to be deployed to be able to take advantage of these new technologies. If standards are not available or the selected tool does not support the standard, code isolation should be used to improve the ability to implement.

Poor change management processes can lead to incorrect or increased software modules being included into a product. This is how developer code is released in a product or why a bug that is fixed in one version shows back up in a later version.

Much of the oldest code relates to where the software interfaces with other software or with users. When new software is written it is often built to match these interfaces, so that the old code will not have to be rewritten, and to avoid breaking this interface. Changes to software interfaces require changes and testing of all of the software that utilizes that interface. Often all of the software that uses the interface is not under the control of one department, so coordinating changes to the interface may require the cooperation and synchronization of developers from many departments.

Re-usable code has increased the productivity of software developers. However, flaws in the libraries of code that is reused get propagated to all the software that utilizes those libraries. Security flaws in common libraries can cause vulnerabilities in all the software that uses the library.

Large software products generally require the integration of software from multiple sources. Communication is key where software is developed by multiple teams of developers. This level of communication can difficult when the software is from multiple companies. Interfaces are built to written specifications that can be interpreted differently by different developers.

Software modules must take control of their own destiny. They cannot depend on external environment to take care of them. They must perform sanity testing of their input and data to be assured that it is reasonable. They must manage their own environment and not be dependent on the environment supplied to them. This leads to a new version of an old adage: *Garbage in – Diagnostic out.*

Software Security Testing

Organizations that are developing software need to include security testing in their software testing strategy. Most software testing tests the accuracy of the results and the exclusion of expected erroneous information. However, it is the unexpected input that can cause software systems to fail and open security vulnerabilities.

The following are a number of common software issues that are exploited and should be tested for:

- **Buffer overflows** are one of the most exploited software vulnerabilities. Applications create a fixed size buffer for data and then they do not validate that the data being put into the buffer will fit. The extra data that overflows the buffer may end up in an area from which the operating system or an application may treat it as instructions to be executed. This allows the attacker to supply instructions to the system. Buffer overflows can come about because of changes in the software, changes to interfaces, or unexpected input. Expect the unexpected and test for the impossible.

- **Race conditions** and other timing issues are problems that are created by instructions not always being executed in the same order. This is an issue with multitasking operating systems or processes that are dependent on resources on multiple computers. Software with timing issues may have been written originally for systems that did not support multitasking and are now being run on systems that do, or the software was developed on systems that perform at a significantly different speed than the production system.

- **Exception handling** is the process of managing unexpected events. These include divide by zero, interrupts, signals, etc. Software that halts due to an exception may leave a debug file that will contain the information that the software was processing, or it may invoke a debug process that will leave the user in complete control of the software and its data. Many programs depend on the operating system to handle these exceptions, but this cannot be relied upon. Different operating systems and different versions (even different configurations of the same operating system) will handle exceptions differently. Software must manage exceptions itself.

- **Software interfaces** are where software is exposed to the outside world. There is no guarantee of the quality or "correctness" of the information that crosses this interface, so software must be self-protective. It must test all the information that crosses the interface. There can be no assumptions.

Normal software testing processes, such as source code analysis and exhaustive source code execution, can be used to locate software security design flaws. However, the testing procedures must be changed to focus on security issues such as testing for unexpected input, processing beyond endpoints, and the handling of invalid input.

Unfortunately, the huge push to deploy software at breakneck speeds in Internet time leads to software systems being released and implemented with inadequate testing. Some software companies view problem reporting and bug fixing as software testing. Many companies that a few years ago would never have upgraded to a new operating system until it had been released for six months or a year are now running their business on beta release operating systems. Time-to-market issues have led some companies to release software without adequate testing. They use their customers as testers. This tactic saves the software company time and money and costs the customer in failures.

Innovative Misuses

Software designers focus on the use and function of the software for which it is designed. Little thought is given to how the software could be misused. Finding ways to misuse software requires a level of creativity that is hampered by being closely involved with the software often. The developers are so in tune with what it *should* do, they cannot see what it *might be able* to do.

Innovative misuses are particularly common with client-server or distributed applications. Often the client-server interface is designed and implemented on both the client and the server by the same people. They do not consider the possibility that any software other than what they wrote will be able to interact with either the client or server, so they will not design, implement, or test for anything beyond what is expected. This creates an opportunity for creative misuse.

Innovative misuse of software is one of the most difficult areas in which to be proactive. It requires that you step out of the box; Do the unexpected; have an understanding of how innovative misuses work and understand how someone could misuse the software.

This is an area where external consultants can be very valuable. A good tiger team, consultants who attack the system as hackers would, is familiar with attack techniques and, being detached from the software, they are not influenced by knowing too much about the proper execution of the system.

Many of the innovative misuses of information systems come from the unknown effects of new protocols. New protocols are generally untested, as is the software to support them.

Systems must work correctly, despite the effects of external influences. Attackers may be able to influence the environment that the system is in thereby affecting the operation of the system. Information systems must be built fail-safe so that when they do fail the information will remain safe.

> Pirate broadcasters have learned how to use the Radio Data System (RDS) to force car radios that implement the standard to stay tuned to the pirates' broadcasts while within range of their transmitters. A radio with active RDS will switch temporarily to any station that broadcasts the appropriate embedded digital signal. This is intended to allow reception of brief traffic announcements, but

> the pirates repeatedly send the signal in their broadcasts to keep such radios tuned to them. The problem can be avoided by switching off the RDS feature on a radio, but then of course one loses legitimate traffic information.[34]

Incorrect Implementation

Incorrect implementation is one of the most commonly exploited vulnerabilities. Implementation issues arise from poorly trained administrators, poorly documented systems, and simple mistakes. Very minor issues such as wrong ownership or permissions on a single file can create a vulnerability that can compromise the entire information network. The level of security of most systems is very dependent on how the system is implemented, installed, and administered.

> Windows Magazine reported that many web sites are unprotected against infiltration. Using standard web search engines, the investigators discovered that many sites allow unrestricted read- and even write-access to files on the web server through ordinary browser programs. An error in the web server configuration made the directories visible.[35]

Initially Unsecured

Most systems come out of the box with minimal security. They may even have known security vulnerabilities in their default configuration. Systems will usually not implement security features by default; security is still viewed as an add-on, leaving the choice of the desired security to the customer.

Securing systems is not always easy or straightforward. The security features may not even be discussed in the manual or, at best, the details on the implementation of the security features are not easily found. Additionally, implementing security features generally complicates system administration.

Enable Security Features

Many times system administrators fail to enable all the available security features. Most systems do not have the security features enabled as a default. It is left to the customer to enable the security features required for their environment. Even when the security features are en-

---

[34]   "Radio pirates steal listeners," *BBC News*, 6 January 2000.
[35]   Methvin, David W., "Safety on the Net," *Windows Magazine*, August 1996.

abled correctly, there are other basic system features that may make the security features ineffective. A common problem is incorrect implementation of basic permissions.

Administration

Security often takes a back seat to other administrative concerns, such as production schedules, user issues, and the day-to-day care and feeding of information systems. System administrators are often not well trained, especially in the area of security. Many system administrators have found themselves as caretakers of the systems that were given to them as tools, spending too much time taking care of their tools instead of the work that they were originally hired to do.

Change management is one of the most valuable tools at the disposal of administrators. Good quality change management procedures track the changes of the environment so that the state of the environment is known for any point in time. This allows for rapid elimination of changes that were not involved in the incident and serves as an indicator to those that might be involved.

Administration logs will track changes made by administrator and facilitate the isolation of administrative errors. Administrator errors are of greater concern than normal user errors. Since administrators have greater privileges than normal users, their errors can be more devastating. Administrator logs should be created and maintained by the information system. However, many of the activities that administrators and operators perform are more peripheral to the system than on the system. These activities should have manual logs that are maintained by the administrators and operators and can be correlated with automated logs, such as physical access logs.

Documentation

Documentation about security features and their administration is usually limited and difficult to locate. Often, the standard administration manuals do not include use of the security features, and in some cases implementing security features changes the normal administration procedures. Sometimes the security manuals are not included in the standard set of manuals and have to be ordered separately.

Patches and bug fixes often have extremely limited documentation. They are viewed as one-time releases with no long-term support, making user level documentation a low priority.

Social Engineering

Social engineering is the ability to achieve a goal through the use of effective persuasion. Social engineers are able to convince someone to do something they shouldn't, much in the same way a con artist would con you. There are a wide variety of methods used, but some of the most common include sympathy (I can't get this to work, can you help?), empathy (I understand. Tell me your problems and maybe I can help), admiration (You are so good at this, can you show me how?), and intimidation (If you don't get me that information, you'll be in big trouble!).

Social engineering relies on the helpfulness and politeness of workers, just as people will dutifully hold open a door for the person behind them when entering a controlled access building. People are very willing to help someone who seems to be having trouble. Surprisingly often, they will supply information if they are asked.

There are a variety of tactics that are employed. One is making an urgent request just before quitting time. Since the employee wants to leave on time, he will be more likely to bypass procedures (such as validating the requestor) to expedite his departure home.

There was a rash of incidents in which companies who owned DEC computers received calls from an individual who identified himself as a software troubleshooter working for Digital Equipment Corporation. He informed the person administering the system that there was a widespread problem and that he was too busy to come onsite and fix the problem, but he would be able to talk the operator through the process if he had remote access. He would then request the dial-up telephone number and the operator's login and password. The attacker was soon able to compromise the system with the assistance of the computer operator. Some of the victims contacted DEC only to discover that there was no widespread problem and no technician by the name that they were given. The FBI was contacted and an investigation was started. However, they were unable to gather enough evidence to determine the identity of the attacker or whether any federal laws were broken. The case was dropped.[36]

Generally, people want to do what is right, so it is vital that everyone knows what the right thing to do is. They must be educated about social engineering, and what to do to protect themselves and the organization from these types of attacks. Awareness programs are important in keeping the information fresh in the minds of those who need to defend themselves against the social engineer.

Technical solutions solve technical problems. People problems require personal solutions.

---

[36]   Murphy, Kim, "Ex-computer Whiz Kid held on New Fraud Counts," *Las Angeles Times,* 16 December 1988.

Checklist

— Examine and test the organization's security policies and processes.

— Perform a social engineering test against your company.

For computer systems:
— Monitor security incident advisory reports.
— Implement security patches.
— Test for known vulnerabilities.

For applications from an external source:
— Monitor security mailing lists.
— Monitor incident advisories.
— Monitor vendor patch list.
— Implement patches.

For applications from an internal source:
— Evaluate software development process for security issues.
— Include security standards in software design.
— Implement software management and control procedures.
— Implement software security testing.

CHAPTER 5

Assigning Safeguards

Seventy-eight percent of organizations were not confident their network was safe from internal attack, while 50 percent were not confident about an external attack.[37]

Every part of the risk analysis up to this point has been focused on determining what to protect, what to protect it from, where to put the protection, and how much protection is necessary. This is the phase where decisions are made on how to best implement safeguards.

Safeguards are applied to reduce risk to an acceptable level. This level is a business decision based on a financial evaluation, weighing the value of the resource, cost of loss, size of threat, and likelihood of vulnerabilities. Once the evaluation is completed, appropriate safeguards for each specific resource can be implemented.

Safeguards must adequately protect the information, addressing it in all of its forms. They must be appropriately installed and maintained and must be cost effective, creating a minimal impact on day-to-day operations. They must be easy to use, difficult to bypass, and interoperable with all other security systems. What good is it to secure information on the computer when printouts are left on desks overnight in plain view, or thrown out in the dumpster without benefit of shredding?

Safeguards can be either protective, protecting the information before there is an incident, or reactive, protecting the information when an incident is detected. Both types of safeguards are required. Protective safeguards prevent most incidents, but, since nothing is completely comprehensive, detective safeguards protect the system when something slips through the protective safeguards. In all cases, safeguards must be consistent, comprehensive and cost effective.

---

[37]   Ernst & Young. *1998 E&Y Global Information Security Survey.*

- **Consistent** so that implementation across different platforms (desktops, servers, network devices), different operating systems (Unix, NT), different locations (network connectivity has made physical locations irrelevant), and different organizations (interconnected systems allow one organization's lax security to compromise others), will run smoothly.

- **Comprehensive** so that every system affords the same level of protection to the enterprise. Information security policies affect all areas of your organization and require both broad-based and top level support. If information security is not corporate priority, its effectiveness will be compromised.

- **Cost-effective** so that the amount of protection reflects the value of the information. The amount of protection required is based on the value of the information that is being protected and the likelihood that the information will suffer a loss. To understand the scope of this issue one must be able to define the potential impact on the business. This requires that a business impact study be performed.

Safeguards reduce risk through one or more of the following methods:

Avoidance

Avoidance is a proactive safeguard intent on keeping security incidents from occurring and is the preferred method of safeguarding information. It is always easier to avoid an incident than to deal with it after the fact.. Security incidents can be avoided by employing a number of processes, including:

Reducing Threats

Reduce threats by changing the perception of the organization. Many threats to an organization, especially electronic threats, are from cyberactivists – individuals who are acting based on beliefs in a cause. These threats are based on the perception that the organization is somehow threatening the cause in which they believe. Sometimes the perception is incorrect, so an education campaign could inform these people of the organization's actual position. Sometimes the perception is correct, so the organization may have to evaluate its business practices or business relationships.

Removing Vulnerabilities

Eliminate vulnerabilities by repairing the vulnerability or changing practices that lead to a vulnerability. This process requires an understanding of vulnerabilities, where they come from, and how they are exploited. It also requires a commitment to constantly monitor for new vulnerabilities and to continuously work to eliminate them. In the data center, for example, this translates to patching the systems and not permitting unnecessary services.

Limit Access

Limit access to reduce the number of entry points into the information system and limit the number of places attacks can originate. This can greatly reduce the complexity of avoiding a security incident.

Adding Safeguards

Add safeguards to further protect the resource from unauthorized utilization. This generally means a more restrictive environment where more identification and authentication is required. This impacts all of those who use the information and must be accompanied with an awareness program so that they will understand the importance of this additional effort; otherwise complaints from valid users may be heard loud enough by management to reduce the security safeguards to mollify the users.

It is important to reduce the risk as much as possible with avoidance. However, risk can never be completely avoided, so it is just as important that other methods be implemented.

Transference

Transference of risk allows an organization to limit losses to a predefined, predictable amount based on legal contracts. Insurance policies clearly define coverage and deductions, and outsourcing contracts stipulate responsibilities and recourse. Service providers define service levels and appropriate remuneration for not meeting these levels.

Transference is the process of shifting the risk to another organization. This can be accomplished by purchasing insurance or other forms of financial relief, or by outsourcing operations.

Insurance

An insurance policy is generally part of an organization's overall risk management plan. The policy transfers the risk of loss to the insurance company in return for an acceptable level of loss (i.e., the insurance premium). Because many computer-related assets (e.g., software and hardware) account for the majority of an organization's net worth, they must be protected by insurance. If there is a loss to any of these assets, the insurance company is usually required to pay out on the policy.

Today, many organizations are offering "hacker policies" to Internet businesses that compensate them from losses caused by hacker attacks. These policies do not cover losses caused from inside attacks.

An important factor is the principle of culpable negligence. This places part of the liability on the victim if the victim fails to follow a "standard of due care" in the protection of its assets. If a victimized organization is held to be culpably negligent, the insurance company may be required to pay only a portion of the loss.

Numerous companies are now offering insurance for e-commerce web sites. The coverage of these policies varies greatly. Some will cover loss from dishonest, fraudulent, or malicious acts committed by an employee; from an intruder who uses stolen credit cards; from computer viruses or break-ins; and from extortion, while others are limited to external attacks.

The Internet presents a whole new risk of exposure. If you had a breach of security at your web site and your web site revenue stream was interrupted for 12 hours, your regular insurance policy wouldn't cover that loss because you had no loss during that breach. It's not like physical damage or money stolen. Traditional insurance covers only physical loss and the net loss of doing business. E-commerce policies need to cover break-ins and theft as well as the downtime that can cost a site business. They need to address both business-to-business and retail e-commerce sites.

Many of these policies require that the applicants be subject to a security risk assessment before being covered.[38]

Outsourcing

Outsourcing can be used to transfer some of the risk of a security incident. Outsourcing data center operations is becoming more prevalent; disaster recovery operations are frequently outsourced. If other organizations are operating the information systems environment, they generally absorb a certain amount of the risk. Contracts with guaranteed service levels, which clearly define the level of risk, are becoming more common. Network connectivity and security are often outsourced to an ISP.

Mitigation

Mitigation is the process of minimizing the impact of an incident. This requires developing and deploying strategies and procedures to rapidly respond to an incident and to reinstate services with a minimum of impact. These are your security incident and your disaster response plans. Everyone must practice risk mitigation since avoidance and transfer will not completely eliminate your exposure to risk.

The key elements to mitigating risk are:

[38]   Patrizo, Andy, "Trouble Indemnity for Web Sites," *Wired News*, 20 January 2000.

Reduce Scope

Reducing the scope of the damage from a security incident is key to risk reduction. Minimizing the interaction between systems and reducing the level of unverified trust will reduce the scope of a security incident. Anything that can be done to segregate or compartmentalize systems will make it more difficult for a security incident to spread from system to system.

Improved Detection

Improve detection so that intrusions will be detected more rapidly and so that no intrusion will go undiscovered. Detection can be improved by increasing the places it can look to find improper behavior. This will improve the coverage of the detection system across the enterprise. Improved detection will also come from improving its ability to more accurately detect malicious behavior by increasing its understanding of new and different malicious behavior. Making more logs available to the detection system can improve intrusion detection since the system will have more information to base its decisions.

Rapid Response

Rapid response minimizes the time that the incident has to cause damage. The response must be planned and practiced so that it will be effective. Speed and effectiveness are key to bringing an incident under control and ending it in a timely and cost effective manner.

The methods used to recover from system outages should be based on what will minimize business losses. These contingencies should be evaluated before an incident, so the process can be understood and practiced. Decisions should be made on when the recovery process should give way to invoking the disaster plan.

Risk mitigation is what disaster planning and preparedness is all about. The disaster response plan is completely focused on how to minimize the incident's impact on the organization. Information security plans should capitalize on the effort already put into a disaster response plan. The evaluations that have been done to determine the cost of downtime and core business processes are directly applicable to an information security plan. An integrated plan should be developed that addresses all form of disasters, even those caused by security incident.

Acceptance

Acceptance is the process of deciding that the risk is small enough to be ignored. This decision should be firmly based on business models and thorough risk analysis to assure that the size and the impact of the risk is fully understood. Some risk acceptance is inevitable. However, the organization must understand the scope of the risk being accepted.

This understanding comes through performing a comprehensive risk analysis and abuse impact analysis. This will create a model for cost, duration, and likelihood of security incidents and is required for sound business decisions.

Checklist

— For each vulnerability that could be exploited to cause a loss to an information asset, determine the safeguards that can be put in place.

— Determine what most needs protection.

— Determine how to best protect it.

— Prioritize based on business objectives.

— Get management buy-in.

— Evaluate methods of safeguarding the information.

   • Proactive safeguards (Phase II - Protection)
   • Reactive safeguards (Phase III - Detection)

CHAPTER 6

Evaluation of Current Status

Ninety percent of companies that were connected to the Internet rated their security as 'poor'
and 43 percent assessed the security of their Internet-based services as no better than 'fair.'[39]

To successfully put a security program into place, one needs to evaluate the current status of information security within the organization. A complete security audit might be too extensive or too expensive, but a security evaluation is certainly called for. This evaluation should address physical security, personnel policies and practices, business process controls, backup and recovery measures, network, and Internet and communications security controls. This evaluation requires an assessment of policies and procedures and testing of security practices.

Assessment

A security assessment evaluates the information security policies and procedures. It looks at the planning and preparedness of the plan to determine how well the security design addresses security issues. If the organization has written information security policies or procedures, this is the best starting place. However, many organizations do not have written polices or procedures, or not ones directly related to information security. Additional information can be found in personnel policies, physical security procedures, and intellectual property statements.

An assessment needs to be a measurable evaluation so that it can be compared to follow-on assessments to determine the effectiveness of changes to the security program. Quantifiable measures should be used wherever possible. Weighting factors may be applied based on the importance of the information to be protected or on management's view of the importance of specific policies.

---

[39] Ernst & Young, *1998 E&Y Global Information Security Survey.*

Comprehensiveness

Information security is a very broad topic and all areas of information security should be addressed. It is important that the policies and procedures address the security of information comprehensively.

Information exists in physical form, electronic form, and biological form. The security program must address all of these. The procedures for physical security must protect written and graphical information and manage its use, storage, and disposal. Electronic security must address recorded information (whether computerized, audio, or otherwise recorded), the transmission of these signals, and the disposal of the physical media that contained the electronic information. The people in the organization are repositories of proprietary information in biological form. The policies must address that these people understand the importance and value of the information that they know, how to protect it, with whom they can share it, and what can be done when the relationship between the individual and the organization is terminated.

The security policies must address all types of threats – physical, natural, human, and automated. The loss of business processing is the same regardless of the source of the losses. It is not uncommon that disaster plans and business continuity plans focus on natural disasters that cause physical damage and have few or no policies that address electronic intrusions. Attacks on information systems are very real and are responsible for significant losses. Most organizations are inadequately prepared.

Security policies must address all phases of security – inspection, protection, detection, reaction, and reflection. An omission in any of these areas leaves a hole in the security. The systems must be continuously inspected for vulnerabilities, which are being discovered and reported daily. Protection systems must be continuously tested. Daily administration and the adoption of new technologies can lead to holes in the system's defenses. The detection systems must be continuously updated to account for new attack patterns and new malicious code. The policies that define your reaction to incidents need periodic review to be assured that they continue to meet the needs of the organization and that they have not been affected by changes in the law. The follow-up procedures need periodic review to evaluate the value of the reports that are produced from an incident.

Policies must address issues throughout the organization. They must be equally suited for research departments as well as sales departments. Of course, the type of information handled in these different areas will be of differing levels, but the policies must be uniform. Information is used throughout the organization so policy must be location-independent to account for information moving throughout the organization. This might be printed material being carried by individuals, or computerized information being transmitted electronically. Global organizations that have different laws about security, privacy, etc. have information that crosses political boundaries. All of these variations must be accounted for.

The information security policies must be equitably enforced to all in the organization. Anywhere throughout the organization that information travels, it should be adequately protected. Geographical or organizational boundaries cannot matter to security policies. It is the information that is being protected and it is the same information in the mailroom or in the boardroom, anywhere in the world.

Industry Standards

In many industries there are organizations that develop information security standards for the specific industry. Some of these standards are mandated by law, or have determined the appropriate level of due care from the monitoring of civil cases. The organization's security standards should be measured against the standards of the industry to which it belongs.

Quality

Quality refers to the ability of the policies and procedures to address the issues they should. They should reflect the security vision and strategies of the organization. The applicability of the policies must be evaluated to determine if they are specific enough to be useful. That is, can they be applied to different situations to address specific problems and yield usable results, or are they so specific as to be useless?

They must address the issues of behavior by adequately describing correct and incorrect behavior as well the repercussions for those behaviors. They require support from both management and users. Users need to support the policies so that they will be followed. Management must support them so that they can be enforced.

The bottom line is policies and procedures must adequately protect the information.

Conformity

Even the best policies are of no value if they are not followed. Conformity measures the level at which the specific procedures are being practiced, how closely the policies are implemented, and how the implementation interprets the policy.

There are a number of places where conformity needs to be measured. Most obviously, information custodians have a large responsibility to be compliant. This starts in the data center where strong adherence to policies is needed. However, it needs to extend to include all information handlers as well as the information consumers. Everyone who interacts with the information must comply.

Conformity is largely based on the individual's knowledge of the policies and procedures and his requirements to support them. Evaluation of the security awareness level in an organization requires interviews with users to determine if they understand the security policies and observations to determine if they are actually following the procedures.

The level of conformity to the procedures is an area that can be measured, and needs to be measured, so that processes to improve the level of security can be evaluated. Changes in the level of compliance can then be attributed to the processes that are implemented.

Testing

Testing evaluates the quality of the implementation of the procedures. It requires evaluation of actual systems in operation and under normal maintenance practices, and will locate shortcomings and omissions.

Static Analysis

Static analysis is a non-intrusive evaluation of the implementation. It looks at configuration files, permissions, software versions, etc., to determine if there are any likely problems. This process generally catches known vulnerabilities and administrative errors.

Static analysis tools review a computer's configuration to determine if there are any areas that are vulnerable to attack. It examines the version of the software products on the system against a database of known vulnerabilities, and evaluates the installation and administration process and privileges to determine if they can be abused to create a vulnerability.

Dynamic Analysis

Dynamic analysis is an active, possibly intrusive, and certainly impactive testing process that attempts to determine vulnerabilities by actually attacking the information systems. This process is usually referred to as penetration testing. Penetration testing tests the security in the same manner that a hacker would attack the system. It is also referred to as ethical hacking.

Penetration testing generally focuses on the following three areas of the security systems:

- **Electronic Security** testing evaluates the ability to subvert the electronic information systems to get unauthorized access to information or to deny access to those who are authorized. Computer intrusion testing can be done either from onsite to illustrate the ability of an insider to be able to attack the system or, more often, offsite, in the same fashion that an external attacker would penetrate the system. Testing electronic security usually includes the testing of known vulnerabilities and standard attack scenarios.

- **Physical Security** testing includes the ability to circumvent physical access restrictions, gather information, and remove it from the premises. Testing physical security requires being at the site. Physical security tests attempt to gain entry by avoiding detection by bypassing safeguards, setting false pretenses, or blending in. It may focus on building access security or computer room access. Any aspect of physical security can be the focus of the test. Physical security also includes protecting information in its physical form. It tests information-handling policies, clean desk policies, and information disposal policies.

- **Biological Security** tests the human factor. Many people in the organization are aware of confidential information and are thereby targets of social engineering. Social engineering is getting information from individuals, usually by means of a ruse. The targets of social engineering are quite diverse. Those that directly handle the information are targeted because of the information that they handle. Computer operations are targeted because they understand the operations of the systems that house the information. The help desk is targeted because they are the organization that is charged with helping people who are having trouble with the system. And those who have no apparent access to information are targeted if they can be used to gain physical access or have contact with those who have access to the information. Many organizations discover that this is the weakest area of their security.

Business Impact Analysis

Organizations that are experienced in disaster recovery (DR) programs may already have completed a business impact analysis. Organizations inexperienced in DR planning may tend to skip the analysis step, and managers will often substitute their view for an analysis. If this happens, some amount of validation of this view will need to be accounted for in the next steps.

Information from the BIA provides insight about the financial and operational impact, current state of preparedness, maximum tolerable downtime, and technology requirements for recovery. It is the BIA which tells us which items are important enough to expend valuable resources.

Checklist

— Review the organization's security policies and procedures.

— Create measurable standards of compliance for these policies and procedures.

— Test the organization's security procedures and practices.

— Evaluate the effectiveness of the procedures and practices.

Given the likelihood of the threats and the value of the information assets, calculate the risk factor for each information asset. (Risk Factor = Value x Likelihood)

Identifier	Value	Likelihood	Risk Factor

The business impact of an incident is based on the cost and duration. The following chart indicates the level of impact based the cost and duration of an incident.

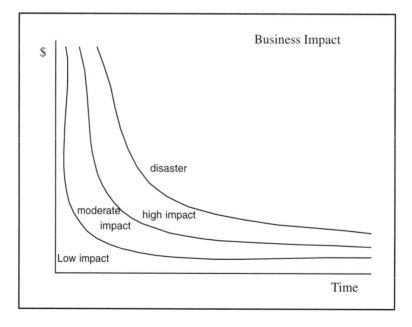

Protection

*Government and commercial computer systems are so poorly
protected that they can essentially be considered defenseless: an
electronic Pearl Harbor waiting to happen.* [40]

– Winn Schwartau

Protection is the reduction of vulnerabilities by the application of safeguards. In the area of information security, protection has received the greatest attention. A great effort has been put into shoring up defenses and plugging security holes. Nowhere is the theory that having one weak link will compromise the strength of the entire chain more true than in information security. A single vulnerability which provides an intruder high-level system privileges can be used to compromise the entire enterprise. Security requires balancing the costs of the security with the possible losses resulting from the theft, destruction, disclosure, or denial of access to the resources being protected. Hence, information protection must be comprehensive (implemented throughout), consistent (implemented uniformly), and cost effective.

A complete and cohesive security design is a lengthy process requiring commitment from management at the highest level and support from all areas of the organization, as information security reaches throughout the entire organization. Anyone who works with company information must understand how to protect it. The more important the information a person has access to, the more important that security measures must be utilized. Those at the top of an organization must stringently abide by security measures – even more so than those at the bottom.

An information security design is a definition at all levels of how an organization plans to build its security. It is built in a hierarchical fashion with increasing levels of details. At the highest level, the design describes the organization's view of how security should work. At each

---

[40]   Testimony before Congress. 1991.
Winn Schwartau is the president of Interpact, Inc. and founder of Infowar.Com, Ltd. and was the Project Lead of the Manhattan Cyber Project Information Warfare and Electronic Civil Defense Team. He has written numerous fiction and nonfiction books about information warfare.

succeeding level, there is more detail and allowances made for technological limits. The final levels describe the process and procedures that the organization will use to implement its security. Information security must be addressed consistently throughout the organization and in a manner consistent with corporate attitudes.

However, information security is only one aspect of running an organization. There are many areas that must work together in harmony to be successful. This harmony is achieved through a common understanding of the organization, its goals, and its values. This requires a consistent vision throughout the organization.

It must be realized that implementing a security design is not trivial and cannot be done by IT alone. Both IT and the business units need to work together to engineer and implement the necessary environment. Broad-based participation and involvement is critical to the success of this venture. This work is highly customized, and is a direct reflection of your corporate culture, making that policy effective and one that your user community will adopt and uphold.

The security design will help your organization institute and enforce information security. A good security design has to balance the often-competing interests of security, operational requirements, technical constraints, and user-friendliness.

The information security design defines a standard toward which your organization will strive. Your comprehensive security design will provide a foundation for procedures that minimize the impact of threats from all sources.

The formal information security design has to be documented, reviewed, and updated on a regular basis. It should be written in a very readable manner to be well received.

The following fundamental aspects of security are used to organize each of these security design documents.

Philosophies

An organization's philosophies set the mood for the entire organization. Sometimes referred to as the corporate vision, these philosophies define the corporate culture – the feel of the organization. They are the fundamental ideas in which the organization believes. They should not change unless there is a fundamental change in the company. This is what makes one company feel like a family-run business, while another feels like a big corporation. They define the openness of the organization, how easy it is to approach management, and the value of individual initiative. They describe the command structure and the level of involvement of those in charge.

Corporate philosophies are often expressed in the form of a series of vision statements. Each of these vision statements address different aspects of the business. One of these areas should be information security.

Security Vision

A security vision is a definition of the ideal security solution. Its broad nature is independent of technology. The language used in a security vision will be similar to that used in the organization's philosophies and principles. Vision statements are high-level executive position statements that give direction and relative importance to the areas addressed. A security vision is based on the company's philosophy, defining the basic concepts of access, authorization, and control. The high-level security vision statements of many organizations will look very similar. However, as the vision is expanded, statements that appear very similar can have very different implications for different organizations.

A security vision will provide a foundation for easy-to-use, business-enabling information services that allow appropriate and secure access to information and resources to anyone, anywhere, anytime, while ensuring protection against unauthorized access. It will define if access is to be freely granted or if it will require extensive validation. It will describe if authorizations will be broadly managed or tightly controlled, and if these controls will be widely distributed or tightly maintained by a limited few. An information security vision encompasses broad concepts such as trust and protection.

- **Trust** is the level of confidence needed in the individuals, applications, equipment, transactions, and business functions that utilize the information. Trust determines who gets what authorizations, what processes have what privileges, who administers the systems, and who monitors which security services.

- **Protection** is the level of control, integrity, and auditing in your business and security practices. Protection determines the level of integrity checking required for transactions and information, the level of access controls, and the use of encryption and cryptography.

Principles

Principles are the standards by which an organization conducts itself. They are the moral grounding – the conscience of the organization. They define corporate integrity. They are a reflection of the organization's culture and environment and must be created and promoted by management. They are often built directly on the beliefs of the founder of the organization.

Principles take philosophy and refine them in specific terms. They create the standards to which all policies must adhere and define the structure in which policies are developed. The statements are broad in nature and address topics. They are often located in the statement of business conduct.

Security Architecture

The security architecture addresses broad topics and serves to ensure a common level of understanding and a common framework for design and implementation. A security architecture is usually defined as a blueprint showing the building blocks of a structure. The information security architecture covers the processes and conceptual aspects of information security, as well as technology, infrastructure, and services. A successful architecture must consider the company culture and the people, in addition to security technology and infrastructure. The culture and people are the supporting foundation of the security. An enterprise's culture has many aspects, which may include business objectives, principles, policies, management processes, and people's belief and practices. The degree of security needed depends on the culture and the people.

A security architecture is a definition of the basic principles that a security implementation can be built with. It is needed to achieve consistent and complete security infrastructure, reduce fragmented and inconsistent efforts while working to meet security objectives that can be qualified and quantified, establish a formal baseline for future audits, and establish duties, responsibilities, and communication paths. An organization's security architecture must be in line with the organization's basic philosophies and principles. It will define the organization's policies.

The information security architecture should be independent of any specific technologies. It should support a heterogenous, multivendor environment.

A good architecture will make security easier for people to use, and will empower the businesses. It improves credibility and visibility for information system initiatives, avoids disputes, and reduces internal political struggles.

Policies

Policies are technology-independent descriptions of the security precautions that are required for different types of information and access. Quite often security policies apply to more than just information; they apply to all corporate resources. They should change only rarely and then only with the endorsement of management.

Policies are the primary building blocks for every information security design, defining the responsibilities of the organization, the individual, and management.

Policies specify what must or must not be done to fulfill the principles. Policies protect information, people, property, and reputation. They should be short, precise, and easy to understand. Creating information security policies and procedures is no small task. It requires evaluation of information and systems, assignment of ownership and responsibilities and, most importantly, it requires support from the top of the company down. It is more important that the CEO of a company support and follow the information security procedures than anyone else in the company. This is because it both shows the importance of the policies, and because the CEO has access to the most valuable information in the company.

It is only through the close alignment of business objectives with sound strategy that a set of policies can be developed to truly enhance the abilities of your organization.

Security Strategy

Security strategy defines how to implement the vision in accordance with the architecture given the technological constraints. A strategy is a documented high-level plan for organization-wide computer and information security. It will define standards to which the security implementation should adhere. Standards should not address specific technologies – this has a tendency to stifle creativity – rather, they should employ general technologies and concepts. Standards define the level of security required for each environment. If a system is unable to implement this standard, an explanation should be required as to why this system should be exempt from the standard or how the system is going to reduce the risk without implementing the standard. It provides a framework for making specific decisions, such as which defense mechanisms to use and how to configure services, and is the basis for developing secure programming guidelines and procedures for users and system administrators to follow. Because a security policy is a long-term document, the contents avoid technology-specific issues.

The security strategy is the approach that is taken to express the management's desire in a coherent manner. A security strategy is built with rules and guidelines.

- **Rules** define specific bounds in which the system must operate. They relate to an entire information systems structure and anyone with access – employees, family members, contractors, clients, vendors, partners, customers, etc.

- **Guidelines** assist in effectively securing the systems. The nature of guidelines, however, immediately recognizes that systems vary considerably, and imposition of standards is not always achievable, appropriate, or cost-effective. For example, an organizational guideline may be used to help develop system-specific standard procedures. Guidelines are often used to help ensure that specific security measures are not overlooked, although they can be implemented, and correctly so, in more than one way.

Procedures

Procedures are definitions of how to implement the policies to a specific technology. They will change when the technology to which they pertain changes. Procedures will also identify those technologies that are unable to implement a policy and where variances are acceptable.

Procedures are the detailed instructions on how to meet the criteria defined in policies. This is essentially an instruction manual to give your user community the confidence to implement your controls successfully. This clearly explains the duties and responsibilities within the security design.

Procedures determine how standards should be implemented. Generally, they are written to apply to a class of systems that have similar attributes or security issues. Procedures must take into account the limitations of both the systems that are implementing them and current technology. Procedures are specific steps to follow that are based on the corporate security policy. They should be reviewed periodically to encompass new technologies.

Security Framework

A security framework is the process of applying the security procedures for an organization, which is largely the administration of security objects. It is a definition of what existing tools are going to be used to implement the strategy.

It should address such topics as retrieving programs from the network, connecting to the site's system from home or while traveling, using encryption, authentication for issuing accounts, configuration, and monitoring.

The framework contributes to asset protection and increased stability, manageability, and reliability. It develops an infrastructure of controls with benefits that outweigh any negative impacts, such as performance degradation and human inconvenience, and it identifies and reduces the frequency and impact of errors and omissions.

Policy should never become static, sitting in a binder on your shelf. This policy and procedure framework must continue to grow and change with your organization.

Standards specify uniform use of specific technologies, parameters, or procedures when such uniform use will benefit an organization. Standardization of organization-wide identification badges is a typical example, providing ease of employee mobility and automation of entry/ exit systems. Standards are normally compulsory within an organization.

- **Standards** are basic security requirements. The define an acceptable level of security to which every system must adhere.

- **Exceptions** are definitions of specific instances where the standards will not be implemented. This may be because of limitations of the information systems themselves or other factors. The exception must define how the security issues, addressed by the standard which was not implemented, will be addressed.

Practices

Practices are the actual day-to-day operations that implement the procedures. They must take into account the business environment, the capabilities and resources of the organization, as well as the budgetary, social, and logistical pressures. However, they need to be consistent to create a consistent level of security throughout the enterprise.

Practices may be specific to a specific system. They are likely to be different for different locations and different types of systems. They identify tasks, individuals, and schedules. They create the basic job definition for the operators.

Security practices must be reviewed and updated often to reflect changes that influence the specific systems to which the practice applies, and they must be tested to assure that they work. These reviews should lead to constant improvement in quality.

System administration practices play a key role in network security. Checklists and general advice on good security practices are readily available.

Security Implementation

The security implementation defines the details on how the framework is implemented. It guides in the selection and development of controls and assists in complying with applicable security policies, standards, and guidelines. It contains detailed steps to be followed by users, system operations personnel, or others to accomplish a particular task (e.g., preparing new user accounts and assigning the appropriate privileges). It includes schedules and responsibilities, as well as specific tools.

Security implementation will assist with the integration of hardware, software, and services in accordance with established standards. It will help justify these tools in your overall framework and help garner budget and human resources that meet your overall objectives.

- **Responsibilities** define who will be performing the actions indicated in the specific practice. They assign accountability to help assure that the work is done.

- **Schedules** indicate when the activities are to be done. This can be used to define when an activity is past due and should be considered delinquent.

Each level of the security design must address the ten fundamental aspects of information security – awareness, access, identification, authentication, authorization, availability, accuracy, confidentiality, accountability, and administration.

These ten aspects are all interrelated and interdependent. To utilize certain information will require specific authorizations, which may dictate the type of identifier and level of authentication required to be granted access, if the access method is appropriate for the information to preserve its confidentiality and accuracy. Accountability is dependent on awareness – the courts have determined that ignorance is an excuse and that the organization is responsible to inform the attacker that he is doing something wrong.

Awareness

Over 50% of companies are dissatisfied with how well information security policies, procedures, and standards are communicated throughout their organization. [41]

Security awareness is the process of making people understand the implications of security on their ability to perform their job. It includes the importance of security, the use of security measures, and the process of reporting security violations.

A security awareness program is critical to any security design. All of the people involved with information must understand the importance of security and what their part is in maintaining the security of the information that is entrusted to them. Increased awareness increases the proper use of security features and the likelihood that a user will report suspicious activities. Employee education in security awareness can be a tremendous advantage to your security program. Employees who understand the value of security and how it affects them are more likely to utilize it.

There are a number of areas that need to be addressed in an awareness program. These include what the information systems should be used for, why security is important, how to use the available security systems, what everyone's part is, how to perform this part, and what the consequences are for not being a good corporate citizen.

Appropriate Use

What is and what is not appropriate behavior must be explained. What one person may think is obvious may not be obvious to everyone. In recent years, appropriate use documents have become common in business. Some organizations will have different appropriate use documents for many different aspects of the information systems, including e-mail, Internet usage, and downloading software. These documents reduce abuse and help protect the company.

---

[41] Price Waterhouse, *Enterprise Security Solutions Survey*, November 1996.

There have been numerous instances in which an individual was confronted after having created a security incident, only to have the individual claim he had no idea that what he was doing was inappropriate. The courts have agreed with this position, deciding that if both parties did not understand the contract, then there was no contract.

Consequently, appropriate use of resources must be clearly spelled out to all involved.

Relevance

The awareness program must bring information security to a personal level. People often think that security is someone else's problem. They do not understand that everyone is responsible for the security of the information they use. Individuals need to understand that security is in place to protect their work. If they do not use the security properly, it will be their work that is lost and they may also be responsible for the loss of others' information. When the costs of a security incident are brought down to a personal level, people will become more interested in following the security procedures.

When a security incident is reported to have cost the organization a large amount of money, employees may not see the personal impact. However, if costs are shown in the number of people who had to redo their work, or man hours lost to repair the problem, or the number of jobs that will have to be eliminated to recover from the incident, then these numbers become much more personal to the employees.

Roles

Individuals have different relationships with the organization's information. These different relationships define the individual's role. Each role has different levels of responsibilities and duties and needs different levels of security awareness.

An individual will have different roles with different information. He may be the owner of some information and the user of other information. He may also have different roles with the same information. He may be a user of the information that he owns. This situation will require procedures to maintain a clear and accountable separation of duties. Roles will dictate the types and levels of authorizations required.

Different levels of awareness may be appropriate for individuals with different levels of responsibility. Following are the basic role divisions. (Further division, such as information creators, information modifiers, etc., may be required for any specific environment.)

- **Information owners** are those individuals who have been given the responsibility of determining the value and the appropriate level of security for the information under their control.

- **Information custodians** are responsible for the management of the information systems that store the information, and for maintaining the integrity and privacy of the information while it is in their control.

- **Information users** are the consumers of the information. They are responsible for the proper handling of the information they utilize.

Responsibilities

Each person's responsibilities in regards to information security are dependent on their role. An information owner is responsible for defining the value of the information, while an information user is responsible for using the information in an appropriate manner. However, everyone is responsible for understanding the organization's security design and their roles in that design. There are a large number of general responsibilities that apply to everyone involved. Everyone needs to know what to do to protect the organization's information, what their requirements are for identification and authentication, as well as their responsibility for maintaining the accuracy and confidentiality of the information.

Awareness is the understanding of the correct security procedures and implications by all who are involved with the organization's information. These procedures often include security incident reporting. Many incidents go unreported because the individuals who have knowledge of the incident are not aware of how to report the problem. A good awareness program should eliminate this issue. People usually want to do the right thing and will generally report problems earlier if they are aware of the importance of information protection. Management should commend those people who report security violations.

Repercussions

Most information resource security problems involve people. Dealing with the human side of a security incident is more treacherous than the technical side. Everyone needs to be aware of the punishment or possible punishment for certain types of transgressions. Knowledge of the punishment and its severity emphasizes the importance of and dedication to information security. The punishment should be proportional to the infraction. The response by management should be evenly enforced, yet flexible enough to handle specific cases.

All entities will be made aware of the organization's security policies and procedures prior to being granted access to any company resources. An awareness program must be comprehensive, including all of the users in the enterprise, continuous, so that the security message will not be forgotten, and cost-effective, so that it can be maintained.

Awareness Program

Awareness is the first step in any security program. It should start before an individual has access to company resources. It has to be made available to everyone in the organization and those outside the organization who will be granted access to information. It must keep the message fresh and in front of its audience so that it is not forgotten. It must be understood by everyone.

Continuous

The security awareness program must be continuous, prior to the individual dealing with the information. "I didn't know," must never be an excuse for improper information handling. New employee orientation provides an ideal opportunity to inform employees about the organization's information security procedures. However, it cannot stop there. Once they are made aware of information security, they must be reminded regularly. An awareness program must support ongoing communication.

The awareness program must have plenty of opportunities to remind people that security is an ever-present concern. The security message can stand by itself or it can be easily integrated into almost any business-related communication. Security awareness should be integrated into every opportunity in which presentations are being given to employees. Orientation and classes about new projects or services offer the opportunity to explain how security impacts these projects and what the users can do to help address these issues.

Comprehensive

Everyone in the organization must understand the importance of information security – from the newest person in the mailroom to the CEO. Everyone in the organization handles information, and they need to know how to handle it appropriately. Even those people who work at the organization and are not employees but have access to proprietary information must be made aware of its value. This includes non-employees, such as contractors and temps.

Awareness programs often start out in the Information Technology (actually, read data processing) department and are focused on computer security – "log off your terminal, don't tell anyone your password." This is important but it is too narrowly focused. Just because someone doesn't use a computer doesn't mean they don't handle valuable and confidential information. The people in the mailroom handle virtually every piece of information that enters or leaves the organization. People with blueprints of upcoming products hung on their walls, or with confidential information lying on their desks, jeopardize the security of the information at least as much as the individual who chooses a poor password.

Coherent

The message must be understood. Different people absorb information in different ways, so your message should use a variety of media – written, visual, audio, in a variety of styles – humor, war stories, etc. With a broad offering of information, each individual will be likely to find one that will catch their interest.

Often, the information security message is not very tangible. People may have a problem understanding how valuable information is, or how a question that may appear to be innocent can be an attempt to gather confidential information. The message needs to be brought into the real world with real world examples, analogies and actual events that put the issues into terms that are familiar to the individuals and can be easily absorbed. The message may need to be personalized to the individual's environment. The potential damages need to be illustrated in money, time, effort, and jobs – tangible losses.

Cost Effective

The goal of an awareness program is to encourage the individuals to be more involved in information security. This awareness allows them to be more rapid and accurate in using security and reporting its misuse. The effectiveness of the program can be increased by adding reinforcements. These can be in the form of rewards for appropriate security behavior, or reminders when security procedures are not being followed. Often small, inexpensive trinkets (a coupon for a candy bar at the cafeteria) can be effective as a reminder for those everyday security practices.

In most organizations, security is viewed as a cost whose services are not used until after there is an incident, instead of a process that continuously reduces losses to an organization by preventing incidents. Because of this, the cost of a security program must be improved by having measurable results.

It is important to be able to measure the effectiveness of an awareness program. This is an area of information security that is difficult to justify since it is hard to show a direct relationship to the safety of the information. Being able to measure the increase in the awareness of people can illustrate the effectiveness of the program. Security must be made important to the individual by making it a measure by which he is evaluated during his performance review. The effectiveness of the program needs to be reviewed, evaluated, and measured to assure that everyone is getting the message. It may be legally prudent to have everyone periodically sign an awareness statement which indicates that they understand their roles and responsibilities and will abide by the organization's security requirements.

Design Choices

A plan should be developed to determine how to make everyone aware of computer security. This will encompass how to get the message throughout the organization, what the message will contain, and how to say it. These choices will, in a great measure, determine the quality of the awareness program. The design must consider the requirements of being continuous, comprehensive, coherent, and cost-effective.

Delivery Method

The selection of methods delivering the security awareness message to the user community needs to be varied and effective. If the user community is largely working online, then computerized security reminders can be very effective. Web sites are useful for reference material – detailed policy and procedures – while a more active delivery method may be required for increasing awareness. Log-on messages and banners can supply some visibility. If your organization utilizes web-casting, the process of pushing web content to the users' desktop, this can be a very effective, enticing method of getting interesting headlines and teasers in front of users.

Not all information users are computer users, however, so the awareness program must deliver its content to those who never interact with the computer system. Security awareness programs should include a variety of communication methods so that everyone has an opportunity to be exposed to the message. It seems as if almost every organization has a newsletter. This is a prime opportunity to have a security forum as a regular column in these newsletters. Posters catch the attention of passersby. Catchy slogans can make a point and be long remembered. Trinkets, like pens, mouse pads, and coffee cups, can hold a message and be in front of the recipient for a long time.

The content of the message is what is important. It needs to convey the importance of security and the implications of not following the security procedures. The message needs to be relevant to its audience. However, unique delivery methods can enhance the message.

Message Content

Just as the method of delivering the message needs to be varied so that it can reach everyone, the style of the message should be varied to appeal to different personalities. People are interested by different styles of information. Some prefer news stories while others will absorb the message better if it is presented humorously. Humor can often relate a concept better and more quickly than presenting the information directly. Space for security information is often limited so the use of cartoons is frequently employed. Real-life stories, too, are utilized to capture the interest of readers. War stories from your own organization and other companies are a good source of real-life crime stories.

Timeliness

Timeliness is very important in capturing the attention and imagination of the audience. Events that took place a few years ago are ancient history in the computer industry. The awareness program needs to focus on current events. It should leverage any reported security incident into an opportunity to remind everyone how important security is.

There is actually an annual opportunity to have a day focused on security. The last business day in November is International Computer Security Day, which was established in 1988 by the Washington, D.C., chapter of the ACM Special Interest Group in Systems Audit and Control (SIGAC). Promoting security awareness through the observation of Computer Security Day can achieve both preventative and detective control objectives.

Implementation Options

When it comes to implementing a security awareness program, the biggest concern to most organizations is the cost. However, a well designed security awareness program will be able to be piggybacked on many existing programs to create an effective program with minimal costs. Integrating security awareness into existing programs, such as employee education and corporate newsletters, can be done with very little additional expense. The use of existing materials, such as posters from security organizations and vendors, trade publications, and books, can minimize the amount of new material that has to be created specifically for your program.

Broad-based Awareness

Broad-based awareness allows for the distribution of general awareness messages to a very large audience. This is a good platform for ongoing reminders and basic security processes. This is the format to be used whenever there are changes to security policy or penalties that affect everyone. New user orientation should contain a section that is focused on broad-based information security. Any regular publication that is received by a large percent of the user base is a good choice for awareness programs. Space should be made available in all of the internal corporate newsletters for security awareness information.

Focused Awareness

People with different roles and responsibilities have different needs in their understanding of specific security aspects. Utilizing a focused awareness message that is specific to a group of specific users, either through a gathering of these users or through a publication specific for this audience, allows one to deliver detailed security information to those who need it. Opportunities include executive briefings, organizational meetings, and specific newsletters. Specific security seminars focused on specific issues can be held to draw in the appropriate audience.

Awards and Rewards

Often security is viewed negatively - as an enforcement organization. Using awards and rewards for appropriate use of security can help with both awareness of security and improving the image of the information security department. Awards can be given out to departments or to individuals in either a formal or informal manner. A little recognition can go a long way. Rewards can be a formal process for reporting violations or an informal process of giving out rewards when individuals are seen performing good security practices. The value of the reward does not have to be great to elicit the response that is desired. Often, candy bars, gift certificates, or logo mugs are ample reward.

Individual Awareness

It is important to be able to measure and verify the quality of the awareness program. Measuring individual awareness is the best way to measure the effectiveness of the overall program. Organizations that have periodic employee reviews have an excellent opportunity to include security awareness into these reviews. Most organizations require that users sign a security agreement prior to having any utilization of information and many require an annual acknowledgment of understanding from each user. Making security a part of the user's review, which has an impact on their evaluation, creates an importance to information security awareness.

Lack of Awareness

Lack of awareness can lead to a variety of security issues. The requirements of a security system often create more work for the users, such as remembering and entering passwords. Users can be very creative in bypassing security features to make their life simpler. Without understanding the implications security features, the users may be unaware of the amount of time, effort, and data that can be lost by not using them.

There have been security incidents that have gone unreported, even though many users knew about them, because they did not know how to report the misuse, or they were not sure that the activity was forbidden.

Prior notification has become a requirement for effective enforcement. Many cases have been dismissed because there was no notification or reasonable expectation of the security policy. This has often been used in conjunction with personal communication and monitoring of e-mail, but it applies to all areas of information security.

Companies need proof of understanding from users that they understand the security policies and will adhere to them. This generally requires a signed acknowledgment that they have read and understand the company's security policies.

> A worker at IBM United Kingdom was dismissed for accessing pornography and other non-business-related material through the Internet. He appealed his dismissal to the London South employment tribunal, which ruled that he had been unfairly dismissed because it wasn't clear that there was a was a breach of company policy sufficient to warrant summary dismissal.[42]

---

[42]   Incomes Data Services, *Employment tribunals grapple with 'cyberliability' in the workplace*, 24 May 1999.

Checklist

—Describe the plan to increase the information security awareness.

—Determine the measures to be used to evaluate its effectiveness.

—Determine the requirements for legal prosecution.
   — Signed current appropriate use document
   — Warning banners at all entry points.

The awareness program needs to address:
— The importance of information security
— How to use the available security features
— The process of reporting misuse

Be sure to consider:
— Physical security
— Information disposal policy
— Clean desk policy
— Internet access policy
— Open access areas
— Portable computers
— Home offices
— Wireless communications

CHAPTER 8

Access

An Internet security survey reports that 30% of the Internet security incidents occur after a firewall is installed.[43]

Access is the manner by which the user gets to the information – the method of communications between information systems and information users. This includes physical and logical access. The type of access that will be allowed to a system is dependent on the security requirements of the information on that system. Decisions must be made regarding access to the system and the information it contains. The care that is taken in this process is a major determining factor of the level of security and control present in the system. The ultimate goal of access security is to control the access to information. All other access controls exist to assist in this goal.

In theory, access should be unrestricted, relying on authorizations to grant access only to those who should have it. Access to computer services and information should be controlled on the basis of need; that is, access will only be granted for a specific purpose based on a need to know. Access to corporate resources should be controlled on the basis of business needs, granted only for specific purposes, and revoked when it is no longer needed. However, in many cases, securing the access to information is easier than controlling authorizations. In any case, it is a belt and suspenders solution that creates the first line of defense against attack.

Different methods of access will require different levels of identification, authentication, authorization, and accountability. The method of access used may also limit the level of authorizations received or what is required to authenticate yourself to the system. All accesses must be able to be audited. This requires that the user, who may be an individual or another information resource, be properly identified. However, some level of anonymous access is required. Before a user can be identified by a system, the user must know of the system's existence and how to make contact with it so the user can identify itself to the system. Knowledge of existence is a form of access in itself.

[43] Computer Security Institute, *1995 Internet Security Survey*, 1995.

Global Access

Access should be allowed to anyone who is authorized, anywhere the information can be safely distributed, and at any time. Therefore, access methods should be unrestricted. The manner by which an information user gets to the information should not matter. Utilization of the information resources should be dependent on authorization and authentication. However, limiting access is an easier task, so it has become commonplace to implement security checks to enforce security policy at access points.

Anyone

Anyone should be allowed access until they reach a point where they are not authorized to proceed. These access checkpoints, or ports of entry, are the points where identification, authentication, and authorization will determine if the individual will be granted permission to proceed. Anything that passes the access point must pass a security check.

The process of authenticating an individual's identity has to be in part based on the access method that is being used. The authentication required is based on the level of trust in both the identification and the communication. The less trustworthy the access method, the more authentication that will be required, since the less trustworthy access method is more susceptible to compromise by eavesdropping and falsified credentials. More public methods of access will require greater levels of authentication than private access methods.

Anywhere

The mobile and interconnected environment in which we live has made it possible to need information from almost anywhere and to have the access necessary to get it. However, the wealth of choices of access options, each with different levels of security and security issues, will affect the ability to get the information.

The security level of the access method has to be a contributing factor in the process of granting privileges. The privileges granted to an individual over an unsecured access method will have to be less than those granted to the same individual when he is using a secured access method. The privileges granted cannot exceed the minimum authorizations of the individual or that of the access method.

Anytime

Global enterprises are an around-the-clock endeavor. It is always "business hours" somewhere and information is needed to conduct that business. Even the concept of business hours is becoming blurred. E-commerce and web-based businesses have created storefronts that are always open for business.

Time of access can play a significant role in identifying misuse, especially when viewed in conjunction with other factors such as location and the resources requested.

Access Methods

Every new method of access creates new security issues. Each access mode has implications to availability (interruption of communications), privacy (eavesdropping on communications) and integrity (interception and replay of communication). Every type of access has different security needs that must be addressed. Other access levels may be appropriate in specific circumstances. Some organizations may have concerns about "visual access" or electronic surveillance.

The changes in access methods define the major phases in the evolution of computing, listed below.

- **Batch mode** computing, where computers run only one job at a time, requires *physical access* to the computer to put punched cards into the card reader and to collect output from the system's printer.

- **Timesharing** or online computing, where a number of users can share the system resources, requires *direct connected terminal access* or possibly dedicated dial-up modem terminals.

- **Departmental computing** puts the timesharing computer into the local department and adds *system-to-system accesses,* generally though a point-to-point connection.

- **Distributed computing** allows desktop computers on a *local area network access* the system resources over the LAN.

- **Global computing** allows desktop systems use the *Internet to access* the system resources.

- **Pervasive computing** uses *wireless communication* to access system resources.

Physical Access

Physical access should be the most restrictive access. Any system can be compromised once physical access is achieved. Physical access is required for only a limited number of processes, usually system updates or the mounting or unmounting of removable media, and should be limited to these.

Physical access encompasses much more than access to the computer room or access to electronic information. Physical access includes written information – papers left unsecured on or in an individual's desk, information in the mailroom, or on the fax machine – awaiting transmission or a recipient to pick it up. Even the blueprints posted on the cubicle wall or the information left on marker boards can provide inappropriate access.

Physical locks that are used to limit physical access should facilitate logging for accountability. Mechanical locks that utilize a physical key can be exploited by creating duplicate keys, while electronic locks can also be exploited; the logging of the access information, however, will indicate what keys have been compromised and when the improper access took place.

Multifactor identification is good in all environments, including physical security. Having locks that require both a physical key and a password increases the level of security. Security cameras are another method of creating a log of physical access for accountability.

Physical access also includes audio information – protecting conversations. Audio communications such as telephone conversations are carried over public carriers with no expectation of privacy. Discussion of confidential information in public areas invites eavesdropping.

A clean desk policy is needed to ensure that information is secured when the office is closed. There are a number of non-employees that have access to an office after business hours – cleaning crews, maintenance crews, work crews, employee family members. Any of these may accidentally or maliciously access sensitive information and later disclose it. Hacker magazines have run articles on how to get a job with a cleaning crew to gain unsupervised physical access to a company.

Clean desk policies are often viewed as an annoyance by employees when the focus is on clean desks and not security. Once employees understand that the information left unsecured in their offices is available to anyone who is in the building when they are not, they are much more receptive to support a clean desk policy.

Additionally, physical security must be extended to information even after it is disposed of, since information is often disposed of while it still has value that needs protection. The information security access policies must address information disposal – both printed and electronic material. Information can be retrieved from the trash. Dumpster diving, the process of climbing into a dumpster to retrieve information, can be very effective. Even items that would not be expected to contain confidential information do. Notes in user manuals may include useful information, even passwords.

Direct access

Direct access is access through directly connected links. This is the classic access path to mainframe computers and time-sharing systems. Terminal-based computing usually employs direct access. System consoles usually require direct connection and are required for some administration procedures, such as rebooting the system. However, the console can be physically separated from the system, which is often located in an adjacent secured computer facility so that physical access is not necessary for procedures that only require console access.

Direct access connectivity gives you the greatest level of control. It also limits the flexibility of connections, since a dedicated wire must be run from the system to every terminal device.

Network access

Network access is access over a computer network owned and managed by the organization. Security is still controlled by the organization, but the diversity of the network opens doors for eavesdropping.

Most network protocols have no level of privacy – the information is sent in clear text across the network where anyone along the way can eavesdrop. Unused network ports in an office that are still connected to the network can be used by merely plugging into them. An attacker may be able to slip into an unused cubicle unnoticed and plug into the private company network.

Even worse, many protocols are broadcast protocols so that the information is sent everywhere. Information may travel farther than expected, leaving the department or even the company. Company networks are no longer islands of communications. Business networks are extended to allow employees to work at home or on the road. These access points create an opening that is a point of attack. Connecting business networks with business partners is becoming more prevalent: this arrangement, in some part, makes the security level based on the business partner's security practices and employees.

Remote access

Remote access is access over public or external communications over which the organization does not have direct control. Dial-up access and Internet access are both examples of remote access. Remote access is also referred to as external access. For an organization to understand what is internal and what is external, they will need to define a security perimeter. The security perimeter defines at what points information can travel into or out of the organization's control. These are the points that need special attention.

Connectivity to the Internet is becoming commonplace. This opens a door to a world where anyone can come to your door and attempt to break it down.

Social Access

Another method to gain access is not technological, but social – the ability to extract information from individuals who know or have access to information. This has been the mainstay of the information-gathering industry for years. Friendly conversations are often a source of information leakage.

Nontechnical attacks require nontechnical defense: awareness. The only defense for social attacks is to educate people so that they will be aware of what is or is not appropriate to share with others.

Access Points as Security Checkpoints

Access should be limited at every place where there is a change in the level of security required, a change in who is responsible for administering the security, or a change in the level of threat. Access is often limited by instituting a number of security perimeters that define the level of security required to pass across these perimeters. Limiting access limits risk.

Security Domains

A security domain is part of an information system that is under a common control and has similar threats and levels of security. A security domain can be managed and controlled independently from other security domains. Security policies are enforced uniformly throughout a security domain. It interacts with other security domains at access points.

Domains of Trust

A domain of trust is part of a security domain that supports a common trust model; that is, it utilizes one authentication and trusts the authentication from anywhere within the trust domain. Often a domain of trust can be viewed as a single information system object. It also implies that if a system in the domain of trust is compromised, all of the systems in the domain must be considered suspect.

Domains of trust have been implemented in a number of different manners in the computer industry. Some allow log-ons without reauthentication from within the domain; others allow access to any resource within the domain.

Security Perimeter

A security perimeter is a demarcation between areas of differing security levels or scopes of control. These security perimeters create multiple rings of security. Within each ring is a domain of trust. Adjacent domains of trust can be combined if they are of the same security level and scope of control. Domains of trust can be connected to other domains of the same level if a connection can be made that supports the same level of security and control.

The points where information penetrates these domains are locations where security processes need to be implemented to control the movement of information into and out of areas of different security levels or controls. All access attempts, successful or not, should produce an auditable record.

Connecting Domains of Trust

Virtual private networks (VPN) create a secure connection between domains of trust. This private network is a cryptographic tunnel over a public or untrusted network. Virtual private networks can connect perimeter devices, like firewalls of one domain to another, or they can connect end-nodes from server to client systems, so that information privacy can be maintained.

By requiring identification and authentication, the VPN philosophy can be extended from static connections between two known points to a more dynamic environment. Authenticated users create a connection from wherever they are to the secure VPN server. These can be for specific purposes, such as allowing secure remote access to specific systems or they can be general purpose systems, that allow the administrator to configure specific users with the authorizations to access specific applications.

Secure remote console access is a service that has long been desired. The use of virtual private network technologies and specialized hardware for connecting to the console can supply all the capabilities of the hardware console securely over the net.

Access Servers

An access server is an information system that facilitates an access method or controls access across an access point. Access servers must create audit logs that can be used to monitor the security of the information system. They need to record the session connections, their duration, byte counts, user names, authentication methods, and other information that is relevant to the type of connection. This information must be able to be integrated into a security monitoring and control system.

Network Security

Network security is based on the ability to limit the flow of information over a specific part of the network, or to limit the connectivity to specific hosts over the network.

- **Switches** are at the lowest level of network security. Switches only transmit a packet to the particular device for which it is addressed. This reduces the ability of one device to snoop the packets that are meant for another device.

- **Filters** are the next step in security. Filters allow for some basic isolation of network traffic based on the destination addresses, so only traffic that needs to cross the filtering device will be allowed to cross. Some filtering devices will block broadcast packets.

- **Routers** The next device is the workhorse of basic network security – the router. A router allows packets to be allowed or denied access based on the addresses of the sender and receiver and the type of packet. Routers also allow for multiple paths for redundancy and for the isolation of traffic.

- **Firewalls** are a collection of computer and network equipment used to allow communications to flow out of the organization and restrict communications flowing into the organization to only those authorized communications from authenticated users. Outbound connections can be monitored to detect disclosure of proprietary information and inbound connections can be monitored to detect intrusion attempts.

- **Proxies** completely isolate connections by becoming both the endpoint for the inside and outside connection. Proxies enable the ability to control access based on the content of the information. The application proxy understands the information and is able to integrate data-inspection to ensure that the information entering and exiting the corporate network is being handled within bounds of the security policy. Application proxies can test files transferred for viruses, scan for inappropriate content, or limit the options of an application. A proxy has to be constructed for each application so that it can understand the content of the information being transmitted.

Host Security

Host-based access security controls access to specific systems. Hosts deny access at the host itself. Every host has to control its own access policy, making host access flexible but administration-intensive. This administrative overhead has led many to use network access control and forgo host control.

- **Connection type** – Limiting specific types of connections can limit the exposure of hosts to certain types of attacks. Hosts can be configured to not allow modems to be used for dial-in connections, or they can require that administrators can only gain access through the system console, which implies physical access.

- **Connection origin** – Limiting the scope of locations from which connections can be made limits the locations from which attacks can be made. It allows for the separation of friendly sites from unfriendly ones.

- **Trust** – Trust is a concept that is common to computer systems. They have been built to enable the sharing of resources, and thereby tend to trust other hosts.

Abuse of Access

The issues of access have historically been built on the assumption that those inside the organization are friendly and those outside are not. This is not always the case. Insiders are not always honest and outsiders may have a need for access.

Issues of access are a primary concern to Internet-based businesses. Such businesses are designed to create as much access as possible so that customers have rapid response. The Internet customer base is assumed to be everyone, creating a need for access from everywhere. However, this means that hostile attacks can come from anywhere.

Attacks focused on disrupting services have been around since the beginning of the computer industry. However, their complexity and scope have continued to grow. They have moved from mere annoyances to causing major financial hardships.

> The first major denial-of-service attacks were launched in February, 2000, when numerous Internet giants, including Yahoo, Amazon, and Ebay, were flooded with traffic bringing response to a crawl and essentially rendering them unavailable.

The attacks were distributed and coordinated. The attack software compromised a number of intermediate sites which all then focused attacks on the target site at once, so the target was overwhelmed by traffic.[44]

---

[44]   Schwartz, John, "Hackers Strike Again," *Washington Post*, 10 February 2000.

Checklist

— Define the domains of trust for the organization.

— Define the level of security within each trust domain.

— Clearly define all access methods for each domain.

— Define the authentication required for each access method.

— Define the level of authorization allowed for each access method.

— Enforce security policy at all access points.

— Access must produce audit trails.

— Access methods can limit authorizations.

— Access methods affect the level of authentication required.

— Define procedures to monitor, enable, and disable access methods.

CHAPTER 9

Identification

Seventy-six percent of organizations surveyed have a security policy.[45]

Identification is the foundation for all aspects of security. All users, whether they are an information resource or an information consumer, must have a unique identifier. An identifier is what a user, which wishes to utilize resources, uses to differentiate itself from all other entities. Without identification there is no basis for granting authorizations or maintaining accountability. Most organizations are primarily concerned with the identification of individuals. However, people are only one type of user. In today's networked client/server environment systems, software, hardware, and networks also need positive identification to assure information security. Information users must have sufficient authorizations to be granted use of the information, and the information resources must provide adequate security for the information. A network must be authorized to transport the information before it can be sent. The computer must be authorized to use the information before it can compute with it. This level of control is necessary to assure information security.

Enterprise Identification

The type of identification used affects all of the follow-up security processes. In a global enterprise there are a number of identification issues that have to be addressed. The sheer volume of items that must be accounted for and identifiers applied causes an issue of name management.

Identification is what a user presents to show who he or she is. Identifiers are usually created by the organization that uses them. However, third-party identifiers are also used (e.g., using driver's licenses to cash checks, not bank-issued check cashing cards). Use of third-party identifiers loosens control of the identification process, namely, knowledge of identifier creation and revocation, and the assurance that the identifier actually represents the user in question.

[45] "The 1999 Information Security Industry Survey," *Information Security Magazine,* July 1999.

Unique

Identifiers must be unique so that the user can be positively identified. Identifiers should be global – that is, an identifier should belong to one user throughout the enterprise. Any specific user should have only one identifier, even if the user performs multiple roles in the organization. This simplifies the association of individual identity for both the user and for the information system. It simplifies management and issuance of identifiers and reduces confusion in tracking the user and controlling which resources he or she uses.

There must be a one-to-one relationship between the individual and the identifier. This allows for individual accountability and ensures that the individual is the person represented by the identifier. Identifiers must not be shared; otherwise it is not possible to promote personal accountability. This is especially important for effectively controlling access to information with high integrity or confidentiality requirements.

Misidentification is a common problem even in the physical world. Identification becomes more difficult in the electronic worlds of the computer where identification must be formal and specific.

In large enterprises name management becomes an issue. Every user requires a unique identifier, or name. Making these identifiers unique, consistent, usable, and widely available can become a difficult task.

Universal

The same type of identifier should be available from all users – individuals, systems, or programs – anything that requires access to the information. This simplifies the process of validating the identifier. It also simplifies electronic storage and allows all users to be controlled in the same manner by having identifiers that are all of the same type and format.

Identifiers must not be context-dependent, meaning the use of one identifier in one circumstance and another identifier in a different circumstance. One identifier should be ample to identify one user anywhere for any reason. This does not mean that there will not be different methods to verify the identifier based on the specific situation.

Verifiable

There should be an easy and standardized process to validate the identifier so that simple standard interfaces can be constructed. The verification process should be highly available, since without verification no privileges can be granted. There should be multiple verification methods that can be used at different times to give different levels of identity assurance or in case a specific method of verification is suspected of being compromised.

Unforgeable

The identifier should be difficult to falsify so that it is difficult to misrepresent oneself as someone else.

Forgery is a problem that plagues everyone. Anything that has value has problems with forgeries. Identifiers that are physically inspected (e.g., company IDs that are authenticated by a building guard) need visual forgery deterrents. The use of holograms, which are difficult and expensive to reproduce, are widely used.

Electronic IDs have a different set of issues since the authentication is done electronically. Cryptographic methods are used to eliminate issues of replay and electronic forgeries.

Transportable

The identifier should be transportable from any location from which the user needs access. However, there are many issues that makes transportability difficult. Infrastructure dependencies will inhibit transportability to those locations where the infrastructure is not available. Laws regarding cryptography will limit the transportability of cryptographic identification across geographical borders.

Easy to Use

The identifier must be simple to use in all the transactions that require it. Its dependency on infrastructure – special card-readers, computer operating systems, etc., – will hinder its acceptance and possibly make it completely unusable, unless the organization plans to supply the necessary infrastructure.

Issuance of Identifiers

An organization may issue identification or utilize an independent issuer. The number of users that need identification and the relationship that the organization has with these users is a factor in determining this decision. The quality of the identifier is in part based on the quality of the authority that issued the identifier.

The level of verification required to authenticate the identity is dependent on the level of trust in the identifier. Cash requires only minimal authentication to verify that it is not counterfeit since everyone trusts the government of the country that issues the currency. Credit cards require more authentication since they are issued by private companies. Personal checks require even more authentication, especially if the bank is not a local bank. The level of authentication required is based on the level of trust in the financial instrument, which is in turn based on the trust in the party that issued it.

Private Issuance

Private issuance of identifiers gives the organization the greatest level of control. They can better control how they are issued, to whom they are issued, and what level of proof is required to receive the identity. These procedures must account for the expected user base. However, if the users are geographically dispersed, then physical contact may not be feasible or, if the volume of identifiers required is large, then it may be overwhelming to the organization. Private issuance also requires an interaction with the individual prior to the transaction where the identifier is needed. This may not be satisfactory, especially in the area of electronic commerce where the customer may not be known to the organization prior to the transaction. So, if there is not a strong relationship between the organization and the users, such as with a retail customer base, the organization may choose to have a trusted third party issue the identifiers.

Public Issuance

Public issuance requires a level of trust in the organization issuing the identification. The issuer must be trusted so that the identifier can be trusted. You must be conformable with the level of verification done to issue the identification. The trusted third party must be able to meet the organization's needs in the level of proof to issue the identifiers as well as being able to handle the volume of identifiers in the locations needed.

Scope of Use

The scope of use indicates how widely the identifier will be used and thereby how widely the identifier is accepted. It is dependent on the trust in the quality of the identifier and its verification process. The scope of use defines in part how it will be administered. An identifier's scope of use will impact the level of verification required to issue the identifier.

Small Scope

A small scope of use for an identifier generally gives more control to the local administration of the systems. However, small scopes will cause the user to authenticate his identification each time he needs resources that are not in a scope in which he has already identified himself.

Large Scope

Larger scopes of use will reduce the number of times that a user needs to be identified and authenticated. The concept of single-sign-on is based on a scope that encompasses everything which any one user may have a need to do. A large scope of use requires more coordination between application administrators that are all within the scope of use of the identifier. It also requires a greater level of trust in the issuance of the identifier.

Administration of Identifiers

Administration of identifiers includes the creation and revocation of the identifiers, the process of distributing the identifier, and the integration of the identifier into the authentication, authorization and administration systems. Name management issues include the ability to create unique names and distribute them via a name service to the system that requires them. The distributed part of the name service is often referred to directory management. This is the process of making the directory of identifiers available to the processes that need them.

Centralized Administration

Centralized administration of identifiers will allow for easy control of the identifiers so that you can be assured that the same standards of proof were required to receive the identifier. It will also help control the uniqueness and universalness of the identifier. It will give you a specific process to verify the identifier. However, having only one authority for identifiers may make the time required to receive the identifier lengthy. It may also slow the process of verifying the identifier. And if you require users from around the globe to be issued identifiers, having centralized administration may create geographical hardships.

Distributed Administration

Distributed issuance of identifiers makes it easier for an individual to have an identifier issued, especially if it requires physical verification. It should reduce the amount of time needed to get an identifier and can facilitate resolving specific issues of a given location. However, it may make it more difficult to maintain verification standards as each location implements the process in its own way.

Distributed administration can cause localized outages and can be used to delegate administrative authority. It can also cause synchronization issues as changes have to propagate through the system. It also increases the number of administrators who might be able to abuse the systems.

Implementation Options

Identification must be available to all access methods. It should be based on an enterprise-wide naming environment to provide uniqueness, and should be based on a public key infrastructure for electronic verification.

Naming Standards

Naming standards are built around X.500, the OSI directory service. X.500 defines a directory structure that is hierarchical in nature and uses keyword value pairs. It defines the Directory Access Protocol (DAP) which is a client/server directory service protocol used when contacting directory servers. DAP is a heavyweight protocol that runs over a full OSI stack and requires a significant amount of computing resources to run. LDAP, which stands for the Lightweight Directory Access Protocol, runs directly over TCP and provides most of the functionality of DAP at a much lower cost. Today, LDAP is widely used as a front end to X.500 directories.

A directory service is the process that is used to manage the unique names that are required to be able to have unique identifiers. This requires a central registry containing user information such as an identifier, public key, digital certificate, and other information. X.500 standards and conventions exist to support the naming of systems, users, and other resources.

Integration into existing systems that do not directly support LDAP requires the introduction of an LDAP to the name service gateway. This is software that emulates older name services, such as NIS, while using LDAP to retrieve the information. Due to the limitations that some of the older systems may have on names, there may be a translation or an alternate name required.

Smart Cards

Similar in appearance to a credit card, a smart card stores information on an embedded microprocessor chip that can be read with a personal identification number (PIN), rather than with a magnetic strip that can be read by anyone. It can be used to secure the storage and processing of the information for a variety of applications.

Smart cards can be used for both physical identification and electronic identification. They can be printed with a photograph of the owner and contain electronic identification within their electronics. It is a physical ID so that possession is required to gain access. When utilized with a password, it easily allows for two-factor authentication.

- **Physical identification** is needed to be able to maintain physical security. It is commonplace to require a physical ID to be granted access to corporate facilities. Physical IDs often contain a photograph of the individual. Smart cards can contain identification for a centralized control or complete access data for local control.

- **Electronic identification** is used for any electronic access. This identification has to be authenticated electronically without any human intervention. The electronic chip on the smart card can contain the individual's private key, stored encrypted, with the PIN known only to that individual. Thus, having the card and knowing the PIN will allow him to use his private key for authentication.

Public Key Infrastructure

A public key infrastructure (PKI) is a system that uses certificates based on public key cryptography for authenticated identification. Public key cryptography is based on a cryptographic method that uses two interdependent keys. What is encrypted with one of the keys can only be decrypted with the use of the other. In this method, one key is made public and the other is kept private.

To send a message privately to someone, one would encrypt it with the recipient's public key and then only the recipient can decrypt it with his private key. To prove identity, one would encrypt it with his private key, then anyone could decrypt it with the sender's public key and be assured that he is the only one who could have sent it.

Identity Errors

Identity errors come from confusing the identifiers of two different individuals. This can be because the identifiers are not unique or through carelessness of the people comparing the identifiers. The problem often goes undetected when the information is stored under the wrong identifier. It is not until that information is needed does the error cause confusion or worse.

We have all been victims of misidentification. Some are harmless–the awkward hello from a stranger at the store who thought you were someone else. Others are annoying–the endless telephone calls for the other John Smith in town. And still others are costly–the state garnishing wages for unpaid child support for someone else's children. These all happen because someone does not perform a thorough enough identification.

Many identity errors occur because the information is stored with an identifier that is not unique or can be misused. It is difficult to create a list of attributes that will uniquely identify a person without issuing a specific ID card. Companies continue to use a name, date of birth, mother's maiden name, etc., to uniquely identify an individual. These are not sufficient. Often, a lazy clerk will merely look at two identifiers and assume they have the correct person when in fact they do not.

> In Australia, two women who have the same identical name, Belinda Lee Perry, also share the birthdate of January 7, 1969 — but that's not all they share. Their records are confused and commingled by banks, building societies, government agencies, the Electoral Commission, and even the local library. One had her library card canceled and her named removed from electoral rolls when the other moved and was refused social security benefits because she was already registered. Meanwhile, the other was refused a student loan because it appeared she already had one, and was billed $300 for the other's bill.[46]

---

[46]   "Hey, Belinda, meet Belinda," *The Sunday Mail*, Queensland, Australia, 10 March 1996.

Checklist

— Determine what will be used for identifiers.

— Decide who will issue the identifiers.

— Set the requirements necessary to be issued an identifier.

— Determine identification requirements for each class of transactions.

  For example:

  Employees and partners will use company-issued identifiers for all transactions.
  Contract customers will use a verifiable identifier issued by a trusted third party.
  Cash customers will need a verifiable credit card to conduct cash transaction.
  Anonymous users will only be allowed minimal abilities.

— Determine how identification will be administered.

— List requirements for issuance.

— Determine reasons for revocation.

— Decide how identification information will be deployed.

  Consider:

  Directory services
  Replication of data

CHAPTER 10

Authentication

Over 85% of companies surveyed said that information security has improved since 1997.[47]

Authentication is the process of validating the identity of an user. Users include individuals, computing devices and resources. Authorization is the first step in information security. Positive identification is needed to ensure that the appropriate user is getting access to the appropriate resource. Even though identification and authentication is usually thought of as pertaining to users, it is important that all information resources be identified and authenticated. Without this authentication it is not possible to be assured that the information being accessed is the actual information requested.

Resource owners want to allow authorized users access to their resources (e.g., electronic data, computers, printers, networks, and applications) and keep out unauthorized users. Authentication is also required by users to ensure that the data and/or software applications they are using are authentic. If they are not authentic, they may contain incorrect data, a computer virus, a Trojan horse, etc. Authentication is a component needed to ensure the confidentiality, integrity, and availability of information resources. The need for dependable electronic authentication is accelerated due to the ever-widening use of electronic communications on a network that cannot identify users physically and/or personally.

Strong authentication is critical to all aspects of security. If the method of authentication is compromised, then you have lost the ability to distinguish who is gaining access. There is the chance of suffering losses of privacy, confidentiality, and integrity by not knowing who is accessing the information and who is changing the information. Consistent methods of authentication are required to avoid a "weak link" attack, where an attacker will take advantage of a weaker method of authentication to gain access to information.

Every type of identifier should have a specific method of authentication identified for it. The process of authentication must be easy, non-intrusive, quick, and accurate. Otherwise, it

---

[47]   "The 1999 Information Security Industry Survey," *Information Security Magazine,* July 1999.

will not be widely accepted. Authentication can be fairly simple, such as a password, or it can be complex, such as smart cards (tokens) or biometrics (e.g., fingerprints, retinal scans, etc.).

Authentication errors can be classified as either false positive or false negative. A false positive authentication means that an entity that should not be allowed access would be granted access. This unauthorized access can lead to information disclosure, corruption, or deletion. It may allow an attacker to gain a foothold to instigate a more devastating attack. One false positive authentication can allow an attacker to gain all the access needed to cause loss. A false negative authentication means that an entity that should be allowed access will be denied access. A single false negative authentication will be a nuisance, making a user reauthenticate, while continuous false negative authentication can lead to a denial of service.

Factors of Authentication

The factors that can be used to authenticate the identity of an entity are those factors that are unique to that specific entity. The factors must be known or derivable to both the entity being authenticated and the process authenticating the entity.

Basic Factors

The following are three basic factors that are used in authentication. These basic factors are available to all types of entities.

- **Something you know** – a shared secret, a password, something both the user and the authenticator know. Password authentication is relatively inexpensive and easy to implement, which is why almost all systems that perform authentication use passwords. The most common password problem is a weak password – if users can select them, they are generally not long enough, not random enough or not changed often enough, to keep them secure. In addition, many systems do not store passwords in a secure location or with strong enough protections to prevent common password attacks.
- **Something you have** – a physical ID (e.g., an identification card).
- **Something you are** – a measurable feature (e.g., fingerprint, facial characteristics, voiceprint). The measuring of a physical characteristic is called biometrics. If the entity that is being authenticated is a program or a system, the measurement can be a crypto-graphic checksum.

Implicit Factors

Implicit factors are entity attributes that can be determined without interaction with the entity. The most common implicit factor is location. Knowing where an individual is may imply that he is who he says he is or that he has already passed other security checks. If a user is in the organization's office, then there is increased expectation that he is a legitimate user. This is the "where you are" factor.

- **Physical location** – Knowing the entity's physical location can increase the likelihood that the entity is trustworthy. If the user is in a secure area, then it is expected that she passed physical security checks. The idea is that once the person has passed a security checkpoint, they have been authenticated. There is work being done in the industry to use GPS (Global Positioning System) to authenticate people.

- **Logical Location** – Logical location is used in much the same manner. If the user is on the internal network, then it is expected that she is in a secured location. Being able to identify the computer that is being used can indicate whether she is accessing the system from her own computer; this, too, increases the likelihood that she is who she says she is.

Multiple Factors

In general, the use of multiple factors in an authentication transaction provides stronger authentication. This is especially true when the nature of the factor, such as a physical hardware device, offers great assurance that only the person being authenticated should have possession of the factor. Two factor authentication – Photo IDs, which are a combination of biometrics (the photograph) and a physical ID, or bank cards, which are physical IDs which require a password or PIN (personal identification number) – is used all of the time.

Authentication Models

Authentication is a verification of identity to prevent impersonation and provide the level of trust necessary to utilize authorizations. The type of authentication required will depend on the quality of the identifier, the access method and the privileges requested. All of this information may not be known at the first contact where initial authentication is performed. As more privileges are requested, more authentication may be required.

Multiple Authentication

In a multiple authentication model each application is in complete control of the identifier used for an entity and the method of authentication. This requires the user to authenticate to every application, system, or network. It also increases administration. Adding or removing a user will usually require updating many identification and authentication databases.

The need for multiple authentication is a result of different systems, networks, and applications each managing their own identification and authentication. A system will perform its own authentication, unless there is a level of trust in the authentication performed by another system. This trust has been limited to systems created by the same vendor. Improvements in security standards and compliance to them has increased this interoperability.

Single Authentication

Single authentication per session, single sign-on (SSO), is a great convenience for users. Historically, every computer, every program, and every service had to authenticate the user individually. This led to an environment where users had to log on to the network, log on again to a computer, and then log on again to an application. With single sign-on authentication, the user authenticates once per session and then presents credentials to each system or application that needs to be able to identify the entity. This requires that the authentication process be known and trusted by all the computers, networks, and applications that would otherwise do their own authentication.

Single sign-on can also be a convenience to administrators, since it creates a standard process for authorization throughout the enterprise. It also creates a centralized database of all of the authentication information. This can simplify the control and management of authentication information. It can also create a single point of administration for management of user authentication.

However, single sign-on does require a distributed authentication process for performance and availability. The biggest inhibitor is that all of the applications must use a standard method of authentication. For new development this is not a big problem, but the modification of existing software and the integration with commercial software can be an extremely costly and time-consuming endeavor.

Multilevel Authentication

Multilevel authentication is the process of requiring different types of authentication based on the method of access, resources requested, or permissions requested. This allows for better implementation of least privileges and can extend access to unsecured locations if the user is sufficiently authenticated.

The level of authentication may depend on the quality of the identifier as well as the method of access. The less trusted the identifier or the more remote the access, the greater requirement for stringent authentication. Access methods may indicate that the individual is in the company's office and has thereby passed some level of physical access security, or it may indicate the security level of the access method – a cell phone is less secure than an office extension. These things all affect the level of authentication required and the level of authorizations granted.

Consider the case of an all-purpose bankcard. It could be a smart card that contains e-cash, an ATM card, and an ID card for other banking transactions. The use of the card as a cash card may not require any authentication above the physical possession of the card, since the amount of money on the card would be limited to a relatively small amount. Use of the card at the ATM would require the physical card and a PIN number to make deposits and withdrawals up to a moderate limit. However, as a bank ID card the authentication process may be more stringent, since it would enable the user to get loans and transfer large amounts of money. It might require a biometric process, such as a fingerprint or photograph, to be verified. The level of authentication based on the level of authorizations requested is not uncommon.

Authentication Options

The level and type of authentication depends on the type of identifier, the access method, the authorizations requested, and the scope of authentication. Adequate authentication should be assured for both local access, from within the corporate firewall, and remote access, from a public network. It needs to be able to handle a wide variety of users who need to utilize information resources. There are users that are not people that need to be authenticated. These users, which include programs, computers networks, etc., must be able to prove that they are the entity that they report to be. The same factors of something you know, something you have, and something you are apply to authenticating nonhuman entities. Nonhuman entities usually rely on either shared secrets or measurable features to verify identity.

Passwords

Using a password to authenticate an identity is as old as a sentry guarding the gate of an ancient city. Passwords require a previously communicated shared secret. Therefore, an out-of-band communication is required before passwords can be used to authenticate an identity. Shared secrets are a common method of verifying the identity of systems. They may utilize an encrypted communication method that requires they know a shared secret to encode and decode the messages sent between client and server.

For a long time this was an adequate method of electronic authentication, but with the increased use of computer systems, each with its own password, requirements for end-to-end authentication, and the implementation of e-business where everyone in the world is a user, passwords no longer live up to the needs of the electronic community.

- **Reusable Passwords** are the most widely used method of authentication today. With reusable passwords you use the same password each time you authenticate your identity. Reusable passwords are simple to use and easy to implement. However, there are a number of issues with reusable passwords. The first problem with passwords is that they must be easy to remember, since they shouldn't be written down, and they must be difficult to guess. Traditionally, security consultants advise choosing "hard to guess" passwords and to "change them frequently."

  The second problem is that reusable passwords are susceptible to two very common attacks – password cracking and network snooping. The power of today's computers has turned password guessing into dictionary searches. Often when a password is compromised it may not be discovered for a very long time, giving the perpetrator plenty of time to cause damage and to cover his or her tracks. Snooping is monitoring the network for passwords from client to server sometimes in plain text; but even if the password is transmitted encrypted, the encrypted password could be "cracked" if the encryption is suspect.

- **Onetime Passwords** is a strategy of using a password only once, so if it is captured, it is not usable again. This is needed due to the advent of networks and distributed computing; having passwords that are used over the net without encryption has lead to snooping packets on the network for passwords. The onetime password strategies are generally based on a pseudorandom number sequence that, given the seed, the password can be computed, but given numbers in the sequence, the next password cannot be computed. Onetime passwords are most often implemented in a hardware device. Computational passwords are often utilized, too, in the authentication of nonhuman entities.

  Onetime passwords have problems with synchronization. That is, if the implementation is time-based, then the clocks in the onetime password device must correspond to the time on the system you wish to access; if the implementation is use-based, if the onetime password device is used without successfully communicating to the host system, the two may get out-of-sync. When this occurs, the password device will need to be resynchronized with assistance from the security administrator.

- **Challenge-Response Passwords** are another method to address the issue of password snooping. The challenge-response system is implemented so that the service issues a challenge to which there is a correct response. This can be implemented with a number of questions that require correct responses or through the use of cryptography. A cryptographic challenge-response method would take the challenge, a random number, encrypt it, and return the encrypted value. The service could decrypt the response to validate that it was encrypted with the key known only to the specific entity.

Handheld Authentication Devices

Handheld Authentication Devices, (HHAD), are portable devices, usually in a credit card-sized format, that have local data storage and computation. They use a variety of techniques to issue unique onetime or challenge-response passwords. The passwords are usually displayed by liquid crystal display (LCD) that is readable by users. These tokens usually require a PIN and contain a built-in keypad. The same algorithms that are used in these handheld devices can be programmed into information systems for authentication.

- **Sequence-based** cards issue a new password each time the card is used. If the card is used unsuccessfully or is activated without making a connection to the server, the server and the card can become out of sync and require some method of resyncing to make the card useful again.

- **Time-based** cards generate a new password every specific unit of time. Incorrect time on the server can render the cards useless. Systems can have incorrect time from clock drift, being rebooted, or accidental or malicious changing of the system clock.

- **Certificate-based** cards contain digital certificates, which are data structures that bind the identities of users and their associated public keys. They are issued by a Certificate Authority (CA). The certificates and associated private keys can be used for authentication and digital signing, as well as other security protocol operations like key exchange. They easily integrate into web-based applications that use the SSL protocol. Certificates and keys can be stored as disc files or in hardware devices like smart cards.

Biometrics

Biometric authentication utilizes the uniqueness of certain physical properties or features of an individual, such as fingerprints, retina map, voice pattern, or facial features. These physical properties or features can be represented digitally as biometric data or biometrics. Biometrics is the only way to be positively sure that an individual is who he claims.

In the past, biometrics has been plagued with the issues of cost and accuracy. New technologies have increased the accuracy and lowered the costs. Today, fingerprint scanners and other biometric devices are widely available and affordable. These products usually store the biometrics of individuals in a server and then use sensors to detect or measure an individual on a real-time basis. If the presented biometrics match the stored data, an individual is authenticated. In order to reduce the risk of a user faking the biometrics (since they are basically electronic data and can be reproduced), sophisticated systems use multiple combined biometrics and enforce signal variations. For example, a good fingerprint authentication device may have to sense finger temperature, skin humidity, and touching-motion pressure, in addition to the scanning of the fingerprint.

However, there is still the issue of personal rights and acceptance. Many people feel that the use of physical attributes, such as fingerprints, retina scans, voice prints, etc., is an invasion of privacy and are concerned about the possibility of misuse. These objections may be overcome if there is adequate security and legal protection of the personal, biometric information.

Nonhuman entities that require authentication can utilize their own personal measurement. Cryptographic checksums can be calculated to determine if the software is the same software it reports to be and hardware systems often have permanent identification, such as serial numbers, that are unalterable.

Authentication Management

The management of authentication information should be easy to use and integrated into the management of identifiers. It should allow for a single point management that can be put into an enterprise management and monitoring system. It should include auditing capabilities to enable the tracking and recording of authentication information (successful and unsuccessful authentication attempts). The needs of the global enterprise require global authentication services.

Authentication Server

An authentication server is a system that controls the authentication for the enterprise. It has a centralized repository of identifiers, and the appropriate authentication methods for each identifier are based on its access method and privileges requested. The authentication service should be replicated for high availability and optimal performance.

Upon request to authenticate an identity, the authentication server will request and confirm the authentication information. The authentication server will then create credentials for the user. The user's credentials are what will be used to confirm authorizations and grant privileges to resources. Use of credentials allows a user to be authenticated once and then present the credentials to all the entities from which it wants privileges.

Subverting Authentication

Authentication requires that the entity being authenticated send credentials to the entity performing the authentication. This action has been plagued with issues, since falsifying authentication is a primary method of impersonating a valid user. There have been both direct attacks to the authentication method itself, such as password guessing, and indirect attacks that attack the communication process.

> In Beijing, a student lost a precious $18,000 scholarship to the University of Michigan because her roommate signed onto their shared account and sent e-mail rejecting the scholarship in her name. A month later, her roommate admitted her misdeed and paid a hefty fine. The University of Michigan reaccepted the applicant.[48]

---

[48]   Kabay, M. E., PhD, "The InfoSec Year in Review," *National Computer Security Association,* 12 July 1996.

Direct Attacks

Direct attacks are attacks the authentication processes directly. They exploit flaws in the authentication method to be able to falsely authenticate.

- **Guessing** is the process of guessing authentication tokens until the correct token is guessed. Guessing can be focused directly at the authentication service by repeatedly attempting tokens until a correct token is found. Other methods include capturing the stored value used to verify the token and then using the authentication algorithm on tokens until the result of the algorithm matches the captured stored value.

- **Cracking** is the process of actually computing the password. However, the term "cracking" is often used when it is actually password guessing. Cracking passwords can only be accomplished when the cryptographic method used to transmit or store the password is susceptible to an algorithmic attack.

Indirect Attacks

Indirect attacks do not attack the authentication process directly; instead, they attack the communication over which the authentication is transmitted. Often indirect attacks can be more successful than direct attacks.

- **Snooping** is the process of eavesdropping while an entity authenticates itself and capturing the authentication information. This is possible if the password is communicated without being encrypted.

- **Capture and Replay** is the process of capturing the authentication communication and replaying it, so that the authenticator thinks that the entity is reauthenticating. Most current authentication methods include a time stamp in the process of authentication so that this is not possible. However, there are many systems and protocols that are being used that rely on old authentication methods.

- **Session Hijacking** is the processing of stealing a session after the authentication has been accomplished. The attacker is able to take control of the communication so that it appears to the server that the attacker is the user who has already authenticated. This process exploits flaws in the communication protocol.

Social Attacks

Social attacks are attacks against individuals in an attempt to get them to divulge the authorization token.

- **Social Engineering** is the process of convincing someone that it is safe to disclose the desired information. It often includes impersonation and false pretexts.

- **Investigation** is the process of delving into an individual's background to gather enough personal information to be able to determine likely tokens.

- **Searching** is the process of physically looking for the token among the individual's belongings. It requires physical access to the individual's workplace to search for information that would lead to the token, or the token itself (e.g., yellow sticky notes under the keyboard or on the mousepad).

- **Eavesdropping** is the process of observing the user entering the token.

Checklist

— Determine appropriate authentication methods for the organization.

— Standardize authentication processes throughout the organization.

— Required authentication will be based on:
    — Access method
    — Information requested
    — Privileges requested

CHAPTER 11

Authorization

Only 65% of organizations surveyed said that information security has "high visibility."[49]

Authorization defines what attributes of which resource an authenticated user is allowed to utilize. They are what provide an entity's privileges. They are used to limit access and create a separation of duties. Authorizations should be multidirectional – all entities (e.g., user, application, systems) that access an information resource should have appropriate authorizations to that resource.

Authorization and Privilege

The concept of authorizations and privileges is often a confusing one. These words are often used interchangeably but they are different, interrelated aspects of security. Authorizations are permissions. An entity is given authorization or granted permission to utilize a resource, but it requires privileges to actually be able to use it. Authorizations are a permission that an entity has that allows it to utilize a privilege to perform a process.

Authorizations are assigned to entities based on the requirements of the entity to utilize the information. This can be based on the job that the entity has to perform.

You are authorized to be granted the privilege to utilize the resource. A privilege is required to perform a process on information. Privileges are granted to entities that have the appropriate authorizations. Privileges are based on many factors. Privileges are often based on appropriateness. A word processor may not be privileged to edit an accounting file. Privileges are often based on legal or policy statements that limit or restrict the activities of authorized users.

---

[49]   "The 1999 Information Security Industry Survey," *Information Security Magazine,* July 1999.

For example, a driver's license is authorization or permission to drive a vehicle. However, the individual with that license may not have the privilege to drive until he has insurance, a vehicle inspection, and other requirements. Therefore, an authorized driver is denied the privilege of driving.

What Authorizations Provide

The use of authorizations provides the ability to control the actions of the users. The authorizations clearly define what resources can and cannot be utilized. They enable the implementation of business practices that limit abuse.

Least Privileges

Authorizations should be granted on the principle of least privileges. An entity's business needs should be demonstrated before any authorizations should be granted.

Least privilege (part of the less rights, less risk philosophy) means that a process should have no more privilege than is required to perform the tasks that it is intended to perform, and that it should have that privilege for the minimum time required to accomplish those tasks. Related goals are to control privilege propagation (to processes and files), and to limit the threat of Trojan horse attacks that attempt to gain privilege in order to do their work.

Separation of Duties

Separation of duties is a basic business process that increases accountability. It implies that different key steps in a process require different privileges that are granted to different individuals. That way, no one person can perform the entire process.

Granular authorizations allow effective distribution of responsibilities. By selectively assigning authorizations an administrator can distribute administrative responsibilities among several users without giving all of them access to all functions. The authorization to administer functional portions of the system, such as the web server or the backup subsystem, can be granted to one or two individuals without granting them administrative access to other portions of the system.

Increased Accountability

Many information systems have administrative accounts that are all-powerful with unrestricted access and unlimited privileges. The power of these accounts is dangerous, since a simple mistake can have broad-ranging implications. They are also attractive targets, since they are all-powerful. These systems often have only one administrator account, so that anyone who has to perform any administrative function has to use the administrative account. With only one account for administrative functions, there is no individual accountability. Being able to assign specific administrative authorizations to individual accounts allows for individual accountability and more granular distribution of authorizations. Authorized users can use their own account to gain the necessary privilege for administrative tasks, so administrative actions can be traced back to the actual user rather than a shared account.

Granularity of Authorizations

The level of detail that is defined by the authorizations determines the ability to limit and separate privileges. A single authorization may enable a number of privileges or a privilege may require multiple authorizations. Authorizations should be defined by functions that need to be performed.

Coarse Grain Authorization

Course grain authorization defines and controls the basic abilities to interact with resources. They can be enforced by the environment (operating system) without concern for the applications. There is no need for cooperation or that the application even have any knowledge of coarse-grain authorizations. The application will either be allowed or disallowed based on things outside its control.

This is the type of authorization that most operating systems utilize, defining a very limited list of attributes and controls.

- **Access** is the ability to see the resource and gather information from/about the resource.
- **Utilization** is the ability to use the resource.
- **Modification** is the ability to change the resource.
- **Creation** is the ability to create a new resource.
- **Deletion** is the ability to remove an existing resource.
- **Management** is the ability to change the authorizations of the resource.

Fine Grain Authorization

Fine grain authorizations define very specific functions. This enables a very specific difference in privileges to be defined. This allows for a better separation of duties and increased accountability. However, data element level authorizations require application awareness. So applications need to be consistent in their knowledge and use of authorizations.

Requirements

Authorization identifies privileges that an entity may be granted. Authorizations can be granted to groups of entities or limited to specific individuals.

Limited Scope

Authorizations need to grant privileges for a specific function. A well-defined fine granularity of authorization allows for very specific differentiation, so that a user can be authorized to perform a task without having to allow him to perform other tasks. The more specific the authorizations are, the greater the accountability afforded. Authorizations can encompass a number of privileges or be very specific to a particular operation. The more specific the authorizations, the greater the ability to enforce separation of duties. Authorizations can apply to an entire application or be granular to the level of individual data items.

Globally Defined

Authorizations should be global. They should have specific use throughout the enterprise. They should not be interpreted differently by different applications. Since authorizations allow an entity to request privileges, not necessarily be granted them, an entity should have the same authorizations regardless of location, time of day, or anything else. Privileges can be restricted at any time for any reason. They are the true controlling mechanism. Authorizations allow an entity to get to the privileges.

Applied to All Entities

Authorizations need to be applied and enforced for all resources that interact with the information. If they are only applied to individuals, they will not indicate what software can be used to manipulate the information (it may be appropriate to use a general ledger program with accounting information and not appropriate to use a text editor), or if the information should be restricted to specific systems. (It may be fine to access payroll information from a PC within the office, but not remotely over the Internet.) All entities – individuals, software, systems, networks, etc. – must be authorized to utilize the information before privileges are granted.

Design Choices

There are a variety of options that are utilized in the implementation of authorizations. These choices affect the manner in which business rules are mapped to authorizations and how they are administered. They all define the association of privileges that a user has to interact with a resource.

Centralized or Distributed

Authorizations can be maintained locally – every resource can have its own authorization process and maintain its own authorization database to associate authorizations to users; or authorizations can be maintained in a centralized database.

Traditionally, each application does its own authorization. However, this often leads to inconsistent implementations, where different software applies different rules to determine authorizations. A global and consistent implementation of authorization is critical to a secure enterprise. This situation can be used to exploit a weak link where a software system that is more lax can allow a user to gain inappropriate authorizations. A weak link can be subverted to compromise the entire enterprise.

The centralized approach can better assure that authorizations are consistently applied. A single database that is available to all applications will give a consistent view of security. A centralized approach can facilitate single point administration. This simplifies the process of adding and modifying authorizations and creates an environment that facilitates consistent administration.

A distributed approach to authorizations localizes the authorizations, which generally improves the performance of the authorization process and localizes outages.

Resource-based or Role-based

Authorization can be considered in two ways: It can be viewed as resource-based—an access control model, such as determining what information an end-user is permitted to access; or, it can be viewed as role-based, such as deciding what information purchasing agents are allowed to access. Authorizations allow you to define administrative roles. The tasks capable of being performed by a given role can be associated with a specific authorization and granted to any user trusted in that role.

List-based or Rule-based

Authorizations can be implemented either with lists, so that each user/resource pair has defined privileges; or with rules so that a user's "attributes" are compared with the resource's "attributes" to determine if privileges should be granted.

List-based authorizations can be organized by either listing all the resources that a specific entity is authorized to use or by listing all the entities that are authorized to use a specific resource. Users or resources can be grouped into named groups to reduce the length of the lists in a list-based authorization scheme.

Rule-based systems are based on a list of rules that determine if authorizations should be granted. The rule evaluates attributes of both the user and the resource. This requires that common attributes be defined that apply to both the user and the resource so that a common comparison can be made. Rules can be extended to include other environmental information like time of day, day of week, or any data value that can detected by the information system.

Authorization Server

An integrated enterprise authorization service requires that all functions that require privileges use a centralized authorization service to determine if the privileges should be granted. Every application has to use the authorization service. Most existing applications aren't designed to use an external authorization service and, of those that are, most are designed for a specific service instead of being written to a generic API.

Creating new applications that utilize a standard authorization service will usually simplify the application by moving the business logic to determine authorizations from every application to the centralized authorization server, reducing the maintenance workload by having a single location to modify business logic as the environment changes. Use of an authorization server will expedite the changes in business policy by having only one place to change it and reduce programming errors based on different interpretations of regulations.

An authorization server combines the centralized security administration and end-user consistency of mainframe-based environments with the flexibility and end-user functionality of distributed computing environments. It improves security by effectively controlling user access privileges and reduces costs through reduced application development complexity and simplified administration. Administration is simplified by providing a graphical user interface (GUI) that manages the security rules and privileges common to all enterprise applications. The authorization server reduces application development complexity by replacing the custom code that must otherwise be developed for each of the many individual applications across the enterprise. Additionally, the authorization server's flexible rule-based application security promotes the enforcement of corporate security policies.

Authorization identifies what privileges a entity has.

Abuse of Authorization

A fundamental step in compromising a system is to gain enough authorization to be able to achieve the intruder's goal. For outside intruders, this can be a major part of the intrusion effort, while inside intruders are often given the authorization. In some cases it is not an issue of gaining the authorizations, rather an issue of being given too much authorization.

> A computer operator at a major Wall Street stock brokerage input a transaction for the sale of 11 million shares – it should have been for the sale of $11 million worth of shares. That mistake was so great that it even caused the Dow Jones index to drop 15 points. It wasn't revealed just how much the mistake cost the brokerage in actual dollars, but it probably cost them a fortune in terms of customer confidence and bad publicity.[50]

---

[50]   Computer Security Institute, "Introduction to Network Security," 1992.

Checklist

— Identify roles based on business functions.

— Determine privileges to perform these functions.

— Define authorizations to be granted privileges.

— Define the least privileges necessary to each authorization.
  Remember
    Authorizations give rights to use privileges.
    Rules determine the ability to use privileges.

— Assure consistency of authorizations throughout the enterprise.

CHAPTER 12

Availability

Fifty percent of the companies that lose those critical business systems for 10 or more days never recover. Ever. Ninety-three percent of the companies without a disaster-recovery plan in place were out of business five years later.[51]

Availability is the state of being able to ensure that users can use any information resource whenever and wherever it is needed in accordance with applicable privileges. Information resources only need to be available when they are needed. Some information only needs to be available at specific times. In this case, it is only necessary to have the information available at these times; having it available when it is not needed for legitimate purposes only makes it available for improper use. Most resources are not utilized most of the time. Understanding the utilization requirements of the information will increase the ability to have greater availability.

Information availability covers a range of issues. The availability of the information depends on the availability of the data, the system that stores and processes the information, the infrastructure that is used to transport and access the information, and the support systems, such as power and air conditioning. All of these systems must be available for the information to be available. Many of the elements that determine availability are not in the direct control of the organization.

Global organizations need access to information around the clock, which limits the availability of time when the information is not needed – meaning that information systems must be always available.

With ever-increasing demands for timely information and greater volumes of information being processed, the threat of information system disruption is a very serious one. In some cases, interruptions of only a few hours are unacceptable. The impact due to inability to process data should be assessed, and actions should be taken to assure availability of those systems considered essential to agency operation. Functional management must identify critical com-

---

[51]   "Will you be ready when disaster strikes?," *PC Week*, 6 February 1995.

puter applications and develop contingency plans so that the probability of data processing and telecommunications support loss is minimized.

Types of Outages

A loss of availability is a loss of productivity. This impacts both direct losses of revenue – the e-store is unavailable to sell goods – and delays in development delayed shipments.

Unscheduled Downtime

Unscheduled downtime is the primary concern of most organizations. Unscheduled downtime has a multiplier effect on lost productivity. Users that were expecting to use the unavailable resource are unproductive while the resource is unavailable, then the work that was not accomplished while the resource was unavailable has to be accomplished when it becomes available, and that catch-up time could have been used for other work.

The entire disaster recovery discipline is built to reduce unscheduled downtime.

Scheduled Downtime

A cause of unavailability that is often overlooked is scheduled downtime. Scheduled unavailability allows an organization to reschedule processes that need the unavailable resources to minimize the impact. Scheduled downtime can be the result of regular processes (such as backups), periodic processes (such as hardware maintenance), and irregular processes (such as system updates, upgrades and failed component replacements).

The difficulty of scheduled downtime is increased with a global business and worldwide offices and customers. Organizations with a web presence have the need for systems with true 24x7 availability to serve their web customers whenever they wish to conduct business.

The total removal of scheduled downtime may be unrealistic. So minimizing the downtime and appropriate scheduling is critical to minimizing the impact.

Peak Usage

Few systems are designed to be able to supply peak usage demands without some level of outage or delays. To minimize the impact of peak usage times, systems should address the needs of those users to whom an outage would have the greatest impact, and delegate the reduced performance to users who will suffer less from the reduced performance or unavailability.

Protecting all Levels

All levels of the information system have to be protected from outages. The interdependencies of the information system makes its availability dependent on all levels operating properly.

Data Availability

The system should support a highly available file system. A highly available file system should eliminate the need for scheduled downtime for routine file system maintenance, such as defragmentation, reorganization, and file system expansion. This should be coupled with a highly available data storage system that can eliminate any single point of failure in the storage hardware. It should be able to repair and replace any part in the system without causing any system downtime. Hardware replication of data can organize the data for optimal performance and minimum impact from hardware failure. Highly available data is often achieved through the use of a storage area network solution (SANS) that facilitates a high level of data protection via disk array technologies and redundant, hot-swappable hardware. The network aspect of the SANS allows copies of the data to be stored in remote locations for disaster recovery.

It should also include an online backup feature that allows applications to continue to access the latest data while the backup process operates on a static snapshot of the data. Backups should be able to perform offline or out-of-band so that they do not affect the availability or performance of the system. Implementing a comprehensive backup strategy can improve system security. It can be utilized to create a consistent implementation of the security policy on all of the systems.

The backups need to be segmented based on security classification. Information with differing security classifications have different requirements for the handling of the media on which the data is stored. Creating backup templates that address specific classifications of information means they can be backed up to specific media at specific times and be maintained separately from backups of differing security levels.

Media retention needs to support the type of information contained on the backup media. Different types of information have different retention requirements. System and security logs have a much longer retention requirement than ordinary data. The retained logs also have a requirement for appropriate custody if they are expected to be useful in the case of an intrusion investigation.

A backup strategy can assist in the adherence of licensing requirements. The specifics of software licenses differ between vendors and products and are quite involved. Many of the software licenses specifically state that the licensee can create one backup copy of the software for disaster recovery procedures. If the backup procedures for this software is not specifically maintained separately, it is likely that the organization will be in violation of the license by having multiple backup copies.

System Availability

All of the hardware systems that support the information system should be designed to be highly available. They should be constructed so that all major components are redundant, including disk drives, power supplies, fans, memory, and controllers. Furthermore, the repair of a failed component should not require downtime. All major components should be hot-swappable, to allow for online replacement.

Rapid recovery of systems from a disaster can be accomplished through the use of a hot site or a rapid replacement service. A hot site has a complete duplicate of the hardware system available at another site to be used in the case of a disaster. Hot sites can be managed internally or with a purchased service. The hot site can be at a remote site or it can be a mobile service that contains the appropriate hardware in a mobile unit that is "rolled" to your area and temporarily replaces your computer center. It is a self-contained "site" equipped with power, environmental controls, communications capabilities, and hardware.

A rapid replacement service is an agreement that provides for the quick replacement of your computer equipment and specified software. The predetermined hardware configuration can be shipped to a customer-specified location. It can also be shipped to the disaster-stricken site or to other locations.

Application Availability

Application availability is just as important an issue as system availability, yet it is often not addressed. Application availability is achieved through application replication where possible and the use of highly available clustering techniques that detect any application outage and restart the application with a minimum of downtime. The information system needs to be able to monitor the business-critical applications for availability and be able to start another copy of them, should they become unavailable. It may be necessary to start the new copy on different hardware than the original. The system should be able to redirect all connections, users, and data to the new copy and terminate the old copy. The users should not experience any difference in the application before or after the relocation.

Peak usage availability is another application availability concern. Application servers may become overwhelmed during times of peak utilization, resulting in a system that is unable to process any application requests. Peak usage issues may be addressed by sizing the information system for that peak usage, which may be cost prohibitive, especially if the peak usage is extreme or rare; or selectively servicing requests during peak usage, so that users with the greatest need will be serviced and only those with the least need will have application availability issues.

Infrastructure Availability

Modern information systems are extremely dependant on infrastructure. The two most important infrastructure elements are power and communication.

- **Power Availability**, or the elimination of power outages for information systems, is well understood. It has been done for almost as long as there have been computers. Uninterruptible power supplies and backup generators can supply power in the case of loss as long as it is cost-justified. Today's distributed systems require that protected power be available outside the data center to support network devices, departmental servers, and desktop systems.

- **Network Availability** is generally based on building in redundancy in the networks and having multiple suppliers to make the networks more available. Networks need to be analyzed from end to end to be assured that networks that are expected to be independent do not utilize the same provider, which could lead to a single point of failure.

Availability Models

Availability is built on the ability to avoid or survive those things that cause outages or to be able to rapidly recover from an outage. Availability is built into all levels of the information system. High availability is built on the following strategies:

Resistant

Resistant systems keep failures from happening. This means that they are designed not only to support the requirements, but also to survive foreseeable extremes. This is sometimes referred to as overengineering and is usually seen in the creation of hardware. However, software systems should also be built to be fault resistant and to operate with unexpected input.

Fault resistant systems are less likely to fail, since they are able to operate in environments that are beyond what is required. Unexpected input or external environment should not affect their operation. Resistant systems will process information regardless of its quality.

Resilient

Resilient systems detect and correct errors before they become failures. In software systems, resiliency is addressed as exception handling or sanity checks. If something unforeseen occurs, then the software corrects or attempts to correct the problem. Resiliency is built into hardware systems too. Hardware systems continuously check themselves for faults before they become errors. Parity memory is an example. It stores parity data so that it can detect single bit errors and corrects them.

Resilient systems are fault tolerant – they tolerate faults, report them, repair them where possible, and continue as best as they can. Resilient systems report problems as diagnostic messages.

Redundant

Redundancy is one of the most common methods of increasing availability. Redundancy can eliminate single point of failure. Today, many information systems are designed with multiple data paths, redundant information storage, and multiple connections to infrastructure. All of these steps reduce the odds of suffering an outage, since the likelihood of multiple outages is slim.

Redundancy is a concept that can be easily applied in many situations and can be used in concert with resiliency so that if an error is detected, the redundant item will be used.

Replaceable

The concept of being able to rapidly replace parts is a key component to resuming services. If replaceable parts are used in concert with redundancy, systems may be able to be repaired without any loss of service. This concept is the basis for what is called hot-pluggable, being able to replace damaged parts without stopping the system. Hot-pluggable systems can be replaced while power is still connected to the system, but they require that the element that is being replaced be deconfigured. On the other hand, hot-swappable systems require no interaction with the system other than removing and replacing the specific element.

Restartable

Restartable systems are designed to be restarted without reinitialization. This is usually accomplished by either saving state information so that when restarted it returns to the state in which it was stopped, or by having an environment that is not dependent on state information.

Many systems are designed to be stateless. That is, it is not necessary to have knowledge of things that have already occurred to be able to function. This allows systems to be brought online without initialization; simply restarting a system will bring it back into service.

Recoverable

Recoverable systems are able to have their state information, usually data in an information system, restored and restarted. The resetting of the state information will allow the system to continue from the point of failure. Some systems will not be able to recover a transaction that was incomplete at the time of the outage.

Availability Classifications

Each resource must be assigned an availability classification to determine appropriate security. The security requirements are based on the availability classification, the value of having the information available, and the costs required to make the information available. Availability is based on the availability of data, systems, applications, and infrastructure.

Harvard Research Group, Inc. (HRG) has defined availability in terms of the impact of an outage on the activity of the business and consumer (end user) of the service. The five Availability Environments (AE) below define availability in terms of the impact on the both the business and the end user or consumer. Each successive level incorporates all the functionality of the previous level. When a failure and subsequent system recovery response has occurred the system is assumed to not be at its original Availability Environment Classification until the failure has been corrected and any failed components have been replaced or repaired. In some cases, there may be system redundancies that support fail over capabilities in the event of an additional failure. The minimum requirement for a system to be considered highly available is that there is a backup copy of data available on a redundant disk and a log-based or journal file system exists for identification and recovery of incomplete transactions -- this represents the AE 1 Availability Environment Classification.

HRG's AVAILABILITY ENVIRONMENT CLASSIFICATIONS (AEC)

- **AE4** - Business functions that demand continuous computing and where any failure is transparent to the user. This means no interruption of work; no transactions lost; no degradation in performance; and continuous 24x7 operation.

- **AE3** - Business functions that require uninterrupted computing services, either during essential time periods, or during most hours of the day and most days of the week throughout the year. This means that the user stays on-line. However, the current transaction may need restarting and users may experience some performance degradation.

- **AE2** - Business functions that allow minimally interrupted computing services, either during essential time periods, or during most hours of the day and most days of the week throughout the year. This means the user will be interrupted but can quickly re-log on. However, they may have to rerun some transactions from journal files and they may experience some performance degradation.

- **AE1** - Business functions that can be interrupted as long as the availability of the data is insured. To the user work stops and an uncontrolled shutdown occurs. However, data availability is ensured. A backup copy of data is available on a redundant disk and a log-based or journal file system is being used for identification and recovery of incomplete transactions.

- **AE-0** - Business functions that can be interrupted and where the availability of the data is not essential. To the user work stops and uncontrolled shutdown occurs. Data may be lost or corrupted.

- * **Disaster Recovery** capability is a horizontal availability feature that is applicable to any of the Availability Environments (AEs). It provides for remote backup of the information system and makes it safe from disasters such as an earthquake fire, flood, hurricane, power failure, vandalism, or an act of terrorism.

Availability Outage

Availability outages cause delays, loss of productivity, loss of sales, and lost opportunities. Not having access to information resources can mean making decisions without needed information.

The Internet has put a light on a seldom considered availability issue – peak utilization outages. Systems can receive so many legitimate requests that they are unable to handle all of them so some go unfulfilled. In some cases, the server itself may fail. Traditionally, only the utility industry has designed systems for peak utilization. But it is a security issue that every organization needs to evaluate.

> The Japan Railroad's ticket reservation and issuing system crashed one November 11 at around 11:11 because of intensive access caused by ticket collectors who were seeking tickets with a string of 10 "1" letters (11, 11, 11, 11,11) printed on a platform ticket. The first two digits indicate the year of Heisei 11 in original Japanese era designation still in use as well as the year in the Christian calendar. Regular train tickets have time stamping printed up to date, but a platform ticket is printed up to the minutes. At that time, the ticket collectors suddenly started purchasing platform tickets through automated system kiosks. The rate of platform tickets issued is usually only about three percent of tickets sold, but it reportedly soared up to 75 percent at 11:11 on that day. Since the system requires 150% more processing time per transaction for a platform ticket compared to for a regular train ticket, this situation caused a massive load on the central computer beyond its ticket issuing capability and crashed the entire ticketing system.[52]

---

[52] "Japan rail ticket system crash due to 11/11/11 11:11," *The Risks Digest*, Vol. 20, Issue 65, 21 November 1999.

Checklist

— Review availability requirements for each information resource.

— Implement highly-available systems.

— Employ redundancy to eliminate single points of failure.

— Determine quality of service requirements.
    Understand utilization profiles.
    Prepare for peak utilization.

— Minimize the impact of scheduled downtime.
    Backups
    Upgrades

— Prepare incident response plan for security incident.

— Prepare and test disaster plan to minimize catastrophic failures.

CHAPTER 13

Accuracy

Consumers Union in San Francisco found that half of credit bureau reports surveyed contained errors, about 20 percent of which were big enough to prevent an individual from buying a home or a car.[53]

Accuracy of information is an issue that is going to become increasingly important. Today we see issues with the accuracy of personal information degrading, partially because that information is not collected firsthand, but purchased through information clearing houses; partially because inaccuracies appear from data entry, actual clerical errors, or inappropriate association with an individual because of poor identification; and partially because information that is given for one purpose is used for another or is commingled with information from other sources to create a more complete picture – however, it often clouds the picture by combining incompatible data sets.

Information Lifecycle

The accuracy of information is important throughout the life of the information. However, the issues that affect accuracy change during its life. Accuracy of information requires that the information be gathered from a known good source, kept in a secure manner so that it cannot be corrupted without detection, and delivered via a trusted method to assure that the message delivered is the same message that was sent. Inside the computer system, this requires using cryptographic methods to create digital signatures, so that the source of the information can be authenticated; checksums, so that the integrity of the information can be assured; and encrypted communication, so that the information cannot be tampered with en route.

---

[53]   "More Consumer Friendly Credit Reporting System Begins," *Consumer Union*, September 1997.

Initially Accurate

Nothing can have a greater effect on the quality of information than the quality of its source. Without being able to verify the source of information, the information itself must always be suspect. This has become very evident in the Internet age. Regularly, there is information available on the Internet that is wrong. It may even cite sources, yet it has no basis in fact.

The quality of information does not improve with age and can never be better than the quality of its source. In today's interconnected world, the concept of independent sources is unrealistic. Receiving the same information from two unreliable sources does not make the information more reliable.

Combining information from multiple sources dilutes the quality of the information, making it only as good as the poorest of the multiple sources and assuming that the subject of the information is the same for all the combined information. This is seen in the personal information sector where an individual's information is attached to someone else, possibly because they have the same name.

Scope of Use

Information is almost always gathered for a specific reason. However, after the information is available it is often tempting to use it for any purpose. Questions that are answered under a specific pretense may be answered differently under another pretense. This is why information that is acquired from information brokers must always be considered suspect, since the context of the information is unknown.

Especially when this information is about individuals, using it for a purpose other than what it was collected for may be a breach of trust. If the understanding of the individual who gave the information was that it was to be used for a specific purpose, or that it was gathered under a specific pretense, then the individual has not given permission for the information to be used for any purpose.

This leads into issues of privacy and misrepresentation.

Correlation of Information

Information correlation is the collection of information from a number of different sources. Correlation can be used for conformation, finding the same information from multiple sources, but correlation is also used to make a bigger picture – putting all the information from all the sources into a result without concern for accuracy. The thought is that combining these diverse sources of information will create a more complete picture. However, there are a number of things that can make this combination of information actually less accurate – introduction of incorrect information, incorrect assumptions, and incorrect association of identifiers to name a few. Poorly chosen identifiers lead to mistaken identities and will cause information that belongs to different individuals to be grouped together.

Information System Accuracy

Accuracy is often focused on the accuracy of the information alone. While this is important, it is only one area of accuracy in the information system. The processing of the information must be accurate. The algorithms must perform correct calculations and the applications must maintain business transaction integrity. The information must be accurately delivered.

Information

The integrity of information is the area of accuracy that has had the most attention. This ensures that the information has not had unauthorized modification while it was in your custody. Integrity is the need to ensure that information is generated or updated in a controlled manner and is protected against corruption or destruction.

All authorized methods of information modification must produce audit records so that accountability is maintained. These audit records must be detailed enough to be able to distinguish not only who changed the information, but what the changes were, so that it can be restored to a known good state. This requires that the applications that provide access to the information be built around a security model that will support this.

Information accuracy must be protected in all of its states:

- **Storage** – Information must be protected from modification while it is being stored. This involves controlling the use of the information based on privileges to thwart unauthorized attempts to modify the information by the storage system. It also requires periodic verification of the information. The storage system should maintain a cryptographic signature or checksum of the information so that any unauthorized modifications can be detected. When a checksum does not match the information, then the information can be restored to a known good state.

- **Transmission** – Information must be protected from modification during transport. It must be evident that the received message is the same as when it was sent. This requires both a checksum that cannot be falsified to prove the integrity of the message, and a signature to prove the origin of the message so that it is known to come from the appropriate source.

In the physical world, tamper-proof packaging is used to ensure that messages have not been altered, and physical signatures are used to prove the originator. In the electronic world this is accomplished with cryptography. Digital signatures will show proof of sender and cryptographic checksums will indicate any tampering. These features are especially important if the message is being sent over a public transportation system.

Message integrity is not assured for any Internet message. The obvious Internet security need is to provide the electronic equivalent of the sealed envelope and to provide assurances that envelope tampering is not possible – not only on the network but anywhere the information travels.

Transaction

The accuracy of business transactions is dependent on the ability to maintain consistency and synchronization between all elements involved in the transaction. Business transactions involve moving money from one account to another, adjusting inventories, and scheduling production and shipping (just to name a few). A single transaction may include a number of these items that all have to be coordinated and committed as a single event, so that the money removed from one account is placed in another and the item removed from inventory is transferred to shipping. Transaction monitoring and control is critical to business integrity.

Transaction monitors, or application servers, are systems that handle this logic so that each application does not have to manage it itself. This reduces the complexity of each application and centralizes the business transaction logic.

The business logic features that will be centralized by the use of an application server include the following:

- **Reservation** – A transaction monitor must be able to reserve a resource (airline seat or an item in inventory) so that it has unique access to the resource until the transaction is completed and cannot be sold to someone else while the transaction is in process.

- **Communication** – In a distributed information service environment, communication to all of the services involved with the transaction can require a number of different methods to a number of different locations. These communications must be reliable and confidential. The complexity in managing these connections in an application is the primary reason for application servers.

- **Control** – The application server has to control the transaction, managing all of the services involved and assuring that all of the transactions with each service are completed. This includes managing the timing issues of handling multiple servers.

- **Rollback** – The removal of a transaction that does not complete successfully. This requires that all of the individual transactions with each of the services are able to be undone if the entire transaction is not completed successfully.

Users

The integrity of a transaction depends on the accuracy of identifying the users involved. This includes the individual who initiated the request as well as the services that are involved with the transaction.

Methods

Accuracy is based on the ability to prevent or detect unauthorized modification. Methods to minimize the risk to the accuracy of the information include limiting exposure and verifying that the information has not changed.

Limited Use

Limiting use of an information resource limits that information resource's vulnerability.

- **Authorizations** – Limiting the users who have authorizations for the information resource to only those who have a business need will reduce the number of individuals who have an opportunity to alter the information.

- **Applications** – Limiting the applications that have privileges to only those that are designed to work with the specific information will tend to increase the appropriate management of the information. They will only perform proper operations on the information and can create verification values to enable validation checkers. General purpose editors should not be allowed since they have no understanding of the appropriate values or the ability to perform sanity checks.

Verification

Verification is the process of validating the accuracy of an information resource. This requires saving state information and then comparing this state information to previously saved versions to determine if the information has changed.

- **Comparison** – The integrity of information can be tested by comparing it to a known good copy of the information. For this method to be effective, the data needs to be static. This works well for detecting viruses and parasites in program files, since program files should not change between updates. It is also a common method of verifying static web pages.

  It is common that the comparison is made, not to a complete copy, but rather to attributes of the known good file. These attributes include at a minimum: file size, owner, permission, and a checksum which is a function of the data in the file. The checksum function returns a unique value for unique input, so that even a small change in the file makes a large difference in the checksum making falsifying the checksum extremely difficult. There is a difference in quality in checksum functions and their ability to be falsified.

- **Calculations** – Information integrity can be maintained by creating a checksum, which is a calculated value that is unique for unique data. Computed checksums can be used with data that is dynamic, recalculating the checksum each time the data changes. If the processes that are authorized to update the information all compute and store a checksum, then modifications to the information through unauthorized methods will be detected.

Loss of Accuracy

Loss of information accuracy has the potential for being the most devastating of all security incidents. The decisions based on inaccurate information can be deadly and often inaccurate information can go undetected for long periods of time.

> During a consolidation of systems effort in a major oil company, it was discovered that the well log data, used by the company's reservoir simulation systems to make million dollar decisions to drill or not to drill for oil, was inaccurate. Investigations showed that it had been changed from the original data, which was available on the original 9-track tapes. Further investigations showed that the data had changed nearly five years prior to its discovery. There was insufficient information to determine how or why the data was altered. But the company is sure that many decisions were made based on results which utilized that faulty data.[54]

---

[54]   SPE Computer Newsletter, 1994.

Checklist

— Review confidentiality requirements for each information resource.

— Adhere to business practices for the industry.

— Adhere to legal disclosure laws for information about individuals.

— Evaluate the quality of the source of the information.

— Determine appropriate scope of use.

— Review data integration practices.

— Perform integrity testing.

— Maintain audit records.

CHAPTER 14

Confidentiality

Nearly 44 percent of respondents said that their organizations have no recovery plans and of those that do, some company plans do not address critical business process.[55]

Confidentiality is the ability to avoid disclosing information to anyone who is not authorized to use it. Information in all of its forms (electronic, printed, spoken), and in all of its states (stored, transmitted, in-use), and in all of its locations (file cabinet, courier, blackboard), must be protected from unauthorized access. The ability to maintain the confidentiality of information is largely based on the quality of managing the sensitivity classifications assigned to the information.

The use of public communications and outsourcing information services makes the issue of confidentiality more difficult. If sensitive data is being transmitted over unprotected communications, e.g., the Internet, it can be intercepted and copies made, or passive eavesdropping can occur if security features are not used that provide message confidentiality and assure privacy. Encrypting the files will make the data unintelligible and port protection devices will protect the files from unauthorized access, if warranted.

Information in the Enterprise

Today's organization contains a huge wealth of information. Maintaining the confidentiality of this information is paramount to the survival of the organization. In addition to the business information, organizations have a great deal of personal information about employees, partners, and customers.

Business Information

Business information is any information that is private to the company. Confidentiality is concerned with the information which, if disclosed, would result in damage to the organization.

---

[55]   Ernst & Young, *5th Annual Information Security Survey,* 1997.

Confidentiality of sensitive data is a requirement of information systems. The level of confidentiality of business information is based on the value of the information. The confidentiality of information is determined by the nature of that information and the impact of wrongful disclosure. The following confidence classifications will indicate the value of the information and its associated confidentiality requirements.

Personal Information

Most organizations have a surprising amount of information about employees and customers. Often this information confidentiality level is evaluated based on its value to the organization. However, this is only one aspect to the total confidentiality requirement for the information. The business is also liable for damages to the individual if it discloses private information.

The confidentiality of personal information is defined by statutes that protect the individual's rights to privacy. The privacy requirements for personal information are also dictated by statute.

The organization must maintain the confidentiality of this personal information to protect the privacy of the individual and also to protect the organization from legal action.

Confidentiality Concerns

Confidentiality requires the same level of protection for all forms of information – electronic or printed. All physical media (tapes, removable disks, printouts, etc.) need to have physical labels indicating their level of sensitivity. This media needs to be handled appropriately for the level of information it contains. This includes making it accessible only to authorized individuals with authenticated identification. This is especially true in the area of disposal and reuse.

Secure Storage

Information needs to be stored in a secure manner. This requires that only authorized users utilizing authorized software over authorized communications should be allowed to utilize the information. System utilities have to be able to manage the file but should not be allowed to see the information.

- **Online** – The confidentiality of stored information is based on the ability of the filesystem to protect the information based on the authorizations of the user or process requesting the information. This works well within a system, but if the information is moved to removable media, e.g., backup tapes, or if the data storage unit is stolen and attached to another system, or if the system is compromised so that the intruder has authorizations then filesystem protections are inadequate. A cryptographic filesystem stores data in an encrypted form, so that the information is unintelligible unless it is requested through the proper manner with the proper cryptographic key. This prevents the disclosure of information unless the cryptographic key was compromised.

- **Offline** – Backups need to be handled with the same level of precautions that the information is afforded online. Removable media should be labeled with the security class of the information and locked up appropriately. Access to backup media will often allow an attacker to circumvent authorizations.

- **Printouts** – Physical copies of the information need to be controlled to protect the information. They need to be locked away when not in use and made available only to those who need access. The transportation of these documents should produce an auditable report.

Secure Communications

Everywhere that information flows must maintain a minimum sensitivity classification of that information. This includes the network on which it travels, the systems that access the information, and the backup media that stores it. In the case where the media contains a number of data items, the aggregate sensitivity level must be the same as the highest sensitivity level of the information contained. It may need to be higher, since the knowledge of the combination of the separate information may be more sensitive than the individual pieces of information.

- **Private Network** – A private network is a dedicated connection between two points. It uses physical security to secure the communications it carries. Since the link is dedicated and only connects two points, constructing private networks to support multiple partners is expensive.

- **VPN** – A virtual private network (VPN) can secure communications between any two points utilizing the public key infrastructure for user-based authentication and strong encryption of information sent over the Internet. With a VPN, businesses can more safely and cost-effectively conduct transactions and share confidential information over the Internet with customers, strategic partners, and employees. The VPN delivers the necessary security, centralized management, and application and network integration for building an extranet.

Secure Disposal

This is a common area for security procedures to break down. Appropriate precautions must be taken when disposing of physical media that contains sensitive information. The disposal process must assure that the information is not retrievable after the physical media is disposed of. Media reuse must also provide the same level of assurance. Since it has been shown that multiple generations of information can be recovered from recordable media, it is imperative that the media only be reused in an environment that affords at least the same level of security.

- **Object Reuse** – The reuse of an information resource must guarantee that a object does not contain any of the information from its last invocation. Any newly created object (memory buffer, file, etc.) cannot contain information "left over" from the last time it was used. The 'object reuse' requirement of a secure system simply states that all user accessible resources are initially cleared or otherwise initialized so that no lingering information can be extracted from them.

- **Magnetic Media** – The disposal of magnetic media has security issues since the media may still contain valuable information. Even when the information is erased, it is likely that it can be retrieved from the used media. Systems rarely write over files, rather they only write over the index. Even when the media is reused, there is a good chance that the file that had been removed can be reconstructed. Used magnetic media needs to be physically destroyed or bulk erased.

- **Physical Forms** – Physical copies of information need to be afforded the same level of privacy as its online counterpart. They need to be locked up when not in use and made available only to those who have a business need. Transactions with the physical copies should create an auditable trail.

Methods of Ensuring Confidentiality

Maintaining the confidentiality of information requires that the information not be available to anyone that is not appropriately authorized.

Compartmentalization

Compartmentalization is the process of limiting the scope of an information resource. This effectively isolates it from any entity that is not authorized. Compartmentalization can be achieved by having separate systems and networks for different levels of security or by using "military grade" systems that enforce compartmentalization.

Encryption

Through the use of encryption, information can be made unavailable to everyone except those with the correct keys. Encryption can be used to protect the information in transit and in storage.

The public key infrastructure also supports confidentiality using a public-private key pair that is different from the one used for signing. In this case, users need to obtain a separate certificate for the confidentiality public key. To send an encrypted message, a user could obtain the recipient's confidentiality certificate from a certificate repository and verify that it is valid.

Then the sender can encrypt the message using the public key. Only the recipient, in possession of the private key, will be able to decrypt the message.

Sensitivity Classifications

Confidentiality is the attribute that defines the sensitivity of the information. This is reflected in the value of the information and is a major consideration in what security measures are to be used to keep the information from being disclosed to unauthorized entities. The basis for information privacy is classification and compartmentalization. It is generally unrealistic to expect every piece of data to have specific authorizations defined for all the entities that can have access, especially with the frequency without which those resources change.

Privacy defines the sensitivity of the information and its relative cost of disclosure. The following are sensitivity classifications:

- **Company Secret** information is the most private company information. It has a very restricted distribution. Its disclosure would have a grave impact on the organization. It must be protected at all times.

- **Company Confidential** information is critical to the ongoing operation of the organization. It has limited distribution. Its disclosure would have a significant impact on the organization. It must not be transported outside a secure area.

- **Company Proprietary** information is specific to the organization and is crucial to the organization's competitiveness. Its disclosure would have a moderate impact on the organization. It must be adequately protected whenever it is transported outside a secure area.

- **Internal Use Only** information is for internal use only. Its disclosure would have limited impact on the organization and is likely to become public in a relative short period of time.

- **Private** information is information that is not directly needed by the organization as part of its business activities; instead, it is information that the company has in its custody. The disclosure of this information would likely result in legal action.

- **Public** information is available to anyone.

Sensitivity classifications are one of the most understood aspects of security. However, the process of assigning sensitivity classifications and the continued use of the classifications is often not done.

Invasion of Privacy

Maintaining confidentiality requires limiting access to authorized users. Adequately protecting the privacy of information resources requires the correct implementation of many aspects of security. Hackers have long taken advantage of common access policies and domains of trust to compromise systems. Once one system is compromised in a trust domain, all of the systems in that domain are easily compromised, since they trust the compromised system.

Information entrusted to an organization has an expected level of privacy. It is expected that the information will not be shared without notifying the individual the information is about. The level of expectation is not always the same as the legal requirements.

Organizations need to be concerned with the handling of this information while it is in their custody and when it is disposed. This concern needs to include the storage media that contained the information, as well as the information itself.

> Beatle and pop star Paul McCartney's financial files from U.K. merchant bank Morgan Grenfell, now called Deutsche Asset Management, recently fell into the public's hands. Files about McCartney's financial account were retrieved from a secondhand computer that Morgan Grenfell had retired. This computer also contained The Cancer Research Campaign and the International Association of Odd Fellows' financial information. The Cancer Research Campaign has ordered an investigation.
>
> The data had not been adequately removed from a PC that was remarketed after its retirement. Forensic computing specialist IRM analyzed the computer and found the data recoverable in a matter of minutes and that no attempt had been made to delete it.
>
> Organizations concerned about information security should not only be concerned about Internet hackers, but also should be focused upon confidential information and "theft" retrieved from improperly retired computer assets.[56]

Technology has enabled eavesdropping in many ways. High tech eavesdropping devices are available that make the activity easy and inexpensive. Computer networks transmit huge amounts of data that can be listened to by anyone along the path of the communications. Eavesdropping has become a major source of security breaches on the Internet.

Wireless communications have fallen victim to the assumption that no one could get access. Wireless baby monitors have been used to gain access to wireless telephones and radio scanners can access cellular services. Wireless communications are susceptible to eavesdropping. Even though laws have been passed to make it illegal it is not technologically difficult to monitor wireless communications.

---

[56]   "Celebrity Victim of Information Piracy," *Computer Week*, 17 February 2000.

Checklist

— Review confidentiality requirements for each information resource.

— Adhere to legal requirements for confidentiality of information.

— Adhere to business practices for your industry for confidentiality.

— Ensure that the same level of confidentiality is applied to information in all its forms.

— Ensure that the same level of confidentiality is afforded to information in all its locations.

— Commingled information should receive the same sensitivity classification as the highest-rated individual piece of information in the group.

— The level of security should be based on sensitivity classification and will be enforced at all times.

CHAPTER **15**

Accountability

Despite the high investment IT managers are making in information security tools and services, 20 percent still have not created security policies, a fundamental step in the implementation of security controls.[57]

Accountability is the ability to positively identify the individual who is responsible for a specific action. This is extremely dependent on the ability to have very strong identification and authentication of the identification. Strong identification and authentication is required to provide non-repudiation (having enough evidence to prove that an individual was not the one who performed the action, even if he denies it). Accountability also requires enough monitoring and auditing to be able to record significant events.

Accountability issues extend beyond employees. Anyone who gets access to information systems, legally or illegally, should be held accountable for their actions. This requires policies for employees, contractual obligations for non-employees who are granted access, and legal remedies for those who access the system without permission. All of these areas must be addressed as well as issues of disciplinary actions and prosecution.

Accountability and Responsibility

Often accountability and responsibility are used interchangeably. However, this is not always the case. Accountability is the ability to identify the individual or program that caused the event. The entity is accountable for its actions.

Responsibility, on the other hand, is an issue of policy or the law. For example, an individual may not be responsible for his actions if he was ordered to perform those actions. There are a number of responsibility modes, including individual responsibility, group responsibility, and responsibility based on the chain of command. Responsibility is used to determine who will receive what disciplinary or legal actions.

[57]   Ernst & Young, *5th Annual Information Security Survey*, 1997.

Accountability Models

Accountability is required for the assignment of responsibility. Use of resources will be monitored and recorded such that an entity can be held accountable for its activities and use of the resources. Anything that affects the accuracy, availability, or confidentiality of information must be accounted for in such a manner that the responsible party can be brought to task.

Individual Accountability

Individual accountability is the most common form of accountability. Every person is responsible for his or her own actions and data and for following security procedures. All security systems should maintain individual accountability and create group and chain of command accountability by aggregating the individual accountability information.

Group Accountability

Group accountability defines a group of people who share the responsibility for the actions of each member of the group. Group accountability is used when each of the individuals are interchangeable; this may be the case when the organization has contracted to be supplied with a number of contract employees.

Group accountability can use peer pressure to control behavior of the group.

Chain of Command

Chain of command means that an individual is responsible for all of the actions of those people who report to him. This is used in the military and in organizations that have strict hierarchical reporting. Often, chain of command accountability is actually shared accountability between the individual and his superior.

Accountability Principles

To be able to hold individuals accountable for their actions there must be a positive means of uniquely identifying each computer user and a routinely maintained record of each user's activities.

Notification

Users must be made aware of their rights and responsibilities. This is done through an acceptable use document, which is acknowledged by all users. This process assures that all parties are aware of their rights and responsibilities.

This is not limited to authorized users; warning signs must be posted so that those who would access the information without authorization know that this constitutes a violation will be pursued through legal channels.

Identification

Positive identification is crucial to accountability. There must be positive identification of the events that are taking place and positive identification of the entity that is evoking the events. A uniform identification system of events and entities can simplify this process, but it is difficult to achieve in a large, multivendor environment. The use of digital signatures, which is a cryptographic checksum of information that can only be created by a single user but is verifiable by anyone, can be used to eliminate the issue of non-repudiation. Non-repudiation is the process of being assured that the entity who has been identified as the entity that utilized a resource, was actually that entity and cannot simply repute that he or she did not do it. Non-repudiation requires strong authentication and auditing.

Monitoring

Accountability is dependent on monitoring and the creation of logs that form an audit trail. The activities of every user must be monitored and recorded so that they can be held accountable for their actions. It requires the judicious use of audit, accounting, and system logs to capture a complete record of the activities in the information system. Consolidating remote logging to a centralized security management system can simplify and improve the accountability process. The centralized system can archive the logs to a non-modifiable storage system, such as a WORM auto-changer, thereby, creating a permanent method of associating an individual with her actions.

All those being monitored need to be informed that their actions may be monitored. When the monitoring of employees includes their interactions with non-employees, then additional levels of notification may be required.

Auditing

From both a control and legal point of view, it is necessary to maintain records of the activities performed by each computer user. The requirements for automated audit trails should be developed when a system is designed. The information to be recorded depends on what is significant about each particular system. Auditing can capture information about every process on the system and allow you to review and process this information to detect unauthorized activity.

While the audit system is a useful analysis tool, using it is a little like sifting through the debris after a burglar has already ransacked your home. Auditing tools help an administrator process the volume of information that is produced by the auditing system, and connect related processes to the individuals who are accountable.

The audit information records the information as it occurs. Auditing tools allow the administrator to find out who broke in and how, and help to track down the culprit. The audit logs are often used as evidence in the prosecution of the culprit.

Alarming

Alarming tools add real-time evaluation of the information that is made available from the logs. They can have thresholds that set off alarms when there is something suspicious occurring. These alarms can be used to attempt to stop the culprit before any damage actually occurs or proactively respond to imminent security problems. Most monitoring tools include notification as well.

Alarming tools are used to alert an administrator that an event is occurring. Notification tools can utilize e-mail, pocket paging, or other services to contact the appropriate person. Notification tools are the first step in implementing countermeasures when the event occurs.

Enforcement

The enforcement of security policies needs to be consistent throughout the organization. Without consistent enforcement, policies may be unable to stand up to legal scrutiny.

Enforcement of security policies may be difficult if they are not reviewed in conjunction with other policies and contractual agreements. Conflicts with other policies or with employee contracts may render them unenforceable.

Contract employees are not bound by employee policies, since they are not actually employees. The issues addressed in the security policies must be addressed by their contract.

Penalties must be well understood. Understanding the penalties or possible penalties acts as a deterrent and reinforces the importance of the policies.

Accounting Events

The audit system can record information events to an audit trail, much like a security camera at an automatic teller machine records everything to a VCR tape. An administrator controls auditing by selecting activities (events) to record during an auditing interval (a session). Session parameters can be configured to specify the duration of a session, and resources can be configured to devote physical resources (memory, disk space, and processing time) to auditing. To analyze an audit session, you can define selection criteria and run the session through them to produce reports.

There are basically three areas of auditing: system auditing, application auditing, and security auditing. In each of these areas the same type of events need to be recorded.

Information Resource Access

Access is the first level of contact that a user has with an information resource. This contact needs to be recorded, successful or not, to be able to monitor the information resource. It will indicate simple scanning of systems as well as concerted efforts to compromise a system. Access logging is difficult to subvert since it is recorded at first contact before there is any chance to be able to alter the logs. All types of access to any information resource should create an auditable record.

Administrative Actions

Administrative tasks involve controlling the behavior of information systems and should be accounted for because of the additional capabilities afforded to administrators. All activities that require administrative privileges should be recorded, successful or not. These include instances when there is a change in the level of authorizations or privileges, or a change in the status of the audit system.

Failure Events

Events which failed are part of the operation of any system. However, failed operations can be an indicator of someone attempting to perform processes for which they are not authorized. Failed events often spread more light on an incident than successful ones.

Accountability System Features

Features should include: auditing capabilities to track and record user authentication events such as log-in attempts, monitoring for operational failures, and basic access control list (ACL) functions.

The audit data itself must be adequately secured. If it is not, a perpetrator could easily perform some malicious action and then "cover their tracks" by modifying or obliterating audit data (the audit trail). The system should protect the audit trail by implementing the audit functionality inside the operating system.

Accountability Failures

The nonphysical nature of information systems makes accountability difficult. The Internet has enabled attacks to come from anywhere in the world. The huge number of systems and networks make tracing these attacks extremely involved. Once an online identity can be determined it can still be quite difficult to match it to a physical person.

None of the tracking can be accomplished it the accountability features are not enabled. Most of the logging systems were not designed to be used to diagnose attacks and create a great deal of information that is not very useful for this. Yet they have to be enabled to be useful.

> The National Archives, who set standards for the rest of the government for the safe storage of information, "lost" at least 43,000 electronic messages (four months' worth) without a useful trace. The audit log features that might have provided a clue had been turned off because they would have hampered the system's performance.
>
> They were supposed to have a backup system that could have replaced the missing information, but they said it was not working

properly. Daily and periodic system backups were supposedly being made by the agency's contractor, but neither was being done. The agency had not verified that adequate backup procedures were in place.[58]

---

[58]   "Archives Loses 43,000 E-Mails" *Washington Post*, 6 January 2000.

Checklist

— Ensure that everyone is aware of their level of accountability.

— All events are accountable to a single user.

— Accountability must be non-reputable.

— Accountability records are maintained such that they can be used as evidence.

CHAPTER 16

Administration

Ninety-three percent of the businesses that experienced a disaster and didn't have their data backed up went out of business.[59]

Administration is a broad term that covers the effort required to manage the security of the information system. It includes the administration of security features in the systems and the software as well as the implications that security has on the administration of the users, networks, systems, and software.

Security administration is an important part of the whole security picture. An information system whose security cannot be managed is not secure, regardless of the level of security of the individual elements. It is not possible to maintain security in an information system with more than a minimum complexity unless appropriate management is possible. The patchwork of security systems in a heterogeneous environment is extremely complex.

Security management is a discipline in which making trade-offs is a continual activity: controls in the system versus controls in the environment, security control versus customer convenience and productivity, strong controls versus implementation and administrative costs, etc. This requires that a security manager adopt a strategic point of view and place more effort in architectural and environmental controls than in controls built into computer systems.

Enterprise Information Security Administration

Security has to be applied throughout the entire enterprise to be effective. This requires integration into computer systems, network systems, communication systems, power systems, and environmental control systems from a wide variety of suppliers. Information security systems must be able to integrate into the control systems of all of these other areas to be able to provide a complete security picture and remain cost-effective to operate.

---

[59] "Disaster Recovery," *Interex 98 Conference*, 12 May 1998.

Security administration systems must be able to interact with a huge variety of heterogeneous systems yet maintain a simple-to-use operator interface that is common across all the varying systems and homogeneous reporting. Centralized management of all security products via an enterprise network and system management framework should support the integration of various middleware technologies and enable enterprise security monitoring for both private and public networks from a single workstation console.

Security administrations systems should be integrated with network and system administration systems so that there is a centralized point of administration and reporting. The centralization of information for management and monitoring allows for a complete view of systems and networks throughout the enterprise, the consolidation and correlation of information from multiple sites, and the ability to have lights-out operations where all of the management and monitoring is done remotely. Some widespread attacks, like worms, my be either undetectable or not confirmable without centralized management.

Centralized management makes the issue of license management easier as well as the distribution of patches, virus signatures, and the like, and reduces the amount of redundancy in the management of the enterprise.

Simplification

The control systems should allow for the reduction, categorization, and prioritization of security events. The system should also do preliminary investigation, isolating the source of the incident.

The system should be able to add problem resolution into the knowledge database so that when another incident occurs the information that was learned from a prior incident will be easily available to expedite the solving of this incident. Predefined suggestions and tips should be available to help lead the operator through processes that have been defined. The knowledge database will lead into the use of expert systems to analyze the information and make determinations about the activities in the enterprise. These systems will be able to spot potentially abusive activities by bringing a wider view of what is going on throughout the enterprise. Based on category and priority, the event can be routed to the person who is the most qualified individual to lead the response to the incident.

Automation

The automation of administrative tasks will increase productivity. Repetitive tasks can be automated so that the system can perform them on a regular schedule.

The automation of multistep processes can make the systems easier to administer and increase the administrator's effectiveness. Tasks involved with installing a new system or adding a new user are often specific tasks that are easy to automate.

The area of monitoring is where automation can be a great help. The logs that are produced by information systems are often quite large, making it difficult to locate the information that is important to the administrator. An automated task that removes the unimportant information or selectively looks for useful information can be of assistance to the administrator.

Administrative Process

System administrators face the dilemma of maximizing the availability of system services to valid users while minimizing the susceptibility of complex network infrastructures to attack. Unfortunately, services often depend on the same characteristics of systems and network protocols that make them susceptible to compromise by intruders.

All administrative job responsibilities must have redundancy to assure that there are always individuals available with the skills and ability to administer the security.

Installation

Security features should be easy to install and enable. They should not have a significant impact on the installation of other software or systems. They should be available in a multivendor environment enabling an enterprise-wide solution. The security systems should be easily integrated into both off-the-shelf software applications and locally developed software systems. Unfortunately, this is not the usual case.

Systems often comes with security features disabled. These need to be enabled and configured. While obvious, this activity is often overlooked. For many systems this is a complex task requiring significant skills.

Configuration

The security features should be easy to customize to meet the needs of the specific organization. Every organization has specific security objectives. The security features should enable easy implementation of the organization's security policies. The configuration should be easy to implement and easy to understand once implemented. There should be a consistent view across all of the implemented security tools to leverage rapid understanding of the specific configuration.

Operations

Operation of a system involves many security activities. Performing backups, holding training classes, managing cryptographic keys, keeping up with user administration and access privileges, and updating security software are some examples. The addition of security features should not significantly impact the day-to-day operations of the system. The changes in standard administrative procedures required to add additional security should be evaluated as to their cost to support the security feature.

Security operations should be integrated into system and network operation tools so that the administration of the systems does not change to facilitate the added security. Administrator tools that encompass the additional security issues should be used to minimize the impact of security on the information systems.

Maintenance

Security is never perfect. Changes in the system or the environment can create new vulnerabilities. Individuals discover new ways to intentionally or unintentionally bypass security measures and procedures, or subvert security. All of these add to the requirement to continuously maintain the system's security.

Change management helps control a stable security environment amid the continually changing environments in which they operate. Change management records the changes that occur in the security environment in response to user complaints, availability of new features and services, or the discovery of new threats and vulnerabilities. Change management should be an integral part of an information security design.

Monitoring

Utilizing security features will increase the level of monitoring required. This monitoring is focused on the issues of exceptions to and violations of security policy. This monitoring will enable better intrusion detection and more rapid response to an incident, reducing the impact of that event. The cost of monitoring should be reduced through the use of automated tools.

Security monitoring must be cost-effective. It must prevent more losses than the cost of the additional system and personnel required to manage it.

Areas of Administration

Enabling security adds administration overhead. The security features have to be administered and the administration of information systems is usually altered, often increasing the administration requirement. Administration is an ongoing process. Information systems require monitoring and management.

Security issues arise from both administration of systems and administration of security. Much of systems administration relates to security, such as the administration of identifiers, authentication, authorization, and accountability.

Identification

User identification is the basis of information security. It enables authorizations and accountability. Administration of identifiers encompasses creation, registration, distribution, revocation, removal, and replacement of identifiers, as well as management of all of the name services.

Authentication

Authentication administration involves managing the authorizations for every identifier for each authentication method. It encompasses managing the users' ability to change authentication values and administration of the authentication services which enable authentication at all the systems that require it.

Authorization

Administration of authorization is the process of defining the capabilities for each user. Administration is often simplified by putting users into groups based on their job function or the role they perform. The granting of privileges to authorized users should be built on business rules that support the business functions. Utilizing a centralized rule-based authorization system facilitates easy changes, which take effect immediately, to authorizations based on the business situation.

Accountability

The administration of accountability is the management of event monitoring. It requires that the accountability features of each of the systems in the information system be enabled and the audit logs that they produce are collected and stored. It requires the proper handling of audit information so that those responsible for specific events can be identified and so that the information can be utilized in any legal actions that may be warranted.

Administration Errors

Administrative errors are partially responsible for a great many security incidents. Incidents based on known vulnerabilities could be completely eliminated if every system had current patches installed.

The lack of administration is not always the administrator's fault. Often there is a shortage of administrators to accomplish the everyday duties of managing information systems. Many systems are administered by end users who have little administration training and no security training. Even full-time administrators are not often trained on security issues and many organizations do not have security administrators.

> The General Accounting Office, with the help of experts from the National Security Agency, used nothing more than public Internet access and commonly known security faults to gain access to several unclassified mission-critical systems, including those supporting the command and control of spacecraft.
>
> Out-of-date information security policies have left significant vulnerabilities in NASA's mission-critical systems that could allow un-

authorized users to steal, modify, or delete important operational data, according to a GAO report. According to GAO, NASA has not created enough awareness among its employees about common security mistakes and vulnerabilities, such as easily guessed passwords. NSA initially breached some systems using passwords such as "guest" for guest accounts and "adm" for system administrators, opening the door for broader access to agency systems.

GAO concluded that it was able to penetrate systems because NASA does not have a consistent information security management policy that the entire agency follows. NASA did not have many policies regarding Internet and network security, and some policies the agency did have were out of date or were not followed.[60]

[60]   Frank, Diane, "NASA systems full of holes," *Federal Computer Week,* 24 May 1999.

Checklist

— Determine a minimum level of security based on business needs.

— Install and test all security patches.

— Enable all appropriate logging.

— Monitor logs for suspicious activities.

— Intrusion detection alerts should be investigated by the duty manager.

Detection

I'm not concerned about the vulnerabilities that I know about –
I've already taken precautions against them – it's the ones that I
don't know about that have me worried. [61]

– Marcus Ranum

Historically, most resources have been spent on protection despite the fact that no matter how well a system is protected, there is always some way to compromise it. No matter the level of protection, security incidents will occur and systems will fail, and detection is the only way of knowing when the system is compromised. This is why rapid detection and appropriate notification are the most important parts of any security strategy. Without proper detection, you may never be aware that a security incident has occurred and thereby continue to use corrupt information to make business decisions. Even worse than having a security incident is having one and not knowing it.

Today, intrusion detection falls into that category that is somewhere between science and art. In the area of science, intrusion detection systems (IDS) are able to continuously monitor activity going on in the information system and can notify someone when there has been activity that warrants concern. These systems can monitor configurations for changes, compare user actions against known attack scenarios (signatures), and distinguish changes in activities that can indicate suspicious activities.

The art of intrusion detection is in the ability to define what it is that distinguishes normal activities from malicious ones – the ability to take the organization's security policies and create software that will determine when they are not being followed. These systems need to be able to

---

[61]   USENIX Security Conference. 1995.
Marcus J. Ranum is the President and CEO of Network Flight Recorder, Inc. and Chief Scientist at V-ONE Corporation, is the principal author of several major Internet firewall products, including the DEC SEAL, the TIS Gauntlet, and the TIS Internet Firewall Toolkit. He has been managing UNIX systems and network security for over 13 years, including configuring and managing whitehouse.gov during its first year of operation. Ranum is a frequent lecturer and conference speaker on computer security topics.

change as its environment changes. All of this requires an understanding of the intruder: where attacks come from, what motivates attackers, how attacks occur, and who these attackers are.

These areas of art and science must be merged to produce a system that is capable of detecting a real intrusion as opposed to some benign activities.

Detection software is an essential part of keeping the system secure. It should monitor the integrity of the system as well as activities that can be considered suspicious. An intrusion detection system attempts to detect an intruder breaking into your system or a legitimate user misusing system resources. The IDS will run constantly on your system, working away in the background, and only notifying you when it detects something it considers suspicious or illegal.

You must have rapid detection to facilitate rapid notification and response. The sooner you are able to identify that your system has been compromised, the less there will be to clean up and the easier it will be to get the hackers off of the system.

The intrusion detection system must have the authority to monitor everything. If it cannot be monitored, it cannot be protected. Having an enterprise view allows detection of multiple minor security infractions that may not appear to be a concern individually, but collectively represent a deliberate attack. Logs from one device, for example a network device like a router, may indicate an attack on another device or system.

To build a successful intrusion detection system, one must first understand the intruder.

Intruder Types

Knowing the enemy is the first step in being able to detect their presence. Computer intruders come from a variety of backgrounds. However, they can be categorized based on a number of the following attributes:

Motives

The types of intruders are as varied as their motives. Motives are generally based on need, actual or perceived. The need can be financial, social, or emotional. It is this need that empowers the intruder to justify his actions.

- **Financial** motives, need or greed, are very powerful. Some intruders are motivated by profit. Some are paid by third parties to compromise an organization's systems, or to acquire information. Others may cause damage expecting to be hired to fix the damage. A sudden financial need can cause an individual to become involved in activities in which he would not otherwise engage. This can make him a willing pawn to someone else.

- **Social** motives are based on rectifying the inequality of social injustices that an organization has done or is perceived to have done. Cyberactivism is growing rapidly, using the anonymity of computer networks to release information about the organization's alleged activities, to cause damage to an organization, or to disrupt the organization's activities.

- **Political** motives are based on advancing a political idealism, usually focused on damaging sites of opposing views or posting political messages on sites.

- **Personal** motives run the entire gamut from hacking into systems for fun to extracting revenge on a company that the attacker feels has wronged him. Personal motives are very strong and will often make the attacker continue fruitless attacks well beyond reason.

Relationship

The relationship between the attacker and the target will often define the type of attack and the possible motive for the attack.

- **Insiders** are those individuals who work for the target organization or have a relationship with the organization that grants the attacker some level of access. This includes employees, contractors, customers, subcontractors, etc. Insiders have more knowledge of the specific working of the systems and processes as well as what information is valuable. Insiders also have the advantage of already securing level of access and trust.

- **Outsiders** are those individuals that have no previous relationship with the organization. They have targeted the organization based on its reputation, directions from a third party (someone who is paying the attacker to attack the company), or random chance. Outsiders have less specific knowledge about the systems, but are usually more skilled at attacking a system.

Intrusion Methods

The next step in intrusion detection is understanding the processes used by intruders to attack an information system. There are a number of intrusion methods that are used successfully against information systems. Intrusion methods are either technical or social. These attacks have been performed by both lone individuals and by groups working a well-orchestrated script.

Intruders tend to follow the path of least resistance, so attacks will be where it is easiest to gather the information or at the sites that information accumulates to give a greater return on investment from the attack. Strongly secured systems will be skipped over for easier targets. Intruders will focus on desktop and laptop computers where the security is often lax. They have a tendency to attack fileservers and database systems, since these systems contain a greater amount of valuable information.

Malicious attacks on information can be either a social intrusion, when information is gathered from a person, or a technical intrusion, when information is retrieved from a computer. When the goal of the attack is information, the form of information is irrelevant.

Physical Intrusions

Physical intrusions require the attacker to come to the organization to make physical contact. They may gain access as part of a tour, or they might impersonate a delivery person or maintenance person. They might physically remove items or just be gathering information. Dumpster diving, which is the pawing through trash looking for some useful information, is a form of physical intrusion.

Technical Intrusions

Technical intrusions use a technical aspect of the information system to gain access and authorization. They will exploit vulnerabilities in technical systems to gain access to information. Computer hacking is a form of a technical intrusion.

Social Intrusions

Social intrusions utilize people to gather information. There are a number of processes used to get people to reveal information. Today, these processes are collectively called social engineering.

Detection Methods

With an understanding of the type of intruders, their motives, and intrusion methods used, intrusion detection methods can be created. These detection methods look at how intrusions occur and how to best detect them.

Profiles

The information that is used by the intrusion detection methods are grouped into profiles which describe specific attributes that are being examined. These profiles include the normal operating attributes of computer systems, networks and users, so that events which are unusual can be detected. Other profiles contain the attributes that indicate vulnerabilities exist or that an attack is underway. These profiles are generally built and maintained by the intrusion detection software which utilizes them.

Offline Methods

Offline methods focus on the known issues that can be repaired before they cause an incident. These include configuration errors and vulnerabilities that can be exploited by the intruder.

Online Methods

Online methods attempt to detect the intruder during the attack by examining the effects that the intrusion has on the system being attacked. Other methods attempt to detect that an incident has occurred by the fingerprints left behind. Some of these methods will attempt to keep the attacker busy, in a safe environment, while he is tracked down; others will lock the intruder out as soon as he is discovered. Both online and offline methods may be used in concert to create a more complete intrusion detection solution.

Detection requires a commitment, a day-to-day administration for maintaining the systems and monitoring the results. Even though monitoring software and data reduction models can reduce the amount of information that the administrator is required to manually process, she must still look at the reports and assess the seriousness of the information. The cost of IDS must remain low, since when it is not needed (hopefully, most of the time) it is overhead, but when it is needed, it is crucial.

It takes both technology (to set up detection software) and procedures (to define the proper time and person to notify when an incident is detected) to respond appropriately to a security incident.

The difference between an incident and a disaster is detection.

This section will focus on intrusion detection – the detection of malicious misuses.

CHAPTER 17

Intruder Types

Surveys of computer professionals show that about half of the attacks of computer systems come from outside the organization. However, an FBI study reveals that disgruntled employees are responsible for nearly 90 percent of computer crimes that result in financial loss to the company.[62]

It is difficult – and possibly dangerous – to try to define the typical hacker. They range from high school students who are experimenting with scripts to disgruntled employees seeking revenge to professionals stealing secrets. Each has his own goals, objectives, methods, and abilities.

The mass media has generally referred to the misuse of computer systems by both authorized and unauthorized users as either "computer fraud" or "hacking." Anything from embezzlement to computer viruses have, at some time, been attributed to the "hacker" community at large. In addition to this, the media often describes "hackers" as being sociopathic or malicious, thus creating a public image of the computer underground ("hackers," in particular) that most researchers would see as an exaggeration of their ability, and, indeed, their intent, to cause damage.

Outside Intruders

Most people perceive the outside world to be the largest threat to their security. This is in part an issue of trust. Those inside the organization have been granted some level of trust. External attacks are frequent and frightening because of the unknown – attacks from unknown locations for unknown reasons. External attacks capture our imagination and attention, since anyone could be the victim of an external attack.

The media coverage of attacks that take place over the Internet by teenage "hackers" has heightened the perception that this is an organization's major threat, even though these are not

---

[62] "1997 CSI/FBI Computer Crime and Security Survey," *Computer Security Issues & Trends*, Spring 1997.

the most damaging types of attacks, and all "hackers" are not minors without an understanding of what is right and what is wrong.

In 1994 a Russian mathematician pulled off the biggest bank heist in the brief history of cyberspace. The St. Petersburg resident attacked Citibank through its money wire transfer system. Transfers were made to accomplices in the U.S., Israel, Germany, Holland, and Switzerland.

According to Citibank, its security system flagged two August 1994 transfers, $26,800 and $304,000, as "strange." Bank officials called the FBI, who observed the electronic interlopers as they made their illegal transfers. U.S. officials were also assisted by telecommunications employees in Russia who helped track the illegal fund transfers to St. Petersburg, according to published reports.

Citibank claims it recovered most of the approximately $10 million in illegal transfers, but says perpetrators were able to withdraw "less than $400,000" before other banks were notified and able to stop the transactions. Officials also say that at no time were any client funds at risk.

The alleged perpetrator was arrested in transit at London's Heathrow airport and, after a 30-month extradition battle, he was extradited to the U.S. Five alleged accomplices in other countries, including Israel, the Netherlands, and the U.S., also were arrested.[63]

Hackers

The classic hacker is a bright young man who is obsessed with technology and the ability to control or master this technology. These hackers hack to improve their skills. Their intentions are not to be malicious or to disturb anyone. Given the cost of computer systems today, hackers have no need to attack an organization's computer system, since capable computers are available to anyone. Most classic hackers have their own systems, or even networks of computers, to practice their craft.

But many of today's hackers are not like the hackers of yore. They do not share the hacker's code of "disturb nothing." They are not seeking to understand the system – in fact, many do not care what type of system they attack – they only want to take control of the system. They do this with tools they did not build or understand, thereby proving not that they are smarter than the organization that they penetrated, only that they have better tools.

---

[63]   "Security on trial in case of online Citibank heist," *USA Today*, 5 March 1999.

Many of these hackers are looking for fame – their fifteen minutes in the spotlight. But to be able to get this visibility, they must hit a site with visibility, one that is expected to have good security and will create notoriety. These hackers will be targeting big businesses and government sites – sites that are able to make headlines. Yet some hackers have been able to make headlines without ever actually doing the deeds that they were reported to have done. Hackers, "leaking" stories to newsmen or over the Internet, have been able to grab headlines without conquering systems.

> The Sunday Business newspaper reported that hackers had seized control of one of Britain's military communication satellites and issued blackmail threats, demanding money to stop interfering with the satellite. The paper, quoting security sources, said the intruders altered the course of one of Britain's four satellites, which are used by defense planners and military forces around the world. A Defense Ministry spokesman said, "There is no basis to the story whatsoever. It's not true." [64]

Cases of blackmailing banks were reported, but never substantiated, as was the report that hackers were responsible for NASA's lost Mars probe. Bragging rights may not be limited to the facts. They may not even be limited to actual hackers.

> The hacking group known as the Cult of the Dead Cow (CDC) published an interview with the leader of a Chinese hacker group called the Hong Kong Blondes. In the interview, elusive Hong Kong Blondes director Blondie Wong said that he had formed an organization named the Yellow Pages, which would use information warfare to attack China's information infrastructure. The group threatened to attack both Chinese state organizations and Western companies investing in the country. For their part, the CDC claimed that they would train the Hong Kong Blondes in encryption and intrusion techniques.
>
> The story was first reported in the mainstream press by Wired magazine, and during the following year it was followed up by numerous publications including US News, the Los Angeles Times, Asiaweek, and Computer-World. In every case, the original source was the CDC's July interview.
>
> However, investigations by Internet Asia have failed to find any evidence that the Hong Kong Blondes ever existed. The Hong Kong

---

[64] "Hackers Reportedly Seize British Military Satellite," *Sunday Business Newspaper*, March 1999.

Police, which is responsible for tracking hacking activities locally, had no knowledge of the group. The Commercial Crime Bureau's Computer Crime Section said that there had been no official reports of the group's activities and that they only knew the group's name through reports in the media. In fact, all evidence appears to indicate that the Hong Kong Blondes report was a highly successful hoax. Ironically, the Hong Kong Blondes have been indirectly responsible for a slew of hacking attacks in China.

Another hacker group, based in the U.S. and calling themselves the Legion of the Underground (LoU), launched a declaration of infowar on China in response to the harsh penalties handed out for computer offenses in the country. LoU members cited the Hong Kong Blondes as an influence behind their short-lived war, which was abandoned following condemnation from other hacker groups after a large number of Chinese web sites were hacked.[65]

Competitors

Corporate information gathering is more aggressive than ever before. Membership in the a competitive intelligence professional societies has been increasing at a rate of 30 percent per year. About 85% of Fortune 500 companies now have a competitive intelligence division. Some call it "strategic planning" or "market research and analysis." Whatever it is called, they use a wide variety of methods to uncover opportunities and flaws in their competitors' strategies. Generally, the competitive intelligence organization within a company will accumulate all possible information on their competitors and analyze patterns and changes in these patterns to discover the underlying reasons for them. Understanding not only what the competition is doing, but why they are doing it, allows the company to better prepare.

Competitive intelligence is the process of gathering information through legal means. However, many of the top professionals in the field have a background in covert intelligence gathering from military or other government organizations.

The new economics have led some businesses to be less ethical in the methods they use to gather competitive information. Corporate espionage is on the rise. In one survey,[66] respondents reported that more than 20% of break-ins were industrial espionage or sabotage by competitors, while 50% of respondents cited that information sought in recent attacks would be of use to U.S.-owned corporate competitors. Political changes have made industrial secrets more valuable than political secrets and have caused professional information gatherers to be looking for work.

[65]   "The Hong Kong Hacker Hoax," *IT Daily* 18/08/1999.
[66]   Zuckerman, M.J., "Cybercrime Against Business Frequent, Costly" *USA Today*, 21 November 1996.

Computer systems help facilitate the process. They bring large amounts of information into one location, and to be useful the information must be accessible. The global network allows spies to work from afar.

Corporate espionage has become such a large concern that on Oct. 10, 1996, U.S. President Clinton signed the Economic Espionage Act into law. It imposes penalties as high as $10 million and 15 years in prison for the theft of trade secrets as well as forfeiture of any property derived from or used to facilitate the crime. The act also provides for preserving the confidentiality of trade secrets during court proceedings. But unfortunately, sanctions against international corporate espionage remain weak.

Inside Intruders

Inside intruders are usually more successful and more damaging than outsiders. Think about it – an insider knows the layout of your system, where the valuable data is, and what security precautions are in place; most importantly, they may have access rights to the data. It is not surprising that an insider would be more successful at attacking the systems and extracting valuable information.

Despite the fact that most security measures are put in place to protect the inside from a malevolent outside world, most intrusion attempts actually occur from within an organization. A mechanism is needed to detect both types of intrusions - a break-in attempt from the outside, or a knowledgeable insider attack. An effective intrusion detection system detects both types of attacks.

To protect a system from someone who is a valid user on the system, you must set up consistency checks to validate the integrity of the system and the information on the system. You will also need to monitor activities to be sure that there are no unauthorized processes running on the system.

Since the inside hacker is already on the system, you must monitor what he takes from it. Data can be copied from the system by electronic means, such as copying a file to systems outside the company. This can be accomplished using FTP or e-mail. Connections that go outside the company should be logged by the firewall as to who made the connection, where the connection was made, and how much data was transferred. This should include e-mail. An employee that e-mails a five megabyte message to a competitor, for example, might be considered suspicious. Data can also be copied from the system through physical means, on printouts, or removable media. Today, gigabytes of data can fit into your pocket. This is why access to removable media and proper data handling procedures are so important.

Insider attacks do not draw the same level of media attention as external attacks. Insider attacks are often handled quietly by the organization that was attacked. If the attacker was an employee, disciplinary actions are taken. If the attacker was under a business arrangement with the victim, then a financial restitution may be sought. Rarely are criminal charges pursued, so most of these attacks never become public knowledge.

> Long-distance telecom carrier MCI is one of the few to concede security problems stemming from its own employees. An MCI employee was charged with stealing 100,000 calling-card numbers that were later used to place $50 million worth of fraudulent calls. The employee, a switch engineer in Charlotte, North Carolina, allegedly wrote software to capture card numbers from various carriers that used MCI's switching equipment. He then sent the numbers to an international hacker ring, according to charges brought against him.[67]

Disgruntled Employees

Disgruntled employees are the biggest risk to an organization. They have personal motives and will not be put off by deterrents that make attacks unreasonably expensive or time-consuming.

They are insiders. This puts them past the first level of defenses. They know what information has value, they know what they are looking for, they understand the information systems, they know where to look, and they are already authorized to some degree.

It is these attributes that make them prime targets of corporate espionage. They may be targeted by competitors or anonymous third parties and enticed with "the chance to set things right" or with financial incentives or revenge. They may offer to help the disgruntled employee with his quest of gathering the information and promise him a new job after the information has been delivered.

Human resources and the security organization need to partner and share information so that the information about employees who are not being good corporate citizens can be used to protect the organization.

> A disgruntled computer technician at Reuters in Hong Kong detonated logic bombs at five investment-bank clients, causing 36 hours of downtime in networks providing market information crucial for trading. The banks switched immediately to alternative services and reported no significant effects on their work; however, Reuters was deeply embarrassed by the incident.[68]

---

[67]   "MCI Worker is Charged in Huge Phone-card Theft," *Chicago Tribune*, p. 4, 4 October 1994.

[68]   Denton, Nicholas and Ridding, John, "Dealing rooms sabotaged by HK Reuters technician," *Financial Times Limited*, 29 November 1996

Contract and Temporary Employees

Businesses are looking for ways to make people more productive more rapidly. Often, this leads to hiring temporary contract employees or to outsourcing – alternate workers. The use of temps has grown enormously. Temps have access to an amazing amount of company-confidential information. Temps in the mailroom handle all of the company's information, and receptionists know who is talking to whom and can eavesdrop. Many security positions, especially guards, are often outsourced.

Many businesses are hiring consultants at very critical positions within the company, where they have access to crucial information, to rapidly gain experience and knowledge in specialized areas. These same consultants may also be working for your competitor where information may be disclosed accidentally. They may be unaware of the proprietary nature or the business-critical nature of the information. Independent consultants may be tempted by monetary gains. Temps and contract employees are often targeted by industrial spies.

A company who is using contract employees loses control of the quality of the employees. It no longer has control over background checks and screening of potential workers. Alternate workers are susceptible to the same factors that cause company employees to be the largest threat to corporate information – money problems, personal stress, fear of firing and layoffs, or just plain greed – and they do not feel the level of loyalty to the company to which they are contracted.

Employee policies do not apply to contract employees. Issues of security, nondisclosure, and appropriate behavior must be spelled out in the contract with them. These contracts are often with a contracting company, not specifically with the contract employee, and the individual's understanding of your company's security policies may be lacking. This may indicate a need for security checks for contract and temporary employees.

Two men admitted guilt in a corporate espionage caper. The bumblers sent Owens Corning a misspelled, ungrammatical note asking for $1,000 in return for secrets stolen from competitor PPG Industries. A supervisor at a company supplying cleaning crews and operators for prototype machines at PPG had access to every office at the PPG research center. He allegedly stole customer lists, blueprints, secret formulas, product specifications, and videotapes of new machinery.

Thanks to the cooperation of the intended purchaser of the information, the FBI was able to arrest the perpetrators. Ironically, two years earlier a similar scam was addressed to executives at PPG Industries offering secrets stolen from Owens Corning; the FBI caught those spies, too. Both companies insisted that it would be crazy, as well as illegal, to accept such information stolen from competitors.[69]

Business Partners

Cooperative business ventures have become a popular business tactic to reduce the risk of entering unfamiliar territory. These ventures generally require sharing a significant amount of confidential information. So even though the financial risk of the venture is reduced, the increased access to company information may increase the security risk.

Ventures into areas of new technologies often require creating close relationships with start-up companies that may have very little history. It may be difficult to get good background information about the company and about the quality of workers that they employ. When you enter into an partnership with another company, you inherit any hostilities that individuals may have toward the other company.

Large, established companies are not immune to problems either. Larger companies may have other business activities that may make them tempting targets. The likelihood of this increases when working with foreign companies where you do not know all the political aspects.

Often companies will find themselves needing to partner with a company on one area, while that same company is a competitor in another area – which means granting access to some while denying access to others in the same company. These complicated business relationships often blur the usual lines of trust and make security issues more complex.

Any of these relationships require intercompany communication that often increases the complexity of data and communications networks. Extending the corporate network to interconnect with the associated companies' information infrastructure opens new doors to security risks. These extended networks allow corporate partners access to internal information through connections that are generally not protected by the company's normal firewall systems, which shelter the company's information from the Internet. These connections need a more flexible solution that allows communication in both directions but still protects both companies from unauthorized activities.

Cooperative ventures may have a tendency to confuse participants, who don't know what information can be shared with what partners. Who actually works for whom? Employees may not understand which information is appropriately shared and which is not. Nondisclosure and confidentiality agreements need to be in place and communicated to all the appropriate people. Even with these precautions, accidental disclosure of information occurs.

The new Extended Enterprise view of business, where a company partners with other companies to share information, expertise, processes, and other resources, opens up a window of vulnerability. Even though you have a good business relationship, you cannot control the qual-

---

[69]   Holstein, William, "Corporate Spy Wars," *U. S. News Online,* 23 February 1998.

ity of employees that your partners hire. Their disgruntled employees now become a threat to your organization.

Other business segments in which your business partner is involved may be controversial or in some way increase their likelihood to be a target and, in turn, increase the threat to your organization.

In addition, your partner's security practices may not be as stringent as yours. This can allow an intruder to circumvent your security measures by attacking through your partner's infrastructure.

Professional Intruder

Professional intruders can be either inside or outside the organization and in many cases are both. This is a new and growing type of intruder. A black market has emerged where the skilled are able to sell their abilities to those who need access to a system. These black webs, as they are called, allow for anonymous communication between buyer and seller.

What distinguishes the professional intruder from other types of intruders it that money is the primary motivation.

Three young men from West Berlin, who had been hacking U.S. sites and passing stolen information to a contact in East Berlin, took a step up the ladder of global espionage when they were introduced to a KGB agent. This agent had a very specific list of information and software that he wished to acquire and he was willing to fund these hackers' activities.

Their hacking business was going very well until Cliff Stoll, a systems administrator at Lawrence Berkeley Laboratory, was assigned the task of finding the cause of an inconsistency in the computer's billing system. His investigation lead to the discovery that the systems at LBL had been accessed and the accounting records altered to remove any record of the access. Cumulative effects eventually became apparent. Stoll soon discovered that his system was just an intermediary on the way to government and military sites that pertained to the star-wars defense initiative.

After an extensive investigation, Stoll was able to trace connections through Tymnet and modem connections, and finally to West Germany. In response to a ruse by Stoll, the intruders requested defense information by mail, giving a name and address of one affiliate of the intruder. At that point, local police, the FBI, and the CIA became involved.[70]

---

[70]   Stoll, Clifford. "The Cuckoo's egg revisited," *Byte*, June 1993.

Hackers for Hire

The lure of easy money and the unlikelihood of being caught and prosecuted have led some hackers to sell their skills. Some have reported to have been contracted by companies to steal secrets, thereby giving the company plausible deniability to the crime. Communications are often anonymous and untraceable. Contact is limited to the electronic delivery of the secrets and the electronic funds transfer. It is difficult to get a good measure of the size of the risk posed by these hackers because of the way that they do business. However, it is known that they have sold their services to college students to change grades, to companies to steal their competitors' secrets, and even to governments for global espionage

> Federal prosecutors seized more than 100 written communications between U.S. subsidiary of Reuters Holdings PLC and a consulting company that investigators believe was hired to steal information via an electronic break-in to the computers of a competitor, Bloomberg LP.[71]

Organized Crime

A Michigan University study[72] reports that "there is an increasing threat of computer crime from organized crime groups from Eastern Europe." There are also reports of strenuous efforts on the part of some foreign intelligence agencies to gather information for the benefit of their national industries; these efforts have included eavesdropping, hotel room burglaries, and the introduction of "moles," as well as other sophisticated intelligence-gathering methods. Our foreign competitors' interest in our information has never been more intense.

New, easy-to-use hacking tools have made it unnecessary to have detailed knowledge about the system being attacked to be successful. This has allowed more people whose business it is to gather information into the world of computer hacking.

> Police in Toronto have arrested 38 members of what they claim is a huge, high-tech Russian organized crime ring. Authorities allege that the mobsters intercepted and decoded vast quantities of credit card data in transit from stores to banks and rigged debit card machines to download and copy encrypted information. The arrests culminated in a two-year investigation.
>
> According to Canadian authorities, the crime ring was based in Toronto but ran operations on four continents. While the ring was

---

[71]   Denning, Dorothy, "Who's Stealing Your Information," *Information Security Magazine,* April 1999.
[72]   Carter, D., "Computer Crime on the Rise" *1995 Computer Crime Study*, Michigan State University, October 1995.

involved in many crimes, it was the sophisticated data theft that most alarmed authorities.

An Eastern European mob kingpin had recruited a computer expert who designed and built equipment that could intercept and decode credit card info as it traveled from merchant to bank to be authorized. According to an international police organization, the mob had to have the cooperation of merchants in order to modify the debit card pads, which they used to download PIN numbers and other data.[73]

Activists

Cyberactivists are a growing concern. The anonymous environment of the Internet enables the activists to participate in their acts of civil disobedience with little fear of being identified. The number of issues which have inspired cyberactivists continues to increase, as does the level of attacks that are being performed. Civil disobedience is giving way to vandalism.

A group of political activists, protesting the Mexican Government's suppression of Chiapas, organized "virtual sit-ins" on Mexico City financial institutions. Protestors were instructed to surf to one of the offending pages and keeping hitting "reload," the theory being that if enough people did this, the site would be effectively blocked. Some of the protestors created a Java applet called FloodNet, which would launch a denial of service attack by repeatedly requesting information from the target web site. The sheer number of requests for information would slow down site traffic to a crawl.

Three months later, 8,000 protestors visited the Electronic Disturbance Theater site over a four-hour period, clicked on the FloodNet button and intermittently blocked Mexican President Zedillo's site. The group organized two more similar electronic events in May and June.

Some of these activists got their start working with nuclear fallout victims in southern Utah, and with Act Up (the AIDS activists group) in the '80s. Their electronic civil disobedience began with phone trees and jamming opponents' fax machines, but after a while those actions weren't getting the response from the media that they did before, so the level of electronic attack had to be escalated.[74]

[73]   "Mob Muscles In On Credit Cards," *Wired News Report*, 10 December 1999.
[74]   Penenburg, Adam, "When Art Meets Cyberwar," *Forbes.com*, 14 December 1998.

Terrorists

Terrorists' use of information has put a new light on security issues. The type of information that is valuable to terrorists may not have obvious commercial value. From a business standpoint, the loss or disclosure of this information may have no direct negative impact on the organization. Generally, the information of interest to terrorists is information about individuals – schedules, relationships with other people, etc. Florists and caterers have been targeted by information terrorists to get information about the future whereabouts of specific individuals.

Information can be used both as a means to an end, such as gathering information that will be used for a terrorist attack, or as the end itself. Information itself can be used as a terrorist attack. Terrorists have illustrated to individuals that they know all about them, their families, their schedules – that they are vulnerable. This in itself is terrorism.

The types of intruders are as varied as their motives. Every organization is a target. There is someone who wants to prove themselves by bettering the organization, or someone who wants to damage the organization, or someone who wants to profit off of the organization. There are always threats. Understanding the types of people who represent these threats can better prepare an organization for them.

Tamil guerillas swamped Sri Lankan embassy computers with e-mail in 1997 in what U.S. intelligence officials said was the first cyber attack by a known terrorist group on a nation's computer system.

Up to 800 e-mail messages a day poured into embassies' computer systems throughout Europe, North America and Asia for two weeks, paralyzing the network.

The Internet Black Tigers, an apparent offshoot of the Liberation Tigers of Tamil Eelam, claimed responsibility for the attack in the e-mail messages. Ethnic Tamils have been fighting the Sri Lankan government since 1983 for an independent homeland.

The CIA has said that terrorists and people who specialize in information warfare are the greatest threats to the world's telecommunication systems.[75]

---

[75]   "Cyber terrorists action reported," *USA Today,* 26 January 1999.

Checklist

—Partner with human resources to share information pertaining to disgruntled employees.

—Evaluate your attractiveness to each type of intruder.

CHAPTER 18

Intrusion Methods

Of the estimated annual $24 billion losses from intellectual property theft for U.S.-based companies, hacking ranked second only to pretext phone calls (i.e., social engineering) as a means of acquisition.[77]

Attacks against information systems are frequent and varied. The method of attack falls into one of three categories: physical, coming onsite and stealing systems or information on physical media; technical, utilizing the information network to get to the information; or they are social, conning the information out of people.

Technical Intrusions

A technical intrusion is the use of technology to gather proprietary information or subvert an information system.

Hacking

Historically, hackers had to be very technically competent to be able to understand the systems well enough to be able to gain unauthorized access. But with the evolution of the hacker culture, the sharing of information about exploits has greatly expanded. It has become easy to get detailed information on how to exploit system vulnerabilities. In addition, there is a plethora of intrusion tools today that allow someone with very limited skill to successfully attack a system. Many of these tools are easy to use – *point-and-hack*. Generally, these tools exploit known vulnerabilities in specific types of systems. However, there are huge collections of tools that utilize a wide variety of vulnerabilities in a lot of different types of systems.

The global Internet allows access from anywhere around the world. This also means that systems can be attacked from anywhere around the world. Geography is no longer a factor. Border guards can no longer keep secrets from leaving the country.

---

[77] American Society for Industrial Security, *Trends in Intellectual Property Loss,* March 1996.

Spying

There are high-tech methods of eavesdropping utilizing miniature cameras or sensitive microphones. It has even been demonstrated that a laser can be bounced off a window and vibrations caused by the sounds inside the building can be collected and turned back into those sounds. The cost of high-tech surveillance has made it available only to the professional information gatherer. But as with all high-tech electronics, falling prices are making it more affordable for a wider audience. As in most other things, security is an economic issue. Security is the process of making it economically unfeasible to compromise the system or information.

A convicted credit-card fraudster on day-parole from prison set up an automated shoulder-surfing operation with an accomplice. They placed cameras in several locations so they could record both the details of bank cards and the fingers of their users as they punched in their PINs. Armed with these details from two weeks of data collection, the two then created fake bankcards using gas station premium-point cards. Apparently, the particular bank victimized was chosen because its bankcards were particularly colorful and showed account information very clearly, even at a distance. The two then stole the equivalent of about $216,000 using stolen account information and PINs. Police finally put the parolee under surveillance on a hunch and correlated the huge number of complaints about unauthorized withdrawals with his presence at cash dispensers. Two years later, the fraudster was sentenced to five-and-a-half years in prison; his accomplice received a four-and-a-half-year sentence.[78]

Physical Security

Physical security is a fundamental aspect of any type of security. If someone can gain physical access to your information systems, they can damage or destroy these systems. Physical access to information systems requires the ability to selectively grant or deny access to a specific individual and that access be auditable (i.e., an access log must be maintained, preferably by an automated system). Information security levels must also be applied to supporting systems. Communications network devices are often housed in unsecured areas, and power and HVAC are rarely held to the same level of security as the computers themselves; without these supporting systems the information systems will not operate.

[78]   *UK Press Associate News*, 4 October 1996.

Physical security is a greater challenge in a widely distributed environment than when information and information systems are totally contained within a centralized data center. Today, the data center still requires the same level of physical security, but so do departmental servers that are scattered throughout the organization. Just because the systems are small, relatively inexpensive, and do not require dedicated power and climate control, does not mean that the information they contain is less important. In fact, most of an organization's valuable information resides on departmental servers at some time. Access to these systems requires the same level of security afforded to the data center.

Business Offices

Most organizations already have some physical access procedures in place and are comfortable with building access (locks on the doors and video surveillance for auditability). However, this security is often not extended to corporate areas outside the office. Shipping and receiving docks and offsite storage areas are often not held to the same level of security. Backup tapes have been stolen at offsite storage locations or in the process of being sent to or from the offsite location.

Today the low price of "color technologies" – scanners, videocapture devices, and printers – has made it affordable for any hacker to produce very convincing company IDs. Quite often companies use PCs and software that is easily affordable to the public to create their official IDs. So, common identifiers may be too common. An ID on someone who acts as if he belongs is not enough to be certain that he does belong.

With the greater distribution of information, physical security becomes even more important. When all the computers and information were in the data center, physical security was easy: it was localized. Now there is sensitive information on departmental servers and PCs on everyone's desktops; information is walking around inside laptop computers. Physical security and security control are much more complicated.

Computers must be secured from both access and theft. A survey reported that most of the laptop computers that were stolen in airports were not random thefts, but were stolen for the information they contained. Almost any security measure can be overcome if the hacker can get physical access to the computer system.

> Crooks stole a personal computer from the Visa International data-processing center in San Mateo, California, which held information on nearly one-third of a million credit card accounts, including those from Visa, MasterCard, American Express, and Diners Club. The information was compressed but not encrypted, according to Visa. As a precaution against the misuse of the stolen information, all of those cards needed to be reissued. Visa agreed to reimburse af-

> fected card issuers – including Citicorp – for costs associated with replacing cards. The total cost to Visa for the pilfered PC may exceed $6 million.[79]

Home Offices

Telecommuters, those employees who work from home, also add additional security issues. They need the same level of security at home as they would have in the office, yet this rarely happens. Homes do not have the same level of physical security or controlled access as do businesses. Family, friends, and neighbors all pass through the door. Home systems rarely enforce strong identification and authentication. They generally do not have network isolation from the Internet, making them easier to attack.

Home systems that connect to corporate networks and to the Internet for private use open the corporation up to attack, even if the connections are not at the same time. Most home office systems will contain proprietary information. Any access to the home system grants access to that information. The home system is vulnerable to attack while attached to the Internet. This can undermine sophisticated private networking schemes that go to great efforts to secure the communication between the home system and the corporate network.

On the Road

Many businessmen spend a great deal of time on the road taking their work and business information with them. Laptop computers are continually becoming smaller and lighter which makes them attractive to the mobile executive as well as the thief. Portable computers contain the information that the user needs to have always at hand. This is the information that is most needed and often most valuable. Mobile computer users must be aware that the theft of their computer compromises all the information on that computer. Many corporate spies have found it easier to steal a portable computer than to break into a company's computer to get the desired information.

> During a 20-minute lunch break at a business seminar in a hotel in Bedfordshire, England, thieves broke into the locked seminar room and stole 11 laptop computers worth about $75,000. That's $75,000 not counting software and data.[80]

Even when laptop thefts occur where there is no critical information on the system, the stolen laptop may contain information that can be used to assist in the compromising of other

---

[79]   *Infosecurity News*, January/February 1997
[80]   *UK Press Associate News*, 25 October 1996.

systems. Portable computers often contain information pertaining to the process of connecting to the corporate network and accessing corporate resources. Everything that is needed to compromise corporate systems is on the laptop computer.

Social Engineering

Today the art of gathering information has nearly become a science – one called social engineering. Social engineering is a confidence game; that is, gaining the confidence of the victim so he or she will give you the information you are requesting. Hackers can accomplish this through a number of methods. They will often start by calling the phone numbers around a modem number to find out what company owns the modem line. Once they identify the company, they will start to work on the employees.

A successful social engineer will leverage people's basic emotions, especially intimidation and preying on people's natural desire to help people who ask for help. He will impersonate new employees to get information from help desks or befriend users who have privileges. Beware of the following –

> "Hi, I'm new with the company and I'm having trouble getting connected. Can you walk me through the procedure?"

He can convince someone that he is a support person or other person in authority and needs the information to solve an important problem.

> "Hello, This is Mr. Laboski, VP of finance. I need a copy of the presentation that you are working on delivered to me at the Midtown Hotel. Now!"

This is often utilized with urgency or "end of day syndrome" (the likelihood that someone will bypass procedures to get it done in time to go home).

Hackers will sometimes pose as an employee who needs assistance or has been given an immense task and desperately needs help to complete it.

> "I've been given a task of compiling a list of all the people who are responsible for databases on the mainframe, and the CIO needs it for a meeting tomorrow."

They will utilize the corporate organization to their advantage. Large organizations are both dynamic and geographically diverse, so it is not surprising to have people you have never heard of in places you have never heard of.

> "Hi, this is Bob in Littletown, and I'm having trouble connecting with this remote software."

These attributes also make it difficult to verify that the person is who he says or to validate that he is an employee without a process in place.

> "My manager? That's Jerry, in Cincinnati, but by now he's already gone home for the day."

Much social engineering will go unnoticed, since a hacker will ask one individual only a few specific questions and then move on. These attacks will include numerous, inconsequential inquiries that add up to a great wealth of information.

Trojan horses can be used as a type of social engineering via software. Games that request passwords so that others cannot pretend to be you while playing the game will surprisingly often yield login passwords. Another common ploy to disseminate a Trojan horse is to disguise it as an exciting new utility that does something very useful while giving your privileges to the hacker. These are just a few ways that a hacker can abuse a user's trust in his software.

Selection

The first step in a social intrusion is selecting the target individual. The selection of the targeted individual of the social intrusion is based on the individual's relationship with the organization whose information is the target of the intrusion, and the willingness of the individual to assist in gathering the information. The willingness is often administered unwittingly.

- **Access** – The social intruder selects those who have access to the desired information. This does not have to be the person who is authorized to have access. It often is someone who is one level removed, such as an administration assistant. This person has the confidence of the person with the information and often as much access as the person.

  The people who handle information without having knowledge of the information will be targeted. This includes telephone operators and people in the mailroom and shipping and receiving. These people transfer information without access all the time. They usually have the ability to gain that access without authorization by listening in on conversations or opening mail.

People with physical access are targeted. This group includes maintenance, cleaning crews, utility workers, etc. These people are generally not directly employed by the organization and lack loyalty.

- **Willingness** – The social intruder may target people that have little company loyalty such as contractors or temporary employees, or people whose jobs have little reward but who have access to information, such as janitors, secretaries, computer operators or people who feel they have an axe to grind with the company. They will offer them what is missing from their lives – money, excitement, revenge, friendship, or recognition.

Motivation

Those mounting a social intrusion will exploit the victim by giving him something that he needs. This is usually a financial or emotional need. The social intruder will determine what type of motivation will inspire the victim to assist in gathering information from the target organization.

- **Greed** – People with a monetary need, especially an unexpected need, are very susceptible. They may be willing to take drastic actions to service this need. In some people the need is only a perceived need – greed. The emotion of greed has always made people easy targets to be exploited.

  Social engineers can exploit a monetary need in a number of different ways. They can offer rewards directly for getting the information, they can convince the individual that the organization's competitors will reward him for the information, or they may convince him that he will become invaluable to the organization if he can show them how they are vulnerable or how he can repair the problem.

- **Revenge** – Revenge is a very powerful emotion used by social engineers. It is a personal motive that goes beyond reason. The social engineer will convince his victim that he will be able to extract his pound of flesh from the organization. He will convince him that the organization or the specific individuals within the organization will suffer greatly because of his actions, thereby offering a level of satisfaction unavailable to the victim without the help of the social engineer.

- **Morality** – Social intruders may convince their victim that the target organization is doing something wrong and that the victim can do something about it. He can bring it to light, make it public, and make the evil organization stop its wrongdoing. They will focus on social issues that the victim is interested in and create a very convincing story, often without the need for facts. People are often very willing to believe the worst about a company or individual.

- **Group Loyalty** – The social intruder will leverage the target's identification and loyalty to a group. This may be in the form of patriotism, ethnicity or other group-identification values. The intruder will convince the target that he or she will benefit from the information that the intruder wants the victim to retrieve.

- **Recognition** – Motivationalists know that a little recognition can go a long way in motivating people to do what is wanted of them. Social engineers know this too. They will pump-up the victim's ego and promise wide recognition when the job is done. This is an effective method when the victim is a disgruntled or unsatisfied employee. These employees often feel that they have been overlooked and have not received the recognition they deserve.

Pretext

The pretext for a social intrusion can be as simple as chatting someone up at a social event or as intricate as impersonating employees and falsifying communications. Social intrusions are limited only by the creativity of the intruder.

- **Socializing** – It has long been said that it is easier to get information by buying someone a drink after work at the local pub than by trying to gather it covertly. Once befriended, people are very likely to talk about what is happening in their life, including office gossip. Why should a hacker steal information when all he has to do is ask for it? This technique requires the hacker to be a sociable person, which many computer hackers are not. However, this is the mainstay of the professional information-gathering industry.

  Information leakage also occurs through socialization on a less sinister level. It is not uncommon that competing companies in the same industry are located in close proximity. Individuals have social interaction with employees of other companies. Whether it is kids on the same soccer team, going to the same church, or spouses who work for different companies, employees have to be aware that social conversations about work can inadvertently leak information.

- **Trusted Advisor** – It is possible that a hacker will know more about the computer system than anyone else, including the system manager. If he is an employee, he has an advantage. He is already trusted, knows the people and the relationships, and can use his knowledge to build relationships with system managers, programmers, and other people who have privileges on the system by helping them with system problems. In this manner he will become a trusted advisor, someone to whom these people turn when they need help. To facilitate this assistance, people will often allow him to access the system with their login, thereby giving him access to their privileges. Every employee should be aware of the importance of information security.

The lion's share of security incidents are caused by either current or former employees. This is why you must know the mood of your personnel. Most employee hackers are disgruntled employees who will cause trouble of some type; the computer is just a handy tool. Occasionally, specific employees generally become disgruntled when there is stress in their life, either personal or business-related. However, if the company is going through change which has the employees concerned about layoffs or strikes, then you must be more alert to the possibility of in-house hacking.

You must impress upon your users the importance of not sharing logins and passwords. If a user needs special privileges, he should be given a special temporary login specific for the function that he is to do. This is required for accountability.

People need to understand the importance of security in their day-to-day life and they need regular reminders, which are available through awareness programs.

Checklist

— Evaluate your susceptibility to different intrusion methods.
- Technical
- Physical
- Social

— Educate employees on recognizing and resisting social engineering.

— Secure systems from both access and theft.

— Perform penetration testing.

CHAPTER 19

Intrusion Process

The Information Warfare Division of the Defense Information Agency found that it was able to gain access to almost 90% of 15,000 Pentagon systems in which vulnerabilities had previously been pointed out to systems managers for correction, by using publicly available techniques. [81]

Regardless of the intrusion method, the intrusion process involves discovering as much about the target as possible, gaining access and authorizations and achieving the attacker's goals. Access is needed to get to the information and authorizations are needed to utilize it. The attacker will utilize physical, technological, and social methods of intrusion to mount a successful attack. Many of the same tools utilized by administrators to evaluate and monitor the security and stability of their systems are the same tools used by hackers to learn about the systems they plan to attack.

Reconnaissance

Technical reconnaissance is the process of using technology to gather information about the targeted organization and the details of its information systems.

There are a number of access levels to information systems. The lowest level is knowledge of the existence of the system, enough to give the attacker a place to start. He may be able to determine the type of system, its function within the organization, and its relationship to other systems. This type of information increases the attacker's chances of mounting a successful attack. Broad-based information of this type can be used for competitive intelligence. Knowing the number, type, and organization of systems within a company can indicate the size and focus of a company's business strategy.

---

[81]   Machlis, Sharon, "Security Experts: Hacker Detection is Key," *Computerworld*, 3 March 1997.

Public Information

There is a wealth of information that is made freely available. Corporate web sites offer information about what the organization does. Companies will brag about the type and number of computer systems they are using. Some will even offer support information over public access methods. Many organizations make their name services (DNS) publicly available. This allows anyone to determine an organization's internal network topology.

Disclosed Information

The disclosure of information is a major security issue that is often underappreciated. There is a tremendous wealth of information that is available just for the asking. This can be asking individuals or asking information systems. Information systems will generally offer enough information about themselves so that an intruder can fashion his attack method for optimal effectiveness. There are a number of processes which will disclose information, including the following:

- **Active Scanning** – Scanning is the process of methodically connecting to each system on the network to determine information about the system. This information will often include the hardware manufacturer of the system, the operating system it is running, and the services that it supports. Each of the services that the system supports will be interrogated to determine if its fingerprints can be used to determine specific system information.

- **Software Fingerprinting** – There are a number of system protocols that supply information to any requestor. Many of these are very common protocol, such as HTTP, SMPT, FTP, etc. They often identify the application that is supporting the protocol and information about the operating systems on which they are running, often to the revision and patch level. This information can be used to construct effective attack scenarios based on vulnerabilities in the specific revision of the software.

SATAN, the first tool to combine the ease of use of a web-based user interface and a rules-based probe engine, caused quite a stir on its release. The system was designed to probe known vulnerabilities and report its findings over the network.

The fear was that the remote probe and report mechanism could be easily converted to a probe and exploit system which, when combined with its ease of use features, would result in global probing of systems by thousands of hackers.

What SATAN did produce was a greater awareness of security issues and a new focus on easy-to-use security tools.[82]

---

[82]   Press Associate News 25 Oct 1996

Gathered Information

Information can be gathered in a number of ways without fraudulent pretense. There are plenty of opportunities to overhear conversations or pick up discarded information, as illustrated below.

- **Shoulder Surfing** – Hackers take every opportunity they can to look over the shoulder of someone who is entering "secret" information, whether it is a phone card number, an ATM PIN number, or a password for a computer system. Crowded areas are a prime location for these types of activities. All of us need education about the handling of information. You need to take the same care with company information as you would with personal information. You must be aware of your surroundings and pay attention to those around you.

- **Dumpster Diving** – Dumpster diving is the term given to scrounging through the trash. A great wealth of information is thrown away by many organizations. This information can be in the form of computer printouts that may contain sensitive information; used carbon printer ribbons that can be unwound so all that was printed can be read; used media that can still be read even if all the data was deleted or the disks reformatted; and computer manuals that not only contain information about the system but quite often contain notes written in the margins by the users of these manuals. This information can be about the systems that are being used, proprietary or confidential information that was disposed of improperly, or even passwords written in the margins of user manuals.

  Such information is thrown away because people don't think of the consequences. Sometimes when a person quits or is transferred, all the material that was in his or her office will be sent to the trash. In many cases no one will review the material to see if it contains any confidential information.

  You need to create an appropriate disposal policy. This policy should address all aspects of data disposal and should be part of a data handling policy. Data classification, access, storage, backup, and removal should also be included. It should define where data of specific classifications can be stored, and how this media, whether it is removable media, disk, or tape, is to be labeled, handled, and disposed of. These procedures will vary depending on the classification or sensitivity of the data. Information classification and handling procedures are important regardless of the format of the information – whether the information is on the computer, printed on paper, or on a markerboard or drafting table. A markerboard in an executive boardroom is no less susceptible to compromise than a piece of paper on a secretary's desk.

- **Eavesdropping on Communications** – Wireless communications is becoming commonplace. In some countries there are more cellular telephones than wired telephones.

The technology to intercept wireless communications is also becoming common and inexpensive. This adds a whole new area for exploitation. Intruders can gain the same level of access to information by eavesdropping on wireless communications without physically tapping into the communications line. Cellular modems and wireless local area networks (LANs) can open the doors to your data communication without a hacker having to physically attach to your network.

> Secret service pager messages were intercepted with a commonly available pager interception program during a presidential visit to Philadelphia. They showed the Chief Executive's movements and messages as he traveled to the Convention Center to deliver a keynote speech. The messages intercepted included ones from the press and daughter Chelsea Clinton awaiting him at the White House switchboard.[83]

Laws that protect some types of communications do not prevent the information from being intercepted. They only give legal recourse if the use of the information causes physical or financial harm.

> Federal authorities charged that a local news bulletin service serving the New York media was tapping into sensitive beeper transmissions by the police, emergency crews, and the mayor's office. Three people and the news service, called Breaking News Network, were charged with mail fraud, conspiracy, and violating the Electronic Communication Privacy Act.[84]

Gaining Access

Gaining access to information through information systems requires gaining access to the systems or to the media that contains the information. Access can be either physical or electronic.

The first level of access is being able to communicate with the system, even if there is no useful information in the communications. At this level the system can be monitored as to when it is running and when it is halted. The system's availability can indicate the importance and use of a system. It may be possible at this level to covertly monitor the systems communication with

---

[83]   "Hackers Intercept White House pager Messages," *Alt 2600*, 16 September 1997.
[84]   "News Service Accused of Pager Eavesdropping," *Los Angeles Times*, 2 August 1997.

other systems. Minimally, this information can be used for traffic analysis: what machine talks with which other machine, for how long, and how often. Even eavesdropping on the communications may be possible. This level may give an attacker the ability to mount a denial of service attack by creating traffic that makes the systems unavailable. It also gives the attacker an opportunity to attempt to gain greater access by guessing passwords or by exploiting vulnerabilities in services that are made available by the system.

The next level of access is to actively be able to enter the system as a user. Unfortunately, in many environments this is considered the lowest level of access. This view leads to systems being compromised without them ever being "accessed."

Breaching the Perimeter

Your goal is to keep outside hackers out, but what exactly is "out?" You must decide what is in and what is out. This is accomplished by defining a security perimeter. A security perimeter is a definition of where information can flow and still be considered secure. It is at all the points where information can cross this boundary — the points of access to the security perimeter — that perimeter defenses must be put into place. These defenses should keep information from going out unprotected and people and processes from coming in unless authenticated and authorized.

Security perimeters are more than just between the corporate intranet and the Internet. There are often many levels of internal security perimeters. The security perimeter is usually closely related to the scope of control of the security personnel. This definition must include computer hardware (computers, networks, terminals, printers, removable media), physical locations (buildings, wiring closets, cable runs), and software (what software can be used with what data). Things that will limit/define the security perimeter include removable media and public communication lines. When any of these perimeter limitations is reached, you have encountered a security perimeter.

You must define the security perimeter to know what is inside and what is outside. Wherever there is interaction between the inside and the outside, monitoring software needs to be put in place to ensure that this entry point is not being subverted.

Implementing multiple levels of security perimeters will reduce security issues. When different levels can be isolated, a security perimeter should be defined. Multilevel security perimeters isolate areas with different security requirements. This isolation increases the difficulty of an attacker gaining access to systems at different security levels. The isolation of network traffic can reduce the possibility of sniffer attacks. Limiting physical access can minimize many security issues.

Many organizations have done a good job of fortifying their public access points. Firewalls are becoming widely deployed and implemented to decrease the success of direct attacks.

Alternate Entry Points

Today's network topology increases the difficulty of being able to secure an environment by securing the network. Networks are replicated for availability and interconnected to partner organizations to improve productivity.

The level of security in a partner's enterprise is different than that of your enterprise. Interconnecting networks with partner networks creates opportunities to exploit. A compromise of a partner's network can lead to a compromise of your network.

Desktop networks and dial-up Internet accounts have created an environment where any system on the network can open the network up to the Internet just by connecting to an ISP account. Modern desktop systems allow multiple networks which are interconnected and supported by routing protocols that communicate the new connections so that they can be automatically discovered. This situation can totally undermine any perimeter security.

Traveling employees often need access to information that is contained on their office desktop computer. If the company does not provide a method for secure access, it is likely that end users will employ an unsecured remote access system. Software that enables remote access to desktop computers is widely available and extensively utilized. This software allows the user to connect to the modem in the desktop and then enables access to the desktop's resources. War-dialers (automated systems that dial phone numbers in search of computer modems) have returned to the attacker's toolkit to locate these unsecured access points within an organization.

Physical Access

Local hackers will often take a field trip to their target's facility. They may appear in a tour of the facilities, or spend late hours going through refuse, or walk right in. Hackers have skirted physical security through a variety of guises. They have impersonated delivery people, telephone workmen, and office equipment repairmen: "I'll have to take this computer into the shop." A hacker newsgroup has even given information on how to get a job as a janitor in order to get uninterrupted, unsupervised access to an entire building.

Gaining Authorizations

Authorizations define what abilities an entity has with a specific piece of information. Authorizations are needed to utilize the information – read, write, delete, etc. Authorizations can be acquired by impersonating another user with more authorizations or by subverting software that has privileges.

Impersonation

Impersonating another user requires being able to authenticate oneself using another's identity. The level of difficulty to impersonate another individual depends on the level of authentication utilized. The type of authentication should be based on the level of authorizations that will be granted. In many cases, however, authentication is often as simple as providing an account identifier and password.

> A group of young hackers managed to break into the servers of as many as 26 different ISPs, businesses, and schools, making off with more than 60,000 users' passwords.
>
> Some of the hackers decided to use the purloined passwords to gain anonymous access to the Net and hack into other sites, and that's how law-enforcement officials got involved. The Sacramento Valley High-Tech Crimes Task Force was mobilized after one of the hackers managed to shut down a Sacramento Internet service provider using one of the ripped-off accounts. A 16-year-old Los Angeles boy has been arrested on felony charges of unlawful access and grand theft. At least five other teens were contacted by police in connection with the case and the circle of hackers may grow even wider.[85]

Session Theft

Session theft is the process of utilizing an existing session that a user has with an information system. The actual user has already identified and authenticated himself to the system to create the session. Sessions can be stolen through a variety of methods, including:

- **Unattended sessions** can be easily stolen by accessing the user's computer or terminal while he is physically away. While the intruder has access to the user's terminal, he has all the privileges that the original user of the unattended session had.

- **Automated sessions** are sessions that are created automatically, usually on behalf of a specific user. Portable computers often have access scripts, that are used to access corporate resources which include both the user's identification and the authentication. When an intruder gains access to one of these laptops, he gains access to the corporate resources through the automated session with all the authorizations of the owner of the automated session.

- **Session hijacking** is the process of intercepting and taking control of an ongoing session. It can occur on the telephone network by reconnecting the call to another number or, more commonly, on the computer network where packets can be redirected to another destination. In either case the user whose session is hijacked will get disconnected and someone else will be connected as the original user with all of his privileges.

---

[85]   "Hackers Force Pac Bell to Seek New Passwords," *San Francisco Chronicle*, C1, 11 January 2000.

A student left his terminal unattended. While he was away, someone used his session to mail a threatening e-mail to the President
of the United States. The Secret Service does not look kindly on
this kind of activity. They arrived at the university and questioned
the student. The system manager was able to convince the Secret
Service, with log information, that the terminal had sat idle for a
long period of time before the mail was sent and then again after
the mail was sent, and that the e-mail program used to send the
threatening e-mail was not the program usually used by the student, that he did not send the e-mail and that the e-mail was sent
by someone else as a prank. The Secret Service is still looking for
this prankster.[86]

Subversion

Subverting software that has privileges can be accomplished by exploiting vulnerabilities
in the software. These flaws may be design flaws, using the software in ways not expected, or
software flaws, misusing the software to get it to accomplish something. Most of the time, they
take advantage of vulnerabilities that have already been exploited. Common exploits are widely
available.

Covert Software

Covert software is malicious code that is introduced into a system in such a fashion that it
will be run by an actual user and thereby gain the privileges of that user. Trojan horses, applications that appear to be useful and harmless, but actually have a hostile intent, are an example of
this type of attack. Viruses are another type of covert software. They insert themselves into
another application and wait until that application is executed. All covert software has to be run
by an unsuspecting user to be able to deliver their damaging payload.

Covert software depends on its ability to go undetected and on having a user run the malicious code.

Achieve Goals

Once an attacker has achieved access and authorizations, he or she is able to perform
whatever actions warranted the attack. Specific goals are numerous and can be personal or
directed by another individual. They are generally driven by ego, believing that they are smarter
than their adversaries and that they are not going to get caught. General goals are based on fame
and fortune.

[86]   "U. of I. Freshman Charged with Death Threats to Clintons," *Chicago Tribune*, p. 2C, 25 February 1994.

Become Famous

It is the goal of many attackers to become famous. Attackers utilize "handles" and refer to themselves as hacker gangs with catchy names to be able to have both their fame and their anonymity. Fame requires that their exploits become widely known, which requires that the target be either a newsworthy site or so widespread that its effects are newsworthy. The press regularly reports on these attackers and their exploits, sometimes without verification, often focusing on the events of their exploits and not on the damage and losses that their exploits create. As commonplace as website vandalism has become, it still gets media coverage.

> After the major denial of service attacks against Amazon, Yahoo, Ebay and others, there were a flurry of copycat attacks on their web sites. The copycat attacks appeared to be mostly teenagers trying to make a statement, stand out within their peer group, or show they could do something cool. One of the most noted was the attack on CNN.com and E-trade. Reportedly the hacker, who calls himself "mafiaboy," had joined telephone conference called with other hackers during which he solicited sites to attack – then those sites went down shortly thereafter. Web site logs contained Internet addresses that indicated that attacks came from a Canadian Internet service provider which suggested that mafiaboy was involved. He had been monitored in hacker-related online chat rooms bragging about his exploits.[87]

Become Rich

It is becoming more common for attackers to attack systems for financial rewards. The evolution of the Internet from an information network to a backbone for electronic commerce has increased the opportunity for attackers to gain access to financial information over the Internet. Financial transactions take place on the Internet. Credit card numbers flow between customer computers to electronic business sites, where a great amount of customer information may accumulate, making them an attractive target.

> An Italian man and his Israeli wife were arrested at their house in the eastern Sicilian city of Catania by tax police after winning about $400,000 from the lottery. The man, an electronics system expert, and his wife, a linguist and interpreter, were charged with illegal

---

[87] Schwartz, John, "Hackers Strike Again," *Washington Post,* 9 February 2000.

use of credit cards. The couple, who allegedly hacked into computers to obtain thousands of Visa and Mastercard numbers, also
went on an online buying spree, ordering clothing, watches, but
most of all books – they set up a library in their Catania studio,
where there were thousands of volumes, mainly novels in Ger-
man.

The tax police said thousands of credit cards were involved. In
most cases, the couple would run about $2,500 worth of charges
on each card. They used thousands of American credit card numbers to place $750,000 worth of online lottery bets.

Investigators in Italy were tipped off by a banking service that became suspicious about bets placed with an online lottery agent in
Bergamo in northern Italy. The Bergamo agent was one of the few
in the country to take bets via computer and has been forced to
shut down.

Without worrying about the expense and playing all possible com-
binations so as to secure the win, the couple was able to win
$400,000, a tax police statement said. The winnings were then
laundered through various bank accounts, including some abroad.[88]

Hackers have discovered ways to subvert e-business systems to change prices on products,
thereby stealing very expensive products for only pennies. Some attackers have even attempted
to extort businessmen by threatening to crash their systems or to release private information that
was entrusted to their custody.

A computer intruder known as "Maxus" hacked into a SQL Server
database at CD Universe and stole 300,000 credit cards. He then
e-mailed CD Universe requesting that they pay him $100,000 in
exchange for details on its security "hole" and the destruction of
the stolen data. When his request was refused, Maxus posted
25,000 numbers on a website on Christmas day which offered to
sell 1,000 unpublished credit card numbers for $1,000.[89]

---

[88]   "Two Accused of Using Stolen Credit," AP, Rome, 4 March 2000
[89]   Stone, Martin, "Mafiaboy Hacker Eyed In Attacks" *Computer Currents*. 16 February 2000.

Checklist

— Limit Information Leakage.
  Minimize information access.
  Minimize distribution of information.   .

— Limit Access.
  Minimize anonymous access.
  Minimize type of access.
  Minimize scope of access.

— Limit Authorizations.
  Restrict privileges to those with need.
  Restrict global privileges.

CHAPTER 20

Detection Methods

Only 41 percent of companies surveyed utilize any method of intrusion detection.[90]

Misuse detection requires the detection of any type of security incident – accidental or malicious. In terms of incident detection there is very little difference between an accidental and a malicious incident. In either case, the information suffers a loss of availability, integrity, or confidentiality. Accidents are usually limited in scope in both the length of the incident and the breadth of the damage. An accident is usually reported relatively quickly and there is not an attempt to hide the fact that it was done. On the other hand, malicious attacks employ a wide range of methods to disguise the activities, and are often broad-based attacks compromising many systems, and, without adequate detection, they can go on for long periods of time.

Detection is composed of monitoring the system and detecting anomalies or a series of activities that indicate that a break-in is occurring and reporting it. It is important that tools recognize not just known attacks, but new scenarios. Detection tools must look for the unusual and the unexpected. When you do detect a security incident you will want to be able to define when the incident started so that you are able to restore the information to a known good state.

Intrusion detection provides the ability to rapidly detect unauthorized hacker activity and respond with a variety of counter-threat techniques. Responses can range from simple security officer notification to dynamic reconfiguration of identified weaknesses or communications paths.

Intrusion detection methodologies are based on three processes:

- **Signature analysis** involves the collection of event log data and the comparison of this data with predefined attack signatures. If the collected data is similar enough to the known attack signature, then an attack is reported. One disadvantage to signature analysis is that they can only detect attacks which have known attack methods that have

---

[90] "The 1999 Information Security Industry Survey," *Information Security Magazine,* July 1999.

a defined incident signature.

Defining the attack signatures is a difficult balancing act. The signature must be specific enough to avoid false indications (reporting normal activities as an attack), and must be broad enough to not overlook an attack because of minor variations (false negatives).

- **Static-state analysis** encompasses various static state checkers. These analysis tools evaluate the system for its ability to withstand an attack and are not dependent on the operation of the system or its involvement in an attack. Vulnerability analysis and configuration analysis fall under this category.

- **Dynamic analysis** evaluates the effects on the system to determine if an attack is underway. Dynamic analysis tools evaluate the activities on the system to determine if there are suspicious activities currently occurring on the system. They will utilize audit trails, network traffic logs, and other system logging information.

These processes are not totally separate. Actually, a complete intrusion detection solution requires both processes. They each have strengths and weaknesses and can complement each other when used together.

Profiles

Many intrusion detection methodologies utilize profiles. The information for these profiles can be gathered from a wide variety of sources, system logs, and network logs. These sources of information are accumulated to create profiles of related information which are used by the intrusion detection analysis software.

Vulnerability Profiles

A vulnerability profile is basically a list of known vulnerabilities. These can be versions of software or hardware or configurations that are known to have vulnerabilities. These vulnerability profiles are compared to the system to determine if it has any of the defined known vulnerabilities. These profiles are generally used by scanners that are run periodically and detect problems after they appear. Some scanners will repair the vulnerability if instructed to do so.

New vulnerabilities are being continuously discovered. Vulnerability profiles have to be updated regularly to be able to detect those newly discovered. These profiles are created by organizations that monitor and track vulnerabilities and are usually the same companies that create the vulnerability analysis software.

System Profiles

System profiles can be very effective if the system is a dedicated server performing a very limited number of specific functions, such as a database server. In this case, the processes that should be running on the system are well known and the resources required to support those processes can be easily defined.

Generally, information systems supply a variety of monitoring tools that can be used to monitor suspicious activities on the system. The logging information from subsystems, such as networking and databases, have a lot of information about connections, where they were from and what they were doing, especially if you utilize some of the additional tools that increase the detail in the logs. System accounting can give a picture of who is using the system and how. Process auditing can give a more detailed look at the processing and data that each user is using. These can also be used as a basis for building user profiles to be used as norms to detect deviations from these norms.

An intrusion detection system may also perform its own system monitoring. It may keep aggregate statistics, which give a system usage profile. These statistics can be derived from a variety of sources such as CPU usage, disk I/O, memory usage, activities by users, number of attempted logins, etc. These statistics must be continually updated to reflect the current system's state. They are correlated with an internal model which will allow the intrusion detection system to determine if a series of actions constitute a potential intrusion. This model may describe a set of intrusion scenarios or possibly encode the profile of a clean system.

Performance analysis tools can also be useful for system security when used to report processing that is out of the normal day-to-day processing. Whether it is an unexpected change in overall system utilization, an increase in a specific user's utilization, or a process that has increased its activity, these all may indicate that the system is being used improperly.

You have to capture a reasonable amount of data – enough to be useful but not so much as to be overwhelmed – and store it for a reasonable amount of time offline. The offline storage of security logs needs its own media, separate from backups, and its own reuse cycle. Security logs have different recovery needs than data.

Many intrusion detection systems base their operations on analysis of operating system audit trails. This data forms a footprint of system usage over time. It is a convenient source of data and is readily available on most systems. From these observations, the intrusion detection system will compute metrics about the system's overall state and decide whether an intrusion is currently occurring.

Most information systems monitor and record a tremendous amount of information about what the systems are doing. These logs can give a lot of insight into the activities on the system, for both appropriate and inappropriate uses.

There are large number of logs (cited below) that contain information that can be useful when you are trying to detect when a system is under attack. Often, the logs are recording information for the purpose of debugging the systems or to account for resource utilization, not necessarily logging the information that you would want recorded for security purposes.

- System accounting logs bill users for the resources that they utilize. These logs have detailed records of what programs are run by what users.

- Audit logs are a more detailed view of specific events. These logs are generally limited to specific users, specific programs, and specific files. They should be focused on interesting events, such as changes to security profiles or attempts to gain additional authorizations.

- Software logs are specific to the programs themselves. Some software programs produce more useful logs than others, and some produce no logs at all. The mark of a good program is its logging of transactions.

Hackers know how to modify logs and hide their tracks, so logs cannot always be trusted. Storing logs on systems other than those about which they report or on write-once media increases the quality of the log information.

Network Profiles

Network profiles illustrate the amount and type of traffic that the network carries, much like highway traffic patterns of direction and volume based on time of day. There are a wide variety of network equipment like routers and bridges that collect information used to create network profiles.

Network profiles can be used to establish normal work patterns and determine when activities are abnormal. Network profiles can indicate broad-based attacks where specific ports are probed on a wide number of systems. Network logs can also indicate when new nodes appear or disappear or when an address is used from multiple physical locations. All of these situations may indicate an attack. They can also spot and report specific connections that are inappropriate.

Hackers will often clean up logs on systems but overlook the logs left on network devices.

User Profiles

User profiles are a statistical model of usage, such as when the system is utilized and what programs are used. Some of these programs even evaluate an individual's typing patterns – speed, misspellings, cadence, etc. In general, these create a behavioral profile of the authorized users of the system.

User profiles are usually created from accounting records, audit logs, and applications logs. Any data source that can distinguish individual users can supply profiling data.

User profiling is built on the theory that an individual doing her job does basically the same thing all the time, and what she does will not be significantly different from anyone with the same job responsibilities. Often user profiles are actually group profiles that are a consolidation of user profiles of many users.

Detection software can monitor the systems for deviations from these standard profiles. These deviations will show when a user has changed how he uses the system, possibly indicating unauthorized activities, or that someone other than the authorized individual is using the account.

Some individuals, however, may not be easily profiled. If they are responsible for multiple job responsibilities they may exhibit different profiles. Requiring different identifiers for each responsibility may allow this person to have multiple profiles.

Administrators and sometimes programmers may also be difficult to profile since what they do may be mostly reactive based on the demands of others. Programmers go through periods of editing and compiling followed by periods of running applications. These different activities may profile quite differently. Administrators are often driven by the crisis of the moment and rapidly jump from one activity to another.

Attack Profiles

Attack profiles are descriptions of the artifacts that are left by an attack. These artifacts can appear in any of the logs that are collected by the information system, and often require the use of multiple logs to identify an attack. Attack profiles are created by monitoring attacks in a controlled environment and recording their effects on the information system logs. There have been enough attacks studied to have a reasonable guess of what is regular errors and what is an attack.

Most attacks today are not created by hand, or even selectively created for a particular target. Most attacks are created by the use of automated hacker tools. The quality and number of hacker tools has grown dramatically in recent years. The use of the Internet and the Web has allowed for the widespread distribution of free hacking tools to those who would otherwise not be able to find them.

Hacker tools allow hackers to attack more sites more successfully with less specific knowledge. Some of these tools can be used in an unattended mode so that they can work around the clock and notify the attacker when they have been successful.

The good news is that attacks that are based on tools leave the same fingerprints (i.e., recognizable entries in system logs) every time it is used. This makes the creation of attack profiles for intrusion detection software easier, and increases the accuracy of identifying an attack.

It is best to have widespread implementation with centralized consolidation of information. Many attacks can go undetected on a single machine, but a large population of machines may reveal similar activities that constitute an attack.

Self-Monitoring Profiles

An intrusion detection system (IDS) must monitor itself to be assured that it is working properly. Whether the IDS is network-based or host-based, these systems are widely distributed throughout the enterprise. Therefore, there will be times that specific components will be unavailable. This situation cannot compromise the quality or integrity of the detection system. It must continue to operate correctly, possibly at a reduced efficiency.

It must also monitor itself to reduce the chance of the IDS itself being subverted. This can happen when an intruder modifies the operations of the IDS so that it will not report his activities. An intruder could use knowledge about the workings of an IDS to alter its operation, possibly allowing anomalous behavior to proceed. The intruder could then violate the system's operational security constraints. A human operator examining the logs from the intrusion detector may discover this, but it would appear that the IDS was still working correctly. However, this is only likely to occur after the intrusion is known.

Another form of subversion error is fooling the system over time. As the detection system is observing behavior on the system, it may be possible to carry out operations, each of which is just slightly outside of normal system usage. When taken individually, the actions could be accepted as legitimate or as slightly suspicious, but not as a threat to the system. What it would not detect is that the combination of these actions would form a serious threat to the system's integrity.

Offline Methods

Offline methods evaluate information which is independent of the operation of the system. The system can be analyzed while it is not operational and the analysis does not change because of the proper operation of the system. Offline analysis can be repeated to assure that the environment has not changed. These analyses should be run whenever there is an update to the analysis programs or profiles. Many security scanners are offline systems, as are virus scanners.

Inside-out systems analyze the system form within the system. They have access to internal information, such as configuration information and can analyze it for flaws. Outside-in systems analyze the information system from the outside and perform tests in the same way an intruder would, gaining only the information the system will supply.

Configuration Analysis

Configuration analysis attempts to detect configuration issues that can lead to a security incident. It will attempt to detect both known configuration vulnerabilities and classes of configurations that may not be a known problem but are likely to lead to vulnerabilities (e.g., too permissive permissions).

This analysis can be performed by frequent, automated scanning of configuration variables and files, or by the continuous monitoring of specific, critical configuration variables and files, or by using a combination of these techniques.

Scanning is a broad-based method used to find classes of problems. Scanning can be implemented almost anywhere as an external process looking at the system configuration. Continuous monitoring is usually reserved for specific, critical configuration variables/files, testing its status every time the variable/file is modified. This method is usually integrated into the audit systems.

Combining these techniques allows for the continuous monitoring of critical files and periodic testing of the entire system. It can reduce the frequency of the scans and thereby reduce the overhead required to monitor the configuration.

Vulnerability Analysis

Vulnerability analysis and response consists of frequent automated scanning of network components for unacceptable (by policy) security-related vulnerability conditions. This includes automated detection of relevant design and administration vulnerabilities. Detection of vulnerabilities leads to a number of user-defined responses including: auto-correction, requesting corrective actions, or simple warning messages.

Vulnerability analysis can be done at a number of different levels. It can examine the software version to determine if it has a known vulnerability, or it can actually test the software to see if it is vulnerable. Most vulnerability analysis software only checks the version and patch level or looks for signatures in the software.

Vulnerability analysis is the most widely used intrusion detection method. Virus scanners are a form of vulnerability analysis. They scan the files on a system searching for signatures of known viruses.

Vulnerability analysis software utilizes vulnerability profiles, which are basically a list of known vulnerabilities. These tools are only effective against known vulnerabilities.

Online Methods

Online methods evaluate state information from the operation of the information system. They must be run continuously.

The wide variety of sources of this information has led to different models for the location of the intrusion detection system.

- **System-based** – System-based detection runs on a specific system and monitors the activities on that system. It can look for anomalies or specific situations that are considered to be security incidents. System-based monitoring must be distributed to all systems that need the monitoring. It can utilize a centralized reporting location to simplify administration.

- **Network-based** – Network-based detection monitors network activity and evaluates connection patterns to discover anomalous connections. It is able to detect attacks that are against many systems that might go undetected by system-based detection.

- **Hybrid Systems** – Hybrid systems utilize both system-based and network-based monitors to correlate as much information from as many sources as possible to get a clear picture of the intrusion and determine if any tampering is going on.

Anomaly Detection

Anomaly detection tools look for unusual activities or statistically anomalous behaviors, and are effective in identifying certain types of misuse, especially masquerading. These tools assume that intrusions are rare and will appear unusual when compared with normal activities. The anomaly detection software generally builds its own statistical norms for the defined profiles while it is operating. It must be able to adjust to changes in behaviors over time.

This requires the construction of normal behavior patterns and acceptable deviations. These patterns can be constructed from policy-based definitions or they can be created from historic information. The detection software then compares actual behavior to this definition of normal behavior. Determining what is a significant deviation is no small task. Some individuals with multiple or varying job functions may not easily fall into a normal behavior pattern.

Anomaly detection generally utilizes real-time monitors to immediately report suspicious activities of incidents that are currently taking place, or anomalous behavior that would indicate that an incident is about to occur. To be effective, real-time monitors require that someone is available to immediately notify who can take action while the attack is underway.

Attack Analysis

Attack analysis and response requires real-time monitoring and detection of attack signatures and other suspicious activities including viruses, probing activity, and unauthorized modification of system access control mechanisms. It depends on the ability to recognize activities that indicate an attack is underway.

Attack analysis is most effective at identifying attacks against known vulnerabilities, since the specifics of these attacks are well understood. Even when these vulnerabilities are already repaired and the attacks do not succeed, the analysis is useful in showing trends in the number and type of attacks that are mounted against your systems.

Attack analysis is very good at detecting the use of tools in an attack. Today, many of the exploits have been built into software tools that are widely available. Since these tools work in a predictable manner, they are easily detectable.

Many attacks have a similar nature that can be detected and reported. These can include port scanning or the same type of failure across multiple systems. These reports are more speculative in nature since the activities do not specifically indicate an attack; rather, that the activities are similar to those that could be used in an attack.

Misuse Analysis

Misuse analysis and response is the real-time monitoring of internal misuse of network resources. Misuse is typically associated with activities not impacting operational effectiveness, but nevertheless counter to documented policy regarding acceptable use of organizational systems and resources (e.g., use of a corporate system for viewing pornography). Automated actions include denial of access, warning messages, e-mail messages to appropriate managers, etc.

Misuse analysis is based on the ability to monitor specific activities that are against company policy and is used to support appropriate use of e-mail or Internet policies. These monitors can track where the connections are made and examine the contents for inappropriate content.

Honey Pots

Honey pots are systems that are configured with vulnerabilities and contain information that appears interesting, but have no strategic value. They are used to attract attackers to an easy target, thereby distracting them from valuable targets.

Honey pots can also analyze the activities of attackers, and have long been used in the educational environment to study how systems are attacked and how vulnerabilities are discovered. These research projects have lead to many of the discoveries that are used as the basis for many intrusion detection technologies. The building and monitoring of a honey pot can be very educational. However, it can also become a time sink for those who are managing and monitoring the honey pot. Balance is the key.

Honey pots are becoming more popular as an intrusion detection device by configuring them (with auditing and alarming with notification and automated responses) to be able to rapidly detect an intruder. They are easy targets and work effectively as an early warning system.

Human Methods

Users represent many eyes and ears and are most often the first to spot a security incident. Most likely it will be a user who is on the system regularly who will notice that the system is running slowly, or that he is unable to access something that he should be able to access, or that the system is running out of free space or some other oddity. In a large organization, their first response will be to contact the help desk. It is these people who are the first to have the information needed to make a preliminary determination that the system may have been compromised. All reports should be taken seriously. Hackers have a tendency to brag, and those they brag to or even the hacker himself may make an anonymous report.

To make human reporting of intrusions effective requires that the users of the system know how to recognize that an intrusion is underway and where to report it. It also requires that the help desk personnel know the appropriate response procedures and can rapidly initiate a response.

Checklist

— Use a variety of detection methods. (Each has its own strength.)

— Create a centralized, consolidated reporting system.

— Require tuning and monitoring.

Reaction

The biggest mistake people make is they underestimate the threat.[91]

– Jeff Moss

When a security incident occurs, the company's reaction is determined based on a set of goals for handling the incident. These should reflect your business practices and keep the business objectives in mind. They must be based on prioritized business objectives. This will determine the company position for handling the incident.

As security incidents occur, management will react to protect the information resources of the company. These information resources include information and the availability of information services. How security incidents are handled can have a profound effect on their impact to the company. The response to a security incident should be well defined in advance. No plan can handle every contingency. However, a general plan can be developed that can handle the majority of incidents.

Your disaster plan must cover security incidents. In fact, you should have a specific security incident plan which details the procedures required.

Preparation is critical to a quick and successful response. The response to a security incident should be planned well in advance of any need for it. While your system is under attack is no time to be trying to make business decisions on what you should do. And it is even a worse time to be creating policies and procedures, which is exactly what you will be doing by default.

Organizations generally spend a significant amount of time and money in the preparation of a business continuity plan that addresses natural disasters. However, it is unlikely that this plan adequately prepares for a disaster caused by a security incident, which is much more likely than a tornado, earthquake, fire, or flood. An incident response plan is a key element of the

---

[91] March 23, 1998. InternetWeek.
Jeff Moss is the founder of DEF CON, an annual computer security/hacker convention in Las Vegas that combines law enforcement, corporate America, and "hackers" from around the world. He is the Director of Assessment Services at Secure Computing and prior to that he was a manager in the Information Security Services (ISS) group at Ernst & Young, LLP, where he successfully performed computer intrusions on large company computer and phone networks to highlight weaknesses and provide solutions.

Business Continuity Plan and requires the same level of attention. This means the same level of preparation and testing. An untested plan is only slightly better than no plan at all. If you haven't tested the plan, you have no assurance that it will be beneficial in the case of a security incident.

Incident Response Philosophies

An organization's response plan will depend on its philosophy of how the incident should be handled. Some organizations wish to fix the problem and quietly get back to business. Other organizations want the guilty party brought to justice. There are basically three philosophies to responding to a security incident. They are as follows:

Watch and Warn

The watch and warn method performs monitoring and notifies someone when an incident is detected. It takes no actions by itself, except the notification of an appropriate individual. It monitors activities and determines what are suspicious activities and reports them so that they can be handled by the appropriate individuals. This is the most passive model of intrusion detection. It is also the simplest to implement. Most information systems supply some level of monitoring capabilities. The output from these standard monitoring facilities can be scanned for incident indicators. It will monitor a number of attributes and report on anything that is out of the ordinary.

This method depends on the ability to rapidly contact someone who can handle the situation. Having people on call and available to respond is critical to effectively implementing a watch and warn system.

Repair and Report

The repair and report philosophy will attempt to close the incident as quickly as possible so as to be back to business as usual as soon as possible. This requires the identification of the intrusion, repairing the vulnerability, or blocking the attack and reporting these actions. This model must be able to distinguish what is an attack and what is not. It must also be able to repair the problem or contain the situation by blocking access without human intervention.

If the specific point of entry has not yet been identified, then a broad-based denial of access may need to be applied. This may be accomplished by disconnecting the system from the local network or by disconnecting the organization from the Internet, if the attack is widespread. If you are fortunate, there will be enough information to be able to use a more limited blocking strategy of blocking a range of addresses or specific services at the firewall.

The affected systems must then be cleaned to remove any malicious code that was involved in the attack and to repair damage to the information on the system. When the system is clean, it can be brought back online.

Finally, the method of attack must be determined so that it can be repaired to prevent the attack from resuming.

Pursue and Prosecute

The pursue and prosecute philosophy requires the monitoring of the attack, the collection and maintenance of evidence, and the involvement of law enforcement and legal counsel to prosecute the attacker. It takes an active role in creating a restricted environment that will minimize the attacker's potential damage, where the intruder is allowed to continue attacking while monitoring systems, and tracking the intruder to collect information to be used as evidence.

This will include exhaustive and difficult processes to determine the origin of the attack when the attack is from outside the confines of the organization. It requires cooperation of the organizations whose equipment is being used to gain access. This includes ISPs, telephone companies, and any company with an Internet connection. Tracking the attacker usually requires that the attack be ongoing, thereby making the systems more vulnerable to an extended attack.

Understanding the organization's response philosophies will direct the incident response plan. Each one will emphasize different attributes and focus on different processes. However, they all have a common core of processes.

Incident Response Plan

Regardless of the philosophy of responding to a security incident, there must be a preplanned response. An incident response plan will establish management procedures and responsibilities to ensure a quick, effective, and orderly response to security incidents. Incident response is not usually a revenue generating activity, so this makes it difficult to obtain necessary resources. However, careful and intelligent planning and justification can be key to illustrating the scope of the issues. All of the business implications should be evaluated and a policy based on business decisions should be created.

The incident response plan should be the best-defined section of security procedures, yet it rarely is. The usual excuse is that the response will depend on the type of the attack. Specific incident handling procedures are often created for specific types of incidents. These usually evolve from best practices and address simple intrusions such as computer viruses, compromised user authentication, or system scanning or probing. This may be true for the specifics. However, in general, the response to a security incident will be the same. Even though you cannot predict the kind of security incident to which you may fall victim, you can prepare for the type of outage you could experience and plan your response accordingly. Your outage will either be a system outage or a data outage. The attack will come from either a live attacker, a programmed threat or both. In any case, the response process will be the same.

The response plan should contain certain topics to adequately prepare the organization for responding to an incident. The following basic steps will have to be taken in any security incident:

Documentation

Documentation is critical to effective resolution and post-incident review of a security incident. The documentation should include the activities of the intruder as well as the activities of those who are attempting to repair the damage. Much documentation which is collected by automated systems can be very useful in the case of a security incident. However, it requires condensing and interpreting to isolate the information that is specific to the security incident and to make it comprehensible to those who need to be informed about the incident.

Determination

Determination that there is a security incident underway sounds deceptively simple. However, it may be very difficult to determine that a security incident has occurred. Hackers can be very adept at hiding their tracks. System administrators may be reluctant in admitting that they are the victim of a security incident. Having an intrusion detection system in place is the first step in detecting incidents.

Notification

Notification must be made of the security incident to the appropriate people (management, legal counsel, law enforcement) at the appropriate time. Some actions cannot be taken until authorized by the appropriate individual. The response cannot begin until those responsible for implementation are notified and mobilized.

Containment

Containment involves limiting the incident to those systems and data that have already been compromised. Minimizing the impact of an incident has to be the primary goal of any response plan and should be put into motion immediately.

Assessment

Assess the scope of the damage. This allows you to isolate the compromised systems and data and begin the process of determining the cause, nature, and extent of the attack.

Eradication

Eradication is the removal of the cause of the incident. All systems affected must be examined for evidence of the incident. Any changes must be corrected and the system returned to its normal configuration. Additionally, any backup media of the affected systems should be examined to determine their state. Eradication involves a complete review of the system and may be time-consuming. Security tools may be used to speed the process.

Recovery

Recovery is the process of returning the system to its normal state. Additional security patches or fixes for the vulnerability exploited may be employed. The system should undergo a complete backup and be placed back into production.

CHAPTER 21

Response Plan

Sixty-four percent of IT Executives indicated that their organizations don't have a planned incident response methodology in place.[92]

A documented response plan is critical to a successful response to a security incident. An advanced plan for security incident handling allows the organization to plan and practice. This preparation allows the participants to have a consistent level of knowledge and expectation when the incident occurs.

Response Procedures

Documentation of incident response procedures will create a common base of information which will facilitate better communication. Everyone knows what is to be done and who should be doing it. The response procedures should indicate which processes have what level of priorities and should receive the greatest attention.

It should document the circumstances that will indicate an incident and determine the direction of your response. Different circumstances can require different responses. You may wish to disconnect the system to avoid further compromise or collect additional information about the attacker, even if it means further compromises.

The response procedures should document procedures involving remote systems and connections to partners and public networks.

This documentation should be used to ensure that everyone on the team understands these procedures.

Authority to Respond

Security incidents are not budgeted items. They create unexpected expenses in overtime, supplies, and information system resources. Predefining the level of approval required to per-

---

[92]   Ernst & Young, *5ᵗʰ Annual Information Security Survey*, 1997.

form response activities will ensure that the appropriate people are involved in the decisions. It also ensures that there is authority for the expenditures that it will entail. Defining which types of intrusion response activities need what level of management approval and what can be considered preapproved will eliminate confusion during the incident and facilitate a faster response.

Describe the approval documentation required. The amount of documentation for approval can increase the time and burden to implement a response, but it reduces miscommunication and fingerpointing. The level of documentation for approval should be commensurate with the level of exposure the response activity will create.

Ensure that everyone on the team is officially empowered to perform the preapproved actions. Some of these actions, such as disconnecting or shutting down a system, will create a denial of service to that system. This will ensure that the proper people will be able to respond quickly without concern for liability issues.

Define roles, responsibilities, and levels authority of all staff involved. This will help eliminate confusion over who is in charge and who should be doing what.

A National Aeronautics and Space Administration employee took it upon himself to track down the hacker gang called Hagis (Hackers Against Geeks in Snowsuits) after they took control of the root directory of some NASA computers, installed hacker tools, and defaced the NASA home page. He belittled the gang on his personal web site, and they retaliated with a vengeance, hacking his personal and home-business sites, having his phone disconnected, bringing down the ISP he was served by, and breaking into his wife's account and threatening her.

NASA ordered him to ignore it. He did stop working on it on company time, but continued the pursuit at home. Meanwhile, the Royal Canadian Mounted Police arrested one of the hackers in the case. The NASA employee says he won't share the information he has discovered on the other hacker involved – he plans to take down that hacker himself.[93]

Financial Limits

The security incident manager is usually a technical manager who may not generally have much spending authority. Due to the time critical nature of a security incident, normal process to allocating funds may not be flexible enough to adequately respond to the incident. It may be necessary to assign different spending limits to individuals during a security incident so that

---

[93]   Penenberg, Adam, "A Private Little Cyberwar," *Forbes,* 21 February 2000.

needed tools or consultants can rapidly be made available. These differences should all be documented in the response plan.

Disabling Services

Services that have been compromised may need to be disabled to keep the attacker out and to repair the service. There should be defined circumstances that warrant disabling services, as well as clearly defining who has authority to shut down services. Different services may require different levels of approval to be disabled based on their business value and if they are internal or external services.

Disconnection from the Network

Disconnecting systems from the network can be used to isolate systems to keep attackers from entering or exiting a network. However, severing connections to partners or remote employees will stop all services to these groups. In addition to defining individuals who are approved to disconnect these networks, a notification process should be established.

Communications

Communication is a very important process during a security incident and should be handled by those who are trained in this area.

Resources

The incident response plan should indicate the resources that are available for an incident response. These resources include people, tools, support organizations, and what is required to assign more resources.

People

People determine how the resources will be structured and staffed. If staffing is coming from other projects, determine the circumstances required to enlist these individuals. Lists of people with necessary skills should be maintained to help get assistance more rapidly.

Tools

Define the tools necessary to adequately respond to a security incident; there are a wide range of tools that may be needed. You will need to capture information about the activities on systems and networks as well as document the configuration information. Support information, such as contact lists and response procedures, will need to be maintained and available during the incident. Documentation on the use of the tools will need to be readily available for reference during the incident.

External Support

Define the process necessary to get external resources involved. External resources may include security response organizations, external consultants, or law enforcement. There are implications with getting any outside organization involved, so the decision to do so will need to be evaluated and approved.

Enlisting assistance from outside the organization has a variety of issues, most notably the issue of making the incident more public. However, there are times when external support is needed. When the response is focused on catching the attacker, private investigators or law enforcement may be required.

Legal Review

The policies and procedures defined as part of a security incident should be evaluated by the organization's legal counsel. They need to be evaluated for compliance with national and local laws to determine if they are enforceable and defensible.

They should be evaluated in conjunction with the organization's other policies and procedures for consistency and compared with the best practices in the industry.

Checklist

— Determine corporate goals.

— Define processes to support goals.

— Define authorized response personnel.

— Define level of authority.

— Determine requirements for escalation.

— Determine requirements for external assistance.

— Determine requirements for invoking disaster plan.

— Have the plan reviewed by legal counsel.

CHAPTER 22

Incident Determination

When asked if their systems were penetrated via the Internet last year, 64 percent of respondents didn't know.[94]

On the surface, determining when there is a security incident seems simple. However, what seems deceptively simple may be the most difficult question to answer: "Is the event that has been detected really a security incident?" It may be the symptoms of an impending hardware failure or a simple error caused by a user or an administrator. Undoubtedly, security incidents will occur when the least experienced personnel are manning the systems, so the incident response plan must have clear definitions of when to invoke the plan or when the appropriate people who can invoke the plan need to be notified.

Information security exists to protect the availability, accuracy, and confidentiality of the information. Anytime any of these attributes are compromised, a security incident has occurred. There is a broad range of security incidents. They can be accidental or malicious. They can be the work of individuals or groups. They can be manual or automated. They can originate inside or outside the organization. They can occur at any time of day or night.

Not all security incidents are of the same magnitude. Nor does the same event constitute a security incident at all locations. Every organization will have to define what constitutes a security incident for themselves. In some secure networks a simple port scan (a process that determines what services a remote system is running) would be considered a security incident, since there should be no unexpected traffic on the network, while in many environments this would not be a security incident until unauthorized access has actually occurred. Information owners are responsible for defining the specifics that determine a security incident based on the criticalness of the resource.

Unless you have active system monitoring in place it is unlikely that you will detect an intruder. That is why it is crucial to develop specific definable events that indicate that a security

[94]   Ernst & Young/CIO *Canada Information Security Survey,* 1998.

incident has taken place and that the security response plan should be initiated. Both users and administrators should be aware of what constitutes a security incident and how to report it.

The greatest advantage that a system administrator has against an attack is the knowledge of the normal behavior of the system. Knowing how the system should behave enables more rapid detection and response.

There are some indicators which, when detected, require more investigation to determine if there is an incident. It is sometimes difficult to rapidly determine the difference between system problems and an actual attack. Making this determination is key to developing an appropriate response.

> The FBI web site was shut down for several hours by a denial of service attack. At the time of the attack the FBI said that it couldn't determine whether the problem was a technical fault or malicious attack. A week later it was confirmed that vandals were responsible. Engineers at IBM, who run the FBI's web site under a federal contract, took the appropriate steps to get the site back and running. Finding the source of the incident was a secondary concern.[95]

The likelihood that these indicators actually represent an incident and the importance of responding to them in a timely manner can be loosely categorized into possible, probable, and definite indicators.

Possible Indicators

Possible indicators of a security incident are those things that are unusual and might indicate that there is a security incident underway. The following four scenarios indicate that an investigation is warranted to discover why they are occurring and if there is a security incident.

Unfamiliar Files

Unfamiliar files on a system, especially in directories that are for programs or configuration files, may indicate that there have been inappropriate activities on the system. These files should be investigated to determine the source of the files, their purpose, and if they are inappropriate.

Procedures can be instituted to compare the files that are on the system with a previously generated list of files.

---

[95]   Schwartz, John, "Hackers hit FBI Web Site," *Washington Post*, p. E02, 26 February 2000.

Unknown Programs or Processes

Unknown processes, especially those that are resident on the system for a long period of time, need to be investigated to determine the origin of the process. Information systems attacks often include installing software on the target site to exploit vulnerabilities or to monitor the system to determine if the intrusion has been detected. Hackers will often attempt to disguise this software by using common software names so that they will not be detected, or they may alter the process monitoring commands so that they do not report the rogue software.

The greatest advantage a system administrator has against an attacker is knowledge of his specific system. This allows him to identify processes that are out of the ordinary.

> A technician at a defense contractor discovered a logic bomb was waiting to run on a system on which he was investigating an unrelated performance problem. It was planted by an ex-employee who was a key developer of the database which stored information about the parts and suppliers for a weapon system that was under development. This developer had discovered that the database was not being adequately backed up, so he planted the bomb to destroy the database, and quit the company, planning to be hired back as a "highly paid consultant" to rebuild the system. The bomb was successfully defused before it caused any damage.[96]

Consumption of Resources

Unexpected consumption of resources, which includes computation, memory, storage, and bandwidth, indicates that there is something utilizing the system in an unexpected manner. During an attack, the attacker will consume some resources. In some cases it will be so great as to cause a denial of service, while in other cases it may be barely noticeable. Unexpected resource consumption does not have to indicate an attack, it can be the result of poorly written software, insufficient allocation of resources, an impending hardware failure, or any of a dozen other things. This situation is minimally a performance issue, if not a security incident. It should be investigated and resolved to fix the performance issue. If the source of the performance issue is a security problem, then a security incident report should be started.

System Crashes

Unexplained system crashes can be an indication of a security incident. When a vulnerability is discovered by a hacker, it will have to be manipulated by the hacker until he can find a

---

[96] "Programmer Accused of Plotting to Sabotage Missile Project," *The Risks Digest*, Volume 11, Issue 95, 28 June 1991.

way to exploit it. These exploits often require fashioning very specific input to the vulnerability to get it to do something useful to the hacker. In the process of finding the precise data, the manipulation of the vulnerability will cause unexpected results. Software and system crashes are one of the most common results. The attack tools that are created to exploit a vulnerability are often crafted for a very specific environment. These tools will frequently crash a system that does not exactly match the defined environment.

Probable Indicators

Probable indicators are those things that could not occur on the system without someone actually instigating them. When these occur without the knowledge of the appropriate administrator, they should be investigated to discover how and why they were done and by whom. Below are four examples:

Activities at Unexpected Times

User connections or activities at abnormal user times are an indication that something unusual is going on. It may be that the user has a special project due, or that the user has had a change in schedule, or it may be that the account is being used by someone else. It is common for attackers to utilize user accounts when not in use by the owner. Often the hours that an attack takes place are when normal users would not be on the system. However, the worldwide nature of the Internet enables attacks from other time zones which obscures the importance of time of day attributes of an attack.

Anomalies should be investigated to determine if they are just an anomaly or if the system is being misused. If the user reports that his account is being used when he is not using it, this must be assumed to be a security incident.

Presence of New Accounts

Attackers need an account on a system to maintain access and utilize resources. They may create an account for themselves so that their activities would not be noticed by the account's actual owner. The process of creating new accounts should be limited to a minimum number of administrators, so when a new account appears that is unknown to the administrators it should be investigated. It is possible that the new account was automatically created by the installation of new software. In all cases, the creation of a new account should be investigated.

Reported Attack

Anytime there is a report by a user who suspects an attack, it must be investigated. Users generally will not make a report unless they feel that it is important and justified. Often, individuals do not want to get involved, so any anonymous reports must also be taken seriously. The perpetrator may also make an anonymous report, either out of remorse or to challenge the organization to find it before it causes any damage.

Notification from Intrusion Detection System

Anytime that the system monitoring software reports a violation, it is likely that there is a security incident underway.

All reports from an intrusion detection system need to be investigated so that the detection system can be better tuned to report all intrusions without reporting activities that are not intrusions.

> The EDAToolsCafe site, which has been in operation for more than three years, was brought down less than three hours after opening its business-to-business e-commerce operation. "The hackers were real pros." said a spokesman for the company, "They triggered one of our 'trip-wires' and alerted us to their intrusion early in the game. In the process, they left their signature, a telltale calling card 'Electro'." The cost to IBS in terms of lost advertising revenues and e-commerce was minimal and the lessons learned will help prevent future situations of this type.[97]

Definite Indicators

There are many situations that can clearly be defined as a security incident. These indicators, listed below, need to be addressed rapidly and with all expectations that there is an incident underway.

Use of Dormant Accounts

The use of dormant accounts is a standard hacker procedure to gain access and authorizations on a system. Any account that is locked should never be accessed or have processing time accounted to it. Anytime that there is activity in an account that should not have activity, someone is misusing the account.

Changes to Logs

Anytime that there is an unexpected change to a system log, it must be considered the result of an attack and investigated. System logs are a primary target for hackers. Any changes to logs are attacks against the auditability of the system and an attack against the required basic business processes.

---

[97] "'Electro' Hacks EDAToolsCafe.com B2B Portal", *Business Wire*, 1 March 2000.

Presence of Hacker Tools

The presence of hacker tools on a system is a clear indicator that someone has been misusing the system. You need to investigate who put the tools on the system and if they have been used. The attack may not be against your system; your system may be being used to attack other systems. The presence of hacker tools can allow you to put a trap on the tools to be notified if they are accessed, thereby being able to catch the hacker while he is using the tools.

Many organizations will define even the possession of hacker tools to be a violation of policy and directly punishable.

Notification by Partner

Often a site is unaware of an attack that is using them as a relay point to attack another site. The telephone call from a partner informing you that they are under attack from your site is often the first an organization will know of the attack.

If a partner has done sufficient investigation to determine that an attack is being directed through your systems, then it has been going on long enough for you to be assured that there is an incident underway.

Notification by Hacker

Whenever an organization receives a report from someone claiming to be an attacker, it must be taken seriously. Hackers are often very bold. Many believe that they are smarter than the system administrators and have little chance of being caught. International hackers are even more confident. They feel that even if they can be located, the effort to extradite them (if possible, since hacking is not illegal everywhere) will deter most organizations from pursuing legal prosecution.

This type of attacker is not generally stealing information. More likely they are demonstrating their computer prowess. Their attacks may affect availability and performance, but with appropriate response, they will have no long-term impact.

> A 17-year-old hacker known as YTcracker, who penetrated several government and military web sites (including those belonging to the Bureau of Land Management's National Training Center, NASA's Goddard Space Flight Center and the Defense Contracts Audit Agency) said he routinely sends messages to government web site administrators insisting that they address vulnerabilities and adopt Unix or other more secure systems, but the messages largely go ignored. YTcracker said in his defacement of web sites he "targeted the systems the government would look at and take seriously." [98]

[98] *Federal Computer Week*, 15 November 1999.

Predefined Situations

In every environment there are specific things that would automatically constitute a security incident. Whenever any of these occurs, it must be considered a security incident.

Loss of Availability

Availability is the primary concern of most organizations. Whenever there is a significant loss of availability an incident should be investigated. A security incident or a disaster can be automatically declared if the information is unavailable to its users for a specific amount of time or at a critical time. Having predefined standards will facilitate a more rapid response to the incident.

Loss of Integrity

A loss of integrity can be devastating to an organization. Whenever information is known to have become corrupted it must be investigated to determine if it is a simple mistake or a malicious act. Whenever there is a loss of integrity in information of a specific integrity classification or higher, a security incident should be automatically declared.

Loss of Privacy

If it is known that the confidentiality of the information has been compromised, there has been an incident. A loss of privacy is not restorable. Whenever the confidentiality of information is lost, it cannot be recovered, only the extent of the damage can be controlled. If there is a loss of privacy in information of a specific confidentiality classification or higher, a security incident should be automatically declared.

Violation of Policy

Any activity that is defined by policy to be a violation must be considered a security incident. All violations of policy must be investigated.

Violations of the Law

Anytime that the information system is being used in the commission of a crime, it is a legal imperative that an investigation be instituted. Cooperation with victim organizations and law enforcement is required to avoid liability issues.

Checklist

— Define what constitutes a security incident for your organization
  In the terms of:
  • level of unavailability
  • loss of privacy
  • loss of accuracy

— Automate determination where possible (integrated into IDS).

CHAPTER 23

Incident Notification

During a Department of Defense information systems test of 8932 computers, 7860 were broken into, 390 detected the attack, and only 19 reported the attack.[99]

It is rare that the first person who notices that there is a security incident is involved with security. Usually, it is the users of the information that notice there is something wrong – information missing, altered, unavailable or that the systems are "running funny." A well-informed user community can significantly increase the likelihood that an incident is noticed and reported rapidly. It is likely that security incidents are not reported as security incidents; rather, they are reported as system problems. The help desk personnel must be trained in order to recognize the difference between a system problem and a security incident. The help desk and system operations are the most logical place for the determination that a security incident is taking place, so it is the best place for notification and response to begin.

Notification needs to be built on a formal set of procedures. Control of information during the course of a security incident or investigation is very important. The right people at the right time need to be notified, but containing information, especially in the early stages, can eliminate the leaking of incorrect information and idle speculation. Release of incorrect information or information to the wrong individuals can be catastrophic. Incident involvement needs to be kept to the minimum number of people necessary to do the job.

- Incident notification procedures should be **prearranged**. (During the response to an incident you don't want any surprises.) You need to determine who will be notified, how the notification will be made, when in the process notification will take place, what will be communicated, and what will be done if notification fails.

---

[99] Defense Information Systems Agency.

- Incident notification should be made **out-of-band**. If a system has been compromised it cannot be used for incident handling discussions. You must be assured that your communications are secure.

In the course of investigating malicious attacks, where the attacker is identified and confronted, it is not uncommon to discover that the attacker has been monitoring the victim's communications, including e-mail, IRC, and even voice mail. Some hackers have reported that the sudden, uncommon use of encrypted e-mail was enough to signal that they had been discovered. So not only do the communications themselves need to be unmonitorable, the fact that the communications exist needs to be unmonitorable – out-of-band communications.

The focus of a computer security incident may be external as well as internal. An incident that affects an organization may also affect its trading partners, contractors, or clients. In addition, an organization's computer security incident handling capability may be able to help other organizations and, therefore, help protect the community as a whole.

Internal

The response team cannot effectively respond to the incident unless they are notified in a timely manner of the incident. Ongoing communication is also very important so that the response team can be apprised of any activities that pertain to the incident.

Initial Notification

It is critical to have rapid internal reporting of the security incident, since in the cases of automated threats, (e.g., virus and worms) the delay of a few minutes can make a tremendous difference in the scope of the necessary recovery.

Incidents can occur at any time, so someone must be available to be contacted when there is an incident. There must be backup people available in case the primary contact is unavailable. These people must have the ability and authorization to proceed without the primary contact. It may be beneficial to have a call list that specifies to move to the next name on the list for notification.

Having specific procedures defined for specific types of incidents can improve responsiveness. Common incidents include virus and worm infestations and network flooding. Other types of attacks can be grouped into more general response procedures.

Response Team

Once the initial contact has been made and the acting incident manager has made an initial assessment of the situation, the rest of the response team, as well as the information owner and custodian, needs to be notified.

It is imperative that the notification is explicit. Information given about the incident must be clear, concise, and fully qualified. It should be given in a calm manner to reduce confusion.

If an incident team is formed, all members must share information. A log should be initiated to record all communication of the incident. This log must include time/date stamps for each event.

Successful incident handling requires that users be able to report incidents to the incident handling team in a convenient, straightforward fashion; this is referred to as centralized reporting. A successful incident handling capability depends on timely reporting. If it is difficult or time consuming to report incidents, the incident handling capability may not be fully used. Usually, some form of a hotline, backed up by pagers, works well.

Incident Manager

Centralized communications are very useful for accessing or distributing information relevant to the incident handling effort. For example, if users are linked together via a network, the incident handling capability can then use the network to send out timely announcements and other information, unless the network is among what is compromised. Users can take advantage of the network to retrieve security information stored on servers and communicate with the incident response team via e-mail.

Understanding the severity of the security incident is imperative to being able to inform the correct level of management.

Management

Once it is determined that a security incident has taken place and the severity is determined, it must be immediately reported to internal management. This should include the information security department, the physical security department, the internal audit department, and the legal department. It is very important to notify the correct level of people at the correct time: too soon may create undue concern, too late may cause embarrassment. Management must be made aware of the incident before the incident becomes public. Managers need to know details about incidents, including who discovered them and how, so that they can prevent similar incidents in the future.

Management needs to be kept apprised of the action plan and the status of the response. A single point of contact with management can streamline communications and minimize the amount of redundancy of communication.

Computer Security Incident Organizations

Many large companies have internal organizations which specialize in managing security incidents. These are teams of people who specialize in the isolation and repair of security incidents. Some organizations focus on specific types of incidents, like virus outbreaks, while others cover all malicious security problems. These organizations should have contacts with industry organizations that specialize in incident response. It is often necessary to require assistance in the process of isolating and repairing a security incident.

Some consulting organizations which specialize in incident response are available to any-one needing assistance, while other organizations exist for specific industries. Some of these organizations are clearing houses for information, issuing bulletins about vulnerabilities that have been repaired and how to repair them, offering training on incident response preparedness and a site to which to send information on an incident to be evaluated. They may determine if it is a known issue or if it is exploiting a new vulnerability. They will coordinate with the vendor on newly discovered vulnerabilities so that the vendor receives a clear description of the issue.

If the source of the attack is from outside the organization, then an outside emergency response team may need to be contacted. There are a number of organizations whose function it is to assist during a security incident. Each incident response organization is chartered to ad-dress the needs of specific communities (government, geographies, etc.). The process of con-tacting these organizations and the information required varies between organizations, so it is best to check their web sites to become familiar with their operations.

Incident Advisory

Incident advisory organizations provide information about security incidents. They may publish newsletters discussing the most recent vulnerabilities and how to repair them. They will have a great deal of contact information for vendors of hardware and software and can assist in getting patches created. They generally do not get involved with the active response to an ongo-ing incident.

Incident Response

An emergency response organization is an organization that has the charter to assist in the response to an ongoing incident and after the incident is under control. They will assist in the diagnosis of the attack and methods to stop and repair the attack.

The best known of these organizations is at Carnegie Mellon University, created in re-sponse to the "Morris Worm" which brought down much of the Internet and demonstrated the growing network's susceptibility to attack. The Defense Advanced Research Projects Agency (DARPA) announced its intention to fund development of the CERT® Coordination Center (CERT/CC) to establish the capability to quickly and effectively coordinate communication among ex-perts during security emergencies in order to prevent future incidents, and to build awareness of security issues across the Internet community.

Since its inception in 1988, the CERT/CC has responded to more than 14,000 security incidents that have affected over 200,000 sites in the Department of Defense (DoD), other fed-eral agencies, and the private sector. Consequently, the time to resolve computer security inci-dents and repair computer system vulnerabilities has decreased. Adoption of practices devel-oped by the CERT/CC have improved resistance to attacks on networked computers and im-proved protection for the information stored on or transmitted by those computers.

In the midst of layoffs, MCI WorldCom's internal business network of NT servers were hit by a new strain of computer virus that corrupts files and encrypts data. Realizing that they were up against something new, MCI Worldcom called in Network Associates' antivirus emergency response team. The virus, dubbed Remote Explorer, wreaked havoc on files in hundreds of desktop computers connected to MCI's large NT-based network. It was the first totally NT-hosted virus that spreads by exploiting a network's features in order to corrupt files or lock them up through encryption. The virus is intrinsically different from any other virus spotted before because it doesn't spread through more traditional means, such as floppies, or through e-mail, as macro viruses do. Instead, it impersonates a network administrator to spread into NT programs over the network. The virus was designed with a time routine that caused it to do damage between 3 p.m. and 6 a.m., as well as all day Saturday and Sunday – times when few people would notice it.[100]

Affected Partners

Most attacks are over a network and, once into a system, a hacker will use the network to broaden his control. Due to increasing computer connectivity, intruder activity on networks can affect many organizations, sometimes including those in foreign countries. Therefore, an organization's incident handling team may need to work with other teams or security groups to effectively handle incidents that range beyond its control. Additionally, the team may need to pool its knowledge with other teams at various times. Thus, it is vital to the success of an incident handling capability that the team establish ties and contacts with other related counterparts and supporting organizations. This must be a predefined process for communications with partners, company- and employee-owned remote systems and other Internet organizations. This way, the involved individuals already know each other and have some level of rapport. They know what to expect and have discussed the type of information that needs to be communicated. They can prearrange authentication processes if necessary. The meetings to do the arrangements for communication are an opportunity to become involved with the partners' security policies. Communications with partners during an incident can be useful in comparing notes or building a consolidated response. It is extremely valuable to work with your partners during an attack (in some jurisdictions it is a legal necessity) but it is also imperative to protect your own assets.

---

[100]   Messmer, Ellen, "Telecom giant calls in Network Associates' emergency response team to stop virus from spreading.," *NetWorld Fusion*, 22 December 1998.

Contractual

Where possible, agreements with partners that establish the company's right to monitor and terminate network activity as well as the process of security incident notification and investigation should be in place. These type of contracts will simplify issues that come about because of an incident that might affect a service level agreement or nondisclosure issues.

Upstream

Upstream sites are those that were involved in an intrusion prior to your system becoming involved. In the attempt to locate the source of the attack, it is likely that one will discover that the attack is coming from a partner's network. This partner who appears to be the entry point for the attack should be contacted since the attacker is utilizing that organization's systems to attack yours. You should share the pertinent information about the origin of the attack and the type of attack so that they can rapidly respond and assist in stopping the attack. Remember, most attacks will originate from locations other than the one that is directly contacting the attacked system, and attackers often use falsified return addresses or utilize other compromised systems as a relay point for the attack.

Downstream

Downstream sites are those that were involved after your site experienced an intrusion. During your investigation you may see that the attacker has moved on to attack another site. You have the responsibility to inform the organizations about the involvement of their systems so that they can take appropriate actions.

You need to be responsive to organizations that inform you that they are under attack from a site under your control. It may be that you have a compromised system that is being used to launch an attack, or it may just be that the attacker is using a falsified address from your domain.

Law Enforcement

Especially important to incident handling are contacts with investigative agencies, such as federal (e.g., the FBI), state, and local law enforcement. Laws that affect computer crime vary among localities and states, and some actions may be state (but not federal) crimes. It is important for teams to be familiar with current laws and to establish contacts within law enforcement and investigative agencies.

Bringing in outside legal involvement must be evaluated as a business decision. This step will usually make the incident public, so the added expertise and investigative resources must be weighed against the issues publicity may bring. Law enforcement agencies may have to be notified, depending on the industry the business is in and the size and type of the incident. Involvement by law enforcement is more likely if an outside attacker caused the incident and/or if you wish to pursue criminal charges against the attacker.

Law enforcement may need to be involved when other companies become involved or legal steps are required to identify the attacker, such as wire taps. Law enforcement is required to collect enough evidence to be able to prosecute the attacker. Even when it is not required, there are times that law enforcement can be of assistance. They can aid in an investigation, especially when external information (such as telephone traces) are needed and in the collection and handling of evidence. However, they choose the cases that they wish to get involved in, and when they do they will be in charge of the investigation.

Security incidents are often difficult to diagnose and it can take a long time to identify the source of the attack. External attacks are often mounted through an innocent third party.

The decision to involve law enforcement or other outside investigative assistance is a serious decision. Outside investigators will often have more investigative experience than the local organization and have skills specific for the job. However, bringing in law enforcement has the tendency to cause the organization to lose control of the investigation. Once a criminal investigation is started, it is the law enforcement organization who is in charge of the investigation and who makes decisions on how the investigation is to be conducted and how it is pursued.

The key is to contact these agencies before there is an incident. Get to know the law enforcement agencies that can help in the event of a security incident. Many offices are willing to assist in awareness events and in defining what type of evidence will assist in the criminal investigation, how it should be recorded and handled, and what type of crimes are prosecutable.

News Media

The organization may suffer loss of business or reputation if the public communication aspects of an intrusion are not properly handled.

Notification of the media is usually only done in response to an inquiry from the media. Security incidents are generally handled quietly, since they can garner much media attention and reflect negatively on an organization's image. An incident handling team may need to work closely with the organization's public affairs office, which is trained in dealing with the news media. In presenting information to the press, it is important that attackers are not given information that would place the organization at greater risk and that potential legal evidence is properly protected.

> A small ISP in Indiana was brought down by a group of persistent and knowledgeable hackers. Although the problems had not yet been made public, the local newspaper was notified by annoyed customers who weren't able to get online to check their e-mail or surf the web. Once the ISP personnel, who had been working 20-hour days for most of a week to eliminate the problems, were able to communicate what happened, customers took it in stride.[101]

[101]   Ward, Joe, "Hackers wreak havoc on Net provider," *The Courier-Journal*, 22 August 1998

Checklist

— Predefine notification contacts.

— Maintain current contact call lists/call trees.

— Predefine information to communicate.

— Maintain detailed contact log.

Organization Information

Contact Name _____

Intrusion Information

Affected System's IP Addresses _____

First Detected: Date _____   Time _____

Number of users affected _____

Downtime _____

Estimated monetary loss _____

Is it ongoing? (Y/N)

Describe the attack: _____

_____

Attacker Information

Suspected origin of attack (IP address) _____

Insider / Outsider

Foreign / Domestic

Availability of Evidence

Availability of log information _____

Was the compromised system preserved? (Y/N)

CHAPTER 24

Incident Containment

A study conducted by the FBI found that 57% of computer crimes were linked to stolen laptops which were then used to break into corporate servers later on.[102]

Incident containment is required to minimize its impact. The more rapidly the incident can be contained the fewer systems will be affected and the easier it will be to repair the damage. Containment decisions must be made rapidly. Having predefined responses based on specific circumstances will expedite the procedures necessary to contain the spread of the incident.

The best approach to containment must be determined and acted on. This may include shutting down the information resource or removing it from the network. Therefore, management must fully support all efforts to contain the incident and contingency planning must incorporate security incidents in the plan.

Stopping the Spread

The first step is to stop the contamination of information and systems. The speed and connectivity of today's information systems increases the challenge of containing a security incident. Automated attack systems are able to scan networks of systems, locate vulnerable systems, and penetrate them without human intervention, so entire networks can be compromised in a matter of minutes. Rapid response is critical to minimizing the impact of an attack. Malicious software like viruses and worms propagate throughout the systems, traveling over the network. Overlooking a single system can lead to the entire enterprise being reinfected. This is well illustrated by the Internet Worm incident.

---

[102]   *SC Info Security News Magazine*, p. 12, May 1999.

The Internet Worm infected about ten percent of the 60,000 systems linked to the Internet within hours of its release. Those who discovered the rogue program on their systems removed the program and its files from the system only to find themselves reinfected from the network. In many systems, the worm consumed all the resources of the system, making it impossible to gain access to the system to kill the rogue program. Many groups whose plan was to use the network to notify others about the problem or to request assistance or even to report the intrusion from detection systems found that the network was saturated by the worm to the point that network communications were virtually impossible. Systems had to be unplugged from the network to deny access to the attacking software, thus avoiding reinfection. Systems had to be restarted in maintenance mode to regain control of the system so that the worm could be purged without the worm restarting and consuming the system.[103]

Determine Affected Systems

In today's large interconnected information systems, it is rare that only a single system is compromised. In this environment, when an incident has been discovered, it is imperative that the scope of the incident be determined so it can be completely removed.

Determining a fingerprint of the incident can aid in the determination of which systems have been compromised. Systems logs, changes to software, entries in configuration files can all be used to indicate a compromise.

Systems that have similar attributes, such as the same version of the operating system or are running the same services are more likely to have been compromised through the use of a vulnerability common to both.

Start with the systems that are known to be compromised. Move outward from them to systems that have communicated with the compromised system based on the connection logs.

Deny Access

Attacks that are under the control of an individual will usually be interrupted when the access to the system is severed. Access can be denied by isolating the system being attacked from where the attack is originating. This may be as simple as denying access at the firewall so an external attacker will no longer be able to enter the network. However, this may only interrupt the attack, since the attacker will often be able to find other routes to the system. Many

---

[103]   Spafford, Eugene H., "The Internet Worm Program: An Analysis," Department of Computer Science, Purdue University. November 1988.

organizations have redundant networks and Internet connections to assure availability. This however, may increase the effort required to isolate systems that are under attack or already compromised.

Since attacks can be either internal or external, isolating the system may require being physically disconnected from the network to regain control. It may even require that the system be completely disconnected from all access points, so that only physical access at the console will be allowed. This will ensure that the individual who is attacking the systems can no longer be causing trouble.

In the process of attempting to deny access to the attacker, access for legitimate users may be interrupted. A balance between the needs of the legitimate users and the need to block the attacker has to be evaluated. This evaluation should include the type and value of the service supplied by the system and the activity of the attacker. If the attacker is not compromising the system, but merely utilizing it, there may not be as much urgency to block his access.

In cases where isolation is not an option – where network connectivity is more important than the accuracy of the information and the integrity of the system – then an ongoing battle is likely. The attacker will be able to continue attacking as you try to block his entry. This situation will be extremely difficult to control. Documentation will be critical to success but difficult to accurately create. The inability to isolate a compromised system will greatly reduce the chances of a successful outcome.

In any case, physical access should be severely restricted and audited. Physical access allows for physical damages to the system and physical destruction of the information it contains. Anyone who is not on the response team and following appropriate security incident procedures should not have any access to compromised systems.

Automated attacks may continue, however, until the system is halted or the attacking processes are eliminated.

Eliminate Rogue Processes

Rogue processes must be stopped before there is any hope of regaining control of the systems that are under attack. Often these processes are disguised as processes that one might expect to see running on the system, or they may be hidden so that they are not visible to casual observation. Some malicious code may bury a copy of itself into the system start-up procedures so that when the system restarts it will reinfect itself. If the system hasn't been sufficiently isolated or if the vulnerability has not been adequately secured prior to putting the system back into service, it may become reinfected from other systems.

There has been an increase in malicious software which comes complete with defensive systems. This software disguises itself, monitoring the system in an attempt to detect its discovery. When it has determined that it has been discovered it will counterstrike, often trying to remove any evidence of its existence by deleting logs, itself, or even the entire system.

Regain Control

Regaining control is bringing the systems back to a state where you can be confident that the repairs that are made to the system will not be subverted. In some cases it has been necessary to stop the affected system and attach its disks to another system as data-only drives to repair the system. Data-only drives do not allow programs to be executed from the drive.

Lock out the Attacker

When discovered, it is common for the attacker to attempt to alter or destroy evidence. This is why it is imperative to lock out the attacker as soon as possible. As long as the attacker has access to the compromised system, it is not possible to fully regain control. The attacker's access must be blocked. This may be achieved by blocking access at the firewall or it may require that the affected system be disconnected from any external connections.

- **Change Passwords** – When a system has been compromised, it is likely that the password information has been compromised. All passwords should be changed. This will slow down the attackers' ability to regain access. If the attack is from within the organization, it may be necessary to restrict access to only the incident response team. In general, this is a good practice.

- **Disable Services** – If it has been determined that the scope of the intrusion is limited to specific services, then they should be disabled. Disabling services will deny the attacker access to the vulnerability of that service he or she is exploiting.

- **Remove Back Doors** – Attackers routinely put back doors into systems to allow them to regain access at any time. They may replace software with code that has the back door or add new services to a system to allow easy reentry. Elimination of back doors is critical to keeping the system from being recompromised after the incident is over.

- **Monitor Activities** – Monitoring the activities of the system can indicate if the attacker is still able to gain access. The attacker must be successfully removed from the system before any attempts to recover the system can be successful.

Scrub the System

You must ensure that all traces of the attack have been removed. A thorough scrubbing of the system is required. Malicious code may lie dormant in a system until an unsuspecting user either runs it or a specific event occurs.

It is not uncommon for an intruder who is not caught to return to the compromised system, and if all of his back doors have not been removed he will regain access to the system. However, this time he will be more cautious and more aware of the response process, so he will be more difficult to detect than first time. There has also been a trend for new hackers to scan systems looking for systems that already have back doors in place. This way, they can gain access to a system without the original compromising of the system and it's a good bet that if it has back doors in it, the system is not well managed or monitored.

Rebuild the System

If cleaning the system is not adequate to remove all traces of the compromise, it may be necessary to reinstall the entire system, even to the point of reformatting the disks. The process of reinstalling is often an extensive process, so it should not be done unless it is absolutely necessary. It does, however, create the opportunity to get a fresh start on a system and institute security policies from the beginning instead of an evolutionary method.

- **User Original Media** – Backups could have been compromised. Install all off-the-shelf software from its original installation media to avoid any issues with compromised software.

- **Apply Security Patches** – Be sure to have all applicable security patches installed on the system. Verify patch lists with all of the vendors for the software on you system.

- **Review Local Customizations** – Re-examine the local customization of the system to be sure that it supports the security policies and does not introduce any security issues.

- **Reload Data** – Only load data files from the backup media. Run any verification software that is applicable to verify that the data is not corrupted.

In a widespread attack when many systems are compromised, incident containment can be extremely involved. Automated attacks can move between systems and replicate themselves so quickly that a complete network-wide shutdown may be the only way to contain the incident.

Containment is only the starting point of bringing an information system back into operation. Damage must be repaired and something must be done to keep it from happening again.

Checklist

— Prepare strategies for incident containment.

— Prepare rapid response team.
      Ensure availability for notification 24x7.
      Create well defined notification procedures.
      Assign authority to respond.

— Develop network disconnect plan.
      Be able to remove specific systems.
      Be able to disconnect entire networks.
      Predefine process to inform network supplier.

— Develop rapid recovery procedures.
      Recover data.
      Verify data.
      Revoke all access.
      Reset all authentication.

CHAPTER 25

Assessing the Damage

Among organizations that suffered financial losses due to computer security incidents, nearly seven out of ten information system (IS) managers were unable to estimate the amount of losses.[104]

Quantifying dollar losses due to the various types of information security breaches is not easy. It is not surprising that much of a company's information is underprotected – the IS managers who are responsible for assigning the level of security for the data in their computer systems are not the business managers who utilize the information. It may also indicate why computer crime is on the rise.

After the incident is contained, the amount of damage has to be determined to anticipate the cost of repairs.

Determining the Scope of Damage

To assess the scope of the damage, you must rigorously determine what has been compromised and what has not. If you do not thoroughly clean your system after a security incident, you will most likely be doing it again.

Compromised Data

If compromised data is never discovered to be compromised and thereby remains so after you have closed the security incident and returned to business as usual, the tampered data could affect business decisions, production processes, and people's lives for a very long time.

---

[104]   "Ernst & Young Information Security Survey," *Information Week*, October 1996.

Compromised Systems

With the interconnection of computers today it is rare that an attack will compromise only one machine. When a incident has been identified, all of the information systems will need to be examined to determine if they have been breached.

Systems that have something in common with the compromised system are more likely to have been exploited by a vulnerability common to both. Those things in common often include: being on the same network, running the same version of the operating system, being administrated by the same administrator, or running the same services. When a system is compromised, the traffic on the same network has a high potential of having been compromised (e.g., network sniffing). Attacks often focus on known vulnerabilities of specific operating systems and services, so systems that are running the same operating system or service are likely to be vulnerable to the same attack and are more likely to have also been compromised. Administrative errors (e.g., not having installed the latest patches, misconfigured permissions on key files) lead to common vulnerabilities, so commonly administered systems are more likely to have the same administrative errors.

The system should be compared to a known good snapshot of the system. This process will identify any files that have been added, deleted, or modified since the snapshot. This will define the scope of the incident. Of the files that have been changed, it will have to be determined what files have been changed with authorizations and which ones have been changed without authorization. The files that have been changed without authorization will often lend insight about the attack process.

Compromised Services

Information systems are very dependent on services for everything from name resolution and correct time to messaging and credit card processing. Minor alterations to services are difficult to detect on the systems that host the services and nearly impossible by the systems that utilize them. However, their effects can be dramatic. Systems can be dependent on services that are supplied by systems from outside of the organization's control. One may not even be aware that his service provider has been compromised. Services also require that they are able to communicate with their clients. This communication can be disrupted or misrouted to another site that may not be trustworthy. Corrupted services can be used to manipulate the client systems and lead to their compromise.

Compromised Privileges

Privileges that the intruder was able to obtain can be used not only to compromise systems, data, and services, they can be used to grant privileges to other users or processes. The use of a privilege that has been compromised needs to be monitored after the incident to ensure that it is only being utilized by properly authorized users.

Determining the Length of the Incident

You must be able to determine how long the security incident has been going on before you can determine what may have been compromised and what has to be restored. If a security incident has been going on undetected for some time, it will be difficult to pinpoint an exact start date. It is generally best to err on the side of caution and select a date that is certainly prior to the start of the incident so that you can be assured that the information that is recovered from that date is not compromised.

Timestamps are a good starting point in determining when files were altered. However, timestamps can be altered. Tracing back through system logs for signs of the intruder can help determine a starting time for the incident, but this can be a lengthy process. If regular backups are taken, finding the modified files in the backups is a very good indicator when the incident started.

Once an incident has been reported, the management team must evaluate it. Information must be gathered to determine the exact nature and scope of the incident. This information can come from interviews of involved personnel, system audit logs, and available security tools.

> For more than eight years a Continental Airlines customer service representative diverted more than 1.4 million frequent flyer miles to relatives and friends. He has been charged by the state of New Jersey with two counts of theft and computer theft by a state grand jury. The theft of the miles apparently occurred over an 8 year period until a specialized computer check revealed unusual computer activity.[105]

Determining the Cause

The cause of the incident must be determined and repaired so that it will not happen again. To be able to determine the cause, there are a number of things that have to be determined. You must be able to identify how the incident occurred, what the basic motive was, and why it was not deterred. All of these questions need to be answered.

At this point you should know the source of the attack and what data and systems have been compromised. Now you must determine how the attacker gained access and privileges to cause the damage. In the containment phase, you should have also identified the hole used to gain access and have repaired it.

An incident may be the result of a number of causes. In this case each cause must be determined and repaired.

[105]   "The Enemy Within," *CIO Magazine,* 15 June 1996.

Vulnerability Exploited

To be able to stop the attacker, one must determine what vulnerability was exploited that allowed the attacker to gain access and authorization to the information, as well as how this vulnerability was exploited. The vulnerability could be a problem with procedures, hardware or software, or inadequate training. Once the exploited vulnerability is determined, then corrective measures can be taken. Once the "how" is known, one should determine if the vulnerability is a known vulnerability, if there is an existing fix and, if so, why this fix had not been implemented. If unknown, it should be reported. The emergency response teams can assist in creating a fix for new vulnerabilities.

Safeguards Bypassed

Re-examine the safeguards that are in place to determine if this situation should have been deterred by an existing safeguard. If there is a safeguard for this situation, determine how it was circumvented and then repair it so that it will catch this type of attack next time. If not, determine what safeguard could be added that would have stopped the attack and add the safeguard that addresses this situation.

See if the process utilized to bypass the safeguards in this case could be applied to any of the other safeguards and determine appropriate remedial actions. Determine if the safeguard needs to be repaired elsewhere in the organization and do so.

Detection Avoided

Determine how long the incident had been going on before it was detected and if this was a reasonable amount of time. Is there anything that could have been done that would have increased the speed of detection? Determine if it is cost-effective to implement the additional detection by determining how much would have been saved from faster detection.

Ascertain if there was an active attempt to avoid detection. If so, what was its level of success and what could be done to prevent it in the future?

Determining the Responsible Party

Identifying the specific individual or individuals who are responsible can be a most difficult task. Often it will be possible to determine what was done, how it was done, when it was done, and from where it was done, but not actually who did it.

Source of the Attack

One will usually be able to locate the source of the attack. Tracing network connections will lead to a point of origin or a location that was being routed through that did not have adequate information to assist with the investigation.

Online Identity

You will probably be able to tell what account was used, even those accounts on other systems that were used during the attack. However, the information from the computer itself will rarely be able to prove who compromised the system. Without stronger authentication methods, there is no proof that this person was the user on the system. It generally takes physical evidence to prove that a specific person was the hacker. It could be possession of the information that was taken, or his bragging of his conquest that is the conclusive evidence.

Attack Fingerprints

One should be able to determine if the attack was a manual attack or an automated attack. In the case of an automated attack it is less likely that the organization was specifically singled out. Other organizations were most likely also victims of the attack. The software controlling the attack is indiscriminate about whose computer it attacks; its concerns are if the systems have specific vulnerabilities that it can compromise.

Manual attacks, on the other hand, are controlled by an individual who may well be selecting his targets based on the owners of the systems or the information that they contain. Motives for the attack are difficult to evaluate. However, they can be divided into those attacks that attempt to gain access to information (whether it intends to sell, compromise, disclose, or destroy the information), and those attacks that are not searching for specific information.

Attacks that are not aimed at information are generally of lesser consequences, even though they can consume resources, deny access, and generally cause havoc. They are not trying to steal the company's secrets. Once this type of attack is removed from the system the incident is over. However, attacks aimed at information may not be solved so simply. Even after the attack is removed from the system, one must determine what information has been violated and what the possible impact is of this information. The hacker's activities will have to be scrutinized to determine the extent of the compromised information, and his use of the information attained may go well beyond the time he is on the system.

In cases when the guilty party is found, it is important to prosecute the hacker as a deterrent to this hacker as well as others. However, prosecution of the party is not easy. Legal proof and bringing forth convincing evidence to a nontechnical jury is difficult at best. This is in part why so many incidents are handled quietly. If the attack was internal, most organizations will opt for disciplinary actions through human resources instead of involving external law enforcement.

Checklist

— Determine the scope of the damage.
  • Number of systems affected
  • Amount of data affected
      Megabytes
      Number of disks
      Number of systems
  • Estimated monetary losses

— Determine the duration of the incident.
  • Earliest evidence of the incident
  • Estimated time to "Return to Business"

— Estimate losses of:
  • Productivity
  • Income

CHAPTER 26

Incident Recovery

Seventy-one percent of organizations have never tested a disaster recover plan for their business units.[106]

Incident recovery is the process of bringing the system back to a known good state, removing any damage caused by the incident and restoring the availability and accuracy of the information. Recovering a compromised system is required to return it to normal operations. Recovery should occur after the incident is contained and there is some idea of its scope. However, it may be a business necessity to return the system to operation before the incident is fully contained. This risk needs to be carefully managed so that the system can be successfully restored. Restoring systems at the same time as containing the incident requires a great deal of coordination so that efforts do not interfere.

Setting Priorities

In most environments it is more important to have accurate information than availability; however, in some environments availability is more important than accuracy. The order and importance of these must be driven by business factors. In either case the primary concern of incident recovery is the minimization of losses. The primary method of limiting losses is to limit the length of the incident. This is achieved through focusing on rapid detection and recovery.

To adequately determine priorities, one needs to understand the costs of having the systems unavailable, the risks of enabling the service when it is not secured, and the timeframe requirements for restoring the systems. The costs and requirements are based on business priorities and contractual and legal requirements.

---

[106]   KPMG, *Information Risk Management Survey*, 1998.

Repair the Vulnerability

Logically, repairing the problem should be the first step in responding to a security incident. However, due to the cost of having the system or data unavailable and due to the time and effort involved, this step is often postponed until services and data are restored. Restoring data and services prior to understanding the cause of the problem can result in the problem reoccurring. This may turn into a lengthy process of repeatedly restoring the system until the problem is isolated.

Once a vulnerability is discovered it must be repaired; to do otherwise is negligent. Most of the time vulnerabilities will be discovered by others who will report them to industry emergency response teams or to the vendor of the systems with the vulnerabilities. Then fixes to the vulnerabilities can be distributed to eliminate the problem everywhere. There is no reason that a system should be compromised because of a known vulnerability that has been repaired. However, most successful attacks are against known vulnerabilities. Every system should have applied all appropriate security patches from the appropriate vendors and keep abreast of new patches as they become available. If you have suffered a security incident the vulnerabilities that were exploited must be identified and repaired to avoid reoccurrence.

For many system administrators this is the most interesting part of the problem. It can take a considerable amount of time and resources. Quite often the exact cause will not be able to be determined; a list of possible causes will instead develop. In this case all of these possible causes need to be addressed and all the related problems repaired.

Repairing a vulnerability entails getting the correct resources. Process vulnerabilities can be addressed by the management responsible for the process. Administration vulnerabilities require that new administration procedures be defined and implemented. Software vulnerabilities must be repaired by those responsible, whether they are in-house or external software suppliers. These suppliers may issue a patch until the fix can be integrated into the software development cycle. If a patch is not rapidly forthcoming, then other methods of eliminating the vulnerability must be investigated. Evaluate how the vulnerability was exploited to determine if it will represent a class problem that could affect other areas of the system. Repairing the vulnerability is always the preferred methods of eliminating reoccurrence.

Vulnerabilities can be repaired in a number of ways.

Apply a Patch

A patch is a piece of software that addresses the specific vulnerability. Generally, it is a small piece of code that has minimal impact on the software system. Patches are used because they can be quickly written, tested and applied. However, they are usually focused on a very specific issue. They may not address other related vulnerabilities or the same vulnerability in other related software systems.

Disable the Service

Disabling the service that has a vulnerability will effectively remove the ability to exploit that vulnerability. If the service is not needed, then its software should be removed from the system so that it is not inadvertently restarted.

Change the Procedure

Changes to procedures may be able to eliminate a vulnerability if the changes in how the system is used affects how the system is misused, or if the vulnerability is a vulnerability in the procedure itself.

Security procedures require continuous review. Changes in technology, business conditions, the law, etc. all relate to the effectiveness of procedures.

Redesign

Redesigning the system is an acceptance of the fact that security really must be designed into the system and not bolted on after the fact. This is the most expensive way to fix a security vulnerability. However, if done correctly, it is the most likely to fix it long term. Redesign is not generally considered until all other options are exhausted.

Redesign does become a viable alternative when new systems are being implemented. Designing a security architecture includes requiring that all new systems and major renovations of existing systems adhere to the architecture. This will in time increase the level of security of the information systems.

Improve the Safeguard

If the incident could have been prevented by implementing safeguards, then those safeguards should be implemented, if they are financially justifiable, even if the vulnerability is repaired. Once a vulnerability is discovered, it is common that other similar vulnerabilities will also be discovered. Implementing a safeguard may prevent incidents based on similar vulnerabilities that have not yet been reported.

Improving safeguards includes changes to existing safeguards and adding new ones. Safeguards can be either technical or procedural.

Review Safeguards

All safeguards should be reviewed and their configurations adjusted based on the information gained from the incident. Evaluate whether there needs to be an adjustment to security procedures to maintain the configurations of these safeguards as new vulnerabilities are discovered or new services are added.

Add Safeguards

Evaluate if there is a need for additional safeguards in locations that were not anticipated, but which the incident brought to light. Determine if there is a need for new safeguards to protect new services or new locations.

Update Detection

If additional detection or changes in existing detection would have reduced the impact of the incident, then those changes should be made. Detection is the last line of defense. If vulnerabilities are exploited and safeguards are bypassed, rapid detection of the incident is the only hope of minimizing the impact of the incident.

Configuration Changes

Make the changes to the intrusion detection systems to better detect intrusions similar to that of the current incident. Review current vulnerabilities and determine if there are changes to the intrusion detection systems that will help account for these. The alerting methods and contacts should be reviewed to be assured that they are the most effective available.

Add Detection

Evaluate the system to determine if additional detection mechanisms are warranted. The addition of new products or plug-ins for the detection system may assist in the rapid detection of incidents. These steps should be made proactively, not just in response to an incident.

Restoration of Data

Generally, the data on a system is the most valuable asset in the data center. Restoring the data on a system that has been compromised is usually of prime importance. However, it may be more important to secure the system first, which will require determining the cause and repairing the problem, so that when the data is restored there will be some level of confidence that the restored data will be able to maintain its integrity.

The restoration of data is based on the type of attack. The level of system compromise may have to be evaluated before a determination of restoration processes begins. The quality of the information that is being resorted will determine the quality of the restored system. This data has to be from a source that is trusted to have not been compromised, or verification and validation tests must be performed. Use of original media is preferred.

Availability

Restoring the availability of data is usually the first step in a recovery scenario. The data must be restored to a known good state, generally from a known good backup, or the data may have to be recreated from processing. If there are changes to be made to make the data current, they then must be applied. The data must be restored before services can be made available to the users.

Integrity

It may be enough to validate the integrity of the online data, or it may be more appropriate to restore the system from a backup. If the data has been changed or altered and not destroyed, it may be very difficult to identify the compromised data. The process of verifying the integrity of the data can be a lengthy one, as every data item has to be checked by comparison to a known good copy or by cryptographic checksum.

Confidentiality

When an information system has been compromised, one must assume that the confidentiality of the information has also been compromised. Once the confidentiality of data has been compromised, it cannot be restored; only the scope of damage can be controlled. Stopping the spread of the data is the prime concern. If the intruder can be caught, it might be possible to limit the compromise to the intruder. If the spread of the information cannot be stopped, then reactive measures must be implemented to limit the impact of the compromise.

Restoration of Services

Every minute that the system is unavailable the company loses money. This may be lost income or it may be lost productivity. However, restoring services may be of little value if the data on the system has been compromised or if the hacker still has access. Restoration of services involves bringing both the specific service and the system that supports it online. The restoration of the system may enable other services, which will need to be verified as uncompromised as well.

Availability

There may be cases where loss of service and user or application downtime may be more important than restoring data. These cases could include systems that control automated environments, factory floors, or where income is based on having the service available, such as service providers or network providers.

Often in these cases restoring services is more important than securing the system. If you restore services prior to determining the cause you may find yourself involved in combat with an attacking hacker. This can turn into a long and painful battle.

If you are planning to restore services or data prior to determining the cause, it is best to take a complete "image" backup, including the entire disks and not just the files on the disk, so that the cause can be determined at a later time.

Integrity

Restoring the integrity of a system requires the verification of all parts of the system. Intruders will often compromise the integrity of a system by planting malicious software, such as back doors and Trojan horses. The integrity of the processes is vital to the accuracy of the results.

Confidentiality

The installation of information gathering software is common in attacks. These programs primarily assist in gathering information that will be used to gain more access or privileges. However, they are also used to gather information from the victim organization. One such tool, a network sniffer, is able to gather information from systems that have not been compromised by monitoring all the information that travels over the network.

The information system must be sufficiently secured prior to restoring services to ensure that restarting the services will not allow more information to be compromised.

Monitor for Additional Signs of Attack

A system that has been compromised is likely to be attacked again. Monitoring the restored systems will help verify that the improvements deter future attacks and can assist in the gathering of information about the attacker if he returns. The monitoring should include the services that were compromised, the processes that were used to compromise the system originally, and the connections for other systems that were compromised. The restored system should be put to the highest level of monitoring for a period of time after the attack to help restore confidence in the system.

Restoration of Confidence

Restoration of confidence is most difficult. Once an impression is made it is difficult to change it. This is why you must be proactively prepared to report on the incident in a very positive light. You must show that you have always been on top of the situation and that you were able to detect the situation and respond quickly to protect the vital information assets of the organization.

This is the area where an incident plan is most useful. A good incident plan will direct what information is released when and by whom. It can keep a loss of confidence from being there in the first place.

There are a number of groups about whose confidence you need to be concerned.

Management

Management has control over setting priorities and allocating budgets. Management confidence is critical to all projects and departments in the organization.

Management must be confident that the situation is being handled quickly, quietly, and in the best interest of the company. They need to be confident in the information security organization and its ability to handle the situation.

Stockholders

Today, many corporate decisions are a reflection of the mood of the stockholders. Ultimately, they are the owners of the corporation and, as the owners, they need to understand the financial impact of security incidents. However, due to the fact that it is a publicly held corporation, any information that is made available to the stockholders is being made public.

Much like the message to management, the message to stockholders should indicate that everything was handled quickly and in the best financial interest of the corporation. They need to be assured that their interests were always being protected.

Users

Users are the people who are directly affected by the unavailability caused by a security incident. It is their work that is interrupted and they are the ones who must trust the system to use the system. Users must be confident that the systems are restored to provide rapid and accurate results.

Without confidence in the systems they employ, users will find other methods to accomplish their work. This may include using other systems that were not designed for the task at hand or going outside the organization for their information systems needs. These choices are often not cost-effective and may reduce the overall security and efficiency of the organization.

Partners

Partner relationships are created to mutually benefit both organizations. They add value to an organization by supplying something the other organization does not have. The partner relationship is built on trust and sharing. These are two attributes that can be severely damaged by a security incident.

Partners must be confident that their trust in another company is well founded and that the information that is shared between the companies is adequately cared for. They must believe that the partnership does not raise their exposure to danger and that the partner's systems will not be used to exploit their own systems.

Public

The public must have confidence in the quality and responsibility of the company. They must feel that the company is capable of handling any situation that arises and that it is safe to do business with the company. The public should feel that the company is doing what is best for the public good.

Checklist

— Determine acceptable limits for returning the systems to operation.

— Restore information from a trusted backup copy.

— Re-enable the restored system.

— Verify the restored system.

— Monitor the system for indications of continued attack.

— Be prepared to implement disaster recovery plans if incident response will not resolve the outage rapidly enough.

CHAPTER 27

Automated Response

An 18-month study conducted by WarRoom Research revealed that of 320 Fortune 500 companies, 30 percent said they have installed software capable of launching counterattacks to security breaches.[107]

Alarms are actually audit events that the administrator considers to have special significance, and for which special notification actions may be defined. Alarms depend on the audit feature, so administrative duties associated with the alarm system are also performed by the audit administrator. Some initial configuration of the alarm system is likely to have been performed by an application developer/integrator with intimate knowledge of audit events generated by the application.

An alarm constantly monitors for alarm conditions and initiates protection and notification actions. The alarm scans the audit trail for defined events. If it detects an alarm condition, it initiates any notification and protection actions defined for the alarm. This mode of operation provides near real-time detection and reporting of incidents.

Automated responses can take many forms, from collecting of information about intruders that can later be used to put the culprits in jail, to the launching of debilitating countermeasures (denial of services or flooding attacks) that virtually shut down an attacker's system. These types of automated responses bring up the question of ethics and legality.

Automated Defenses

Automated defenses are more than just notification; these systems must be able to spot certain abusive acts and take corrective measures before they result in major losses. They require the integration of monitoring and control systems. They have to be able to determine that an incident is underway, evaluate how it can be stopped, and then implement the response. Automated defenses are focused on rapidly deterring the attack to minimize damage. Automated

---

[107] WarRoom Research, *Information Systems Security Survey*, 1996.

defenses should be limited to the systems under the control of the organization or those of participating partners. Extending beyond this point constitutes an automated counterstrike.

Many detectable security incidents may not be able to be completely blocked, but they can be stopped through a predictable response. Being able to automate the response to particular incidents can significantly reduce the damage caused by the incident.

This is a major issue with Internet businesses, for whom everyone is a customer, and packet flooding attacks. These attacks cannot be prevented. However, they can be stopped by:

- Blocking the source of the attack so the attacker cannot get to the site.

- Temporary disabling the service which is being attacked. This is effective if the service is not critical to the business process. Some attack software will stop when the service becomes unavailable.

- Disconnecting from the net will cause a loss of availability to all users including the attacker. This, however, may well be the intent of the attack.

Known scenarios can be defined with their predefined response. The process of expanding from specific attacks to a more general class of attacks and then devising effective automated responses for them remains a true challenge.

Gathering Counterintelligence

When a system manager suspects her system is under attack or has been compromised, it is likely she will try to gather information about the hacker. There is, however, a question about how much information gathering is legal. This will vary if the system being examined is managed by the system manager or if the computer is owned by the company that is gathering the information. If the hacker is coming in from another system, gathering information from that system creates a whole new set of issues. Of course, you don't have to worry about what is admissible in a court of law until the hacker is caught and goes to trial.

Is it proper for a system manager to use counterintelligence techniques? The answer to this question may end up being defined in a court of law based on the policies and procedures you have in place. Adherence to and consistent interpretation of your policies are key to presenting a successful court case.

Collect all the information available about the intruders from your system. Your company policy should indicate that to diagnose problems in response to a security incident it may be necessary to collect information and examine files that would otherwise be considered private. This can include an examination of user files and e-mail.

Remember, the hacker is often using someone else's system to attack you, so the system manager of that system may have no idea that the attack is underway. She may just be experiencing system problems. If you are trying to gain information from counterintelligence measures in which you may use the same information-gathering commands as an attacker would use, the system manager of the system from which you're being attacked may interpret your activity as an attack. Therefore, automated counterintelligence measures should be discouraged. You should contact the system manager of the attacking system and enlist her support in tracking down the intruder.

> In the wake of highly publicized Internet attacks, many new tools have been introduced that give corporations the ability to track hackers across Internet boundaries, enabling them to rapidly respond to intrusions and automatically determine an attacker's network entry point. These tools will help companies protect their e-business infrastructure so they can conduct secure, uninterrupted business.
>
> The distributed, fault-tolerant design of the Internet makes it difficult to track attackers across global network boundaries. These tools detect attacks against computer networks and aggressively respond, tracking the attacker back across numerous Internet "hops" to the source of the attack. They should enable authorities to quickly locate and gather forensic evidence, supplementing the computer forensic expertise which is in short supply.
>
> It takes an enormous investment in time and personnel to manually track down these computer attacks. The process is grueling and complex. There is a desperate need for better automated incident response tools.[108]

These are just a few of the questions you and your legal staff will have to decide. During a successful attack in progress, is it justified to penetrate the attacker's computer system under the doctrine of immediate pursuit? Is it permissible to stage a counterattack in order to stop an immediate and present danger to your property? These questions will also have to be answered by the courts.

Counterstrike

The concept of retaliation is not new. It is a basic military strategy to eliminate the opponent's ability to wage war. This appears to be the stance of a growing number of large companies that have been victimized by hacker attacks.

Countermeasures include tools that disable an attacker's browser, block TCP/IP connections, or launch debilitating countermeasures such as denial of services or flooding attacks. However, it is difficult to be assured that the attack is coming from the location it appears to be.

---

[108]   "Turning the Tables on Hackers," *Business Wire*, 23 February 2000.

Even though the concept of counterstriking is intriguing, the problem with getting involved in a cyberspace shootout is being certain that you are targeting your attacker. It is common for an attacker to route the attack through other sites on the way. Hackers can also forge packet headers to make it appear that an attack is coming from a completely different location. If a company is shooting first and asking questions later, innocent people could be hurt. And the organization that returns fire may open itself up to civil, criminal, or physical risk.

> An activist hacking group known as the Electronic Disturbance Theater simultaneously attacked web sites owned by the Mexican Government, the U.S. Pentagon and the Frankfurt Stock Exchange. However, during this attack the hackers were counterattacked. Pentagon programmers set up a program to detour the attacker's traffic through an application which caused the attacker's browsers to crash.[109]

The net-based counterattack described above, although minor in scope, raises important legal and political issues. Does an organization have the right to counter any of the hundreds of hacker attacks they receive everyday with counterattacks of their own? Will this depend on whether the organization is a government or military organization or a private company? Will the source of the attack, being either foreign or domestic, affect this question?

All of these questions will have to be answered in the coming digital years.

---

[109]   Schwartau, Winn, "Cyber-civil disobedience," *Network World,* 11 January 1999.

Checklist

— Include automatic notification in any automatic response system.

— Confine automated responses to systems within your scope of control.

— Determine requirements to autodisconnect systems or networks.

— Notify any partners who might be affected by the automated systems.

— Consult with legal counsel before implementing automated systems.

Reflection

We are now worse off, with respect to protecting our critical infrastructure, than we were a few years ago.[110]

– E. Eugene Schultz

Once the chaos of the situation has subsided and all the systems are restored to a normal mode of operation, it is time to take a clear look at the incident and perform a follow-up postmortem analysis. This follow-up stage is one of the most important phases of information security, yet, since the incident is under control, it is often not done, or not done well. This process will document the incident, evaluate the handling of the situation, and determine what further actions are required. Every incident is different and brings unexpected issues, so there is always something new to be learned. But the process used to review an incident should remain consistent.

This process should include a cross section of the organizations that were, or should have been, involved in the incident and monitored by management. This group will not only perform a postmortem of the incident, they will plan the implementation of remedies to prevent recurrence and open up communication with users and others affected by or involved with the incident. They will need to determine the business impact of the incident. All in all, they are responsible for total quality process improvement. They should take this opportunity to develop a set of lessons learned, improve future performance, and inform management of the steps taken during the incident. Additionally, the development of postmortem improvements will provide the opportunity to organize any documentation that may be necessary should legal action be required.

---

[110] Testimony before Congress, May 1999.
Dr. Eugene Schultz is a Trusted Security Advisor for Global Integrity Corporation (an SAIC Company). An expert in Unix, LAN and network security, and security administration and management, he has co-authored several books, and has published over 70 journal articles.

Postmortem Documentation

Possibly the most important step following a security incident (and certainly one of the least done) is the process of writing the security incident postmortem. Postmortem follow-up requires documentation of the incident as well as reports for specific audiences, such as management and emergency response teams. These reports will be used to adjust the level of security that is implemented.

This report is crucial for bringing all the issues together. It is a chance to review the incident calmly, after the crisis has subsided, bringing together the views and insight from all involved parties to create a single, consistent description of the incident for all those who have a need to know.

This report is needed if any follow-up actions are going to be taken against the perpetrator. If the actions are warranted, this report will serve as the foundation of the prosecution. If the actions are disciplinary, management will need this report to determine the severity of the punishment. The report has three parts: the timeline, the technical summary, and the managerial summary.

The technical summary will be fundamental to improving processes and creating best practices. This summary can be shared with other technical groups within the organization to educate and increase the awareness throughout the company.

The summary for management will give them the insight needed to understand the size and scope of the incident and its impact. This knowledge is crucial to the process of making sound business decisions about the need for security, especially as it relates to budgets and personnel.

The scope of a postmortem report may, on the surface, seem overwhelming. However, most of the information should have already been gathered and documented in the individual logbooks of those who were involved in the incident. Documentation from a security incident will be plentiful. Everyone involved must keep a logbook that details his or her activities during the incident. Security monitoring systems generate a tremendous amount of information that was probably utilized during the incident. Information systems can monitor and log in the most excruciating detail. It is because of this overwhelming amount of detailed and technical information that condensed and summarized documentation of the incident is required.

Process Management

A security incident tests the procedures that are in place to manage an incident. Once the incident is over, then it is time to review the processes and evaluate corrective measures. Security incidents impact a wide variety of departments and processes. All of the processes that were involved with the security incident should be reviewed and any that need improvement based on this incident should be fixed accordingly.

Risk Analysis

Risk analysis encompasses the area of risk identification and evaluation. It is the ability to determine what components are critical to the business processes and to effectively quantify the impact of the loss. These estimates are untested until a loss occurs; it is at this time that the quality of these estimates is realized. The descriptions include which products and processes would be impacted and to what extent.

Business Impact

The business impact analysis determines the financial impact a security incident has on the organization. It is based on product revenues and the impact of peak seasons. It also takes into account the upstream and downstream implications and includes estimated costs associated with implementing determined recovery strategies. The comparison of actual losses to the estimates will help improve the ability to better predict the business impact of future disruptions.

Emergency Response

Emergency response procedures include all of the aspects that are invoked because of the security incident. This includes the response team's ability to react to the situation, contact the appropriate people including infrastructure providers and partners, and handle any situation that may develop.

Emergency response teams have to coordinate with other emergency response teams when the incident is caused by a physical disaster. Disaster response teams will control and manage physically damaged sites. In a physical disaster scenario, information becomes just one aspect of the disaster. Personal safety and those things that jeopardize physical safety are the priority.

Incident Management Program

Incident management is the process of controlling the incident. It defines the incident declaration criteria and the recovery escalation sequence. It includes coordinating all of the teams (e.g., Damage Assessment Team, Site Security Team), facilitating communications, and reporting. It handles issues of allocation of resources and personnel management.

Business Recovery Program

A business recovery program is an ongoing program that ensures the prudent reduction of risks and the resumption of key business operations following a major disruption. The recovery process is based on the mitigation of the impact of the incident. It encompasses disaster planning and recovery for production, information, sales, and services in both the short term and the long term. The key goal is the restoration of productive capacity and capability.

External Follow-up

Follow-up communications should be handled by those individuals who have been identified to coordinate with outside organizations. These may include affected partners, emergency response personnel, the news media and law enforcement.

Follow-up communication is as critical to the perception of the incident as any other aspect.

Required Financial Reporting

In many industries, especially financial services, security incidents have to be reported to the governing body if they cause a significant financial impact.

In any case, a financial impact analysis will generally be required so that the appropriate information can be presented to the owners of the organization.

News Media

If the incident is made public, the channel of communication to the news media is paramount to the public perception of the incident. Only a designated spokesperson with experience handling the media should speak to reporters – preferably the chief public relations officer of the organization.

Law Enforcement

In the case where legal prosecution is desired or required there will be extensive interaction with law enforcement. It is also prudent to have the organization's legal department or even outside legal counsel involved. The laws that cover intellectual property and computer crime are quite new and relatively untested. The interpretation of these laws are still being defined, so legal professionals are a necessity.

Management must evaluate and prioritize efforts to identify the individual or individuals who were responsible for the security incident (even though in most cases it is not possible to identify the actual individual) and determine the level and type of punishment to pursue, which may include disciplinary actions or legal remedies, either civil or criminal.

CHAPTER 28

Incident Documentation

Seventy percent of companies now view security as "mission critical." [111]

Incident documentation is one of the most overlooked aspects in responding to a security incident. Record keeping is crucial. Events should be recorded immediately after they have been observed. Detailed record keeping is required during a security incident for both prosecution and for review, so that the quality of the response plan and the effectiveness of the actual response can be evaluated.

Incident documentation should never be kept on the system that was compromised. This information must be protected from modification. It is best if the logs are kept on a non-modifiable media, such as CD-R, or at least media where alterations are obvious. Proper handling and chain of custody are important in assuring the quality of the documentation.

Incident Source Information

Incident documentation comes in a number of forms from many different sources. Computer systems record a great deal of data about their operations. Security systems monitor and record when individuals access systems, both electronically and physically. Video surveillance tapes may be a valuable record of activities. Administrator's handwritten journals and service logs provide information. Even telephone logs are document sources for an information security incident.

Incident Logbooks

Incident logbooks should be started as soon as an incident is reported. Everyone involved should have his or her own logbook and be responsible for maintaining it during the incident. Logbooks record the activities as they happen. They present the situation from the perspective

---

[111]   "The 1999 Information Security Industry Survey," *Information Security Magazine,* July 1999.

of each of the individuals involved. They are a necessity for reviewing and recalling specifics. If the incident becomes a legal matter, these logbooks become the central narrative of the incident.

The logbook should be a bound book, not looseleaf pages, so that the information is contained and not lost. Handwritten entries in logbooks are the easiest way to take notes at the time of an observation and are difficult to alter. This will also expose any tampering with the information. Audio or video recordings may also be useful and a time saver.

Logbook entries should contain date and time, system identification, and a detailed description of the event, even details that you may think are obvious. If the incident results in criminal prosecution, you may be using these details six months or a year after the fact. You must keep to the facts in the logbook. Speculation and reasons for your actions are useful information, but they must be appropriately annotated to distinguish them from the facts.

Record the names of all the people with which you had conversations about the incident. Summarize the conversation, highlighting the major points and any conclusions that were drawn. Tape-recording conversations can be useful. This creates a complete record without a personal viewpoint. Even with taped conversations, the fact that there was a conversation and a reference to the tape should be entered into the logbook.

Cross-references to the original sources of the information are invaluable when it comes to reviewing and verifying information. These cross-references must be specific enough to be able to locate the original information after some time has passed. They are especially useful when they refer to other log entries. Important facts from systems logs must be able to be located and confirmed.

Help Desk Logs

Help desk logs are a focal point within an organization. Any significant problems will be reported on the help desk. Since most security incidents are identified by the organization's help desk, it is natural that their logs became the starting point for the incidents. Any organization large enough to have a help desk will have automated call tracking or customer care systems. They track calls to completion and usually utilize databases of previous problems and solutions to help resolve the current problems. They can recognize patterns that are in their database that were previous attacks and can correlate calls from throughout the organization to recognize widespread trends.

The help desk can be a very helpful adjunct to the security organization. However, it will take some effort to integrate security processes. The help desk will require training on how to identify security issues and appropriate reporting procedures. Additional information may need to be logged to optimize the logs for security incidents.

Network Logs

Many network devices log network activity – which machine started the communication, to which machine it went, the type of communication, and the amount of data transmitted. This information can be used for traffic analysis and determining specific security violations. Logs are also useful in tracking down the route an attacker took through the network.

The network operations team should have a network management system that is a central location where information is consolidated and accumulated. Information may be able to be extracted or forwarded from here for security operations. Some discussion may be required to determine what information is available and important to the information security operation.

Security monitoring and management is often integrated with network monitoring and management. Some of the network management systems have security modules that plug in to the system to gather and consolidate security information. A consolidated network view of security may be able to throw a light on an incident before it becomes visible to any specific system. Network sweeps to gather information often go undetected by any one system, but are obvious to network monitoring systems.

Network logs are often overlooked by attackers who modify system logs to cover their tracks.

System Logs

System logs record the activities of the system. Originally designed to aid in the diagnosis of system problems and capture data about system failures, they do contain some information that is valuable to security. System logs generally contain user logon/off timestamps, system configuration information, boot-up messages, shutdown/restart timestamps, and failure messages from subsystems (file I/O errors, network errors).

System log monitoring is usually one of the first steps taken for securing an information system. The main problem with system logs is the volume of information they contain. The effort to monitor these logs is high for the return of information gathered, so many automated tools are available that process these logs and eliminate data that is not useful.

System logs are very common among computer systems. The format of the information that they contain is also well known, so it is common for hackers who wish to cover their tracks to alter the information in these logs. There are a number of tools built specifically for this purpose. The information in any logs on a compromised system must be considered somewhat suspect.

Administration Logs

Administration logs are written logs that are maintained by those who administer the system. These logs contain details about the day-to-day activities on the system including backups, changes and modifications, reconfigurations, etc. Anytime there is administrative action there should be a log entry. Since these are manual logs, the quality of the administrator will dictate the quality of the logs. Larger organizations with data centers and full-time administration staffs generally have good administration logs. Departmental servers need the same level of monitoring.

These logs are useful to determine if there was an administrative procedure that introduced the security issue. They will highlight any administrative change that was not logged. These changes should be considered suspect. Administrative logs will intersect with all of the other logs (backup, security, etc.), and can be used as a common thread to connect activities in these other logs. They also act as an index to these logs.

Physical Access Logs

Physical access has the potential of being the most devastating security breach. No system can be completely impervious to physical attack. This is why physical access logs are so important.

Physical access to information systems require auditability; therefore, there must be a log of when the systems were physically accessed and by whom. This includes not only computing systems but removable media, backup storage sites, and disaster recovery standby systems. The importance of these logs would imply that automated logging should be implemented. This requires electronic locks that create an activity log. Simple mechanical locks are insufficient for security.

Physical access logs can be useful in tying together other logs, since much of the system administration and incident monitoring and repair requires physical access.

Accounting Logs

Accounting logs track the resources utilized by specific individuals or processes. These are often a good indicator of unusual activity and can indicate when a user or process first appeared on a system. They are often used to create user profiles.

Due to their widespread use and their well-known format, there are many hacker tools which can alter these logs. They are a common target for hackers to alter. This is the primary reason that remote storage of information systems logs is so important. When the logs are stored on a system other than the one that they are monitoring, then it is more difficult to locate and alter these logs.

If accounting records are consolidated across multiple machines they may be able to locate broad-based network attacks that will produce similar log entries on many separate machines.

Audit Logs

Audit logs record very fine grain information about specific users, files, or system attributes. They record both successful and unsuccessful attempts. Unsuccessful attempts to change security attributes may be more important than successful attempts.

Audit logs can generate a great deal of information; for this reason, many organizations do not utilize auditing and those that do use it sparingly, enabling it only for very specific (usually powerful) users and critical files. However, judicious use on key accounts and critical configuration elements can yield valuable results.

Auditing has to be enabled for specific events. It should be enabled for any changes that affect the security of the systems or the operations of the system, as well as those changes that change the authorizations required to perform an operation, especially when the restrictions are lowered.

Since auditing records are created at the time that the event is taking place, and generally they are enabled only for important activities, they can be used to trigger alarms. Many network or security monitoring systems will be able to configure alarms from specific audit events.

Security Logs

Security logs track the changes to security settings. They accumulate information from security software and changes in systems that affect the security settings of users, data, or systems. Security logs are less common and less utilized than the other types of logs. However, they are a consolidated location of security specific information when they are used.

Default security logs are often focused on only those changes to the security system itself and not the changes that can affect the security of the system. To be effective, security logs must record all changes that affect the behavior of the system (system configuration files) and privileges of the users (permission on files).

Security logs overlap with administrative logs to a large extent. However, when there are changes to the security of a system it needs to be recorded, even in multiple logs, because of the serious impact it can have.

The process of changing security attributes is one of the areas where a hacker, especially an inside hacker, is most likely to expose himself. Hackers need to gain unauthorized privileges to get access to protected information. The ability to change privileges should be limited to a very small group, and anyone who attempts to change security attributes should be investigated.

Backups

Backups are a snapshot-in-time of the state of your systems. They contain a complete image of the system that can be used to recreate the system at that point in time. Information cannot be lost if it is backed up.

Backups are offline, so usually the attacker is unable to cover his tracks by modifying the information on a backup. Backups generally have a good chain of custody – you know where they have been and who has had access to them. This gives a high level of integrity assurance to the information on the backup. It also makes them useful in legal proceedings.

Backups are extremely useful in determining when an incident started and what was affected. Files that have been modified can be examined on the backup to find when the file was first altered.

Incidents may require restoring information from backups; and security incidents can go undetected for a long time.

Different types of information require different backup and retention schedules. Computer software may require limited backup copies in its licensing agreement. Transient information should not be retained for any significant period of time. Business information should be backed up and retained based on its value and security classifications. System security logs may require longer retention periods and should be kept in their complete form in the case that a security event occurs and has to be investigated.

When an incident is first discovered, an image backup of the affected systems should be taken. This image backup is a complete backup of all the disks attached to the system, including unused disk space. Hackers will often use unused disk space to hide tools and other information to avoid detection. Forensic software can be used to locate and recover this information.

Incident Timeline

The incident timeline is a detailed description of the events that took place during the security incident. Time is the only constant by which events can be tied, so the incident timeline becomes the focal point to which all the other postmortem documentation are associated. This is often the first chance to bring all the information together. It is a sanitized, chronological consolidation of each individual's incident logbooks with extensive footnotes to the original source material. The response team should review the timeline. This will help ensure its accuracy and completeness. It will also create a consistency in the final perception of the incident.

The timeline includes the activities of the attacker, how the incident was discovered, the actions taken to determine that there was an incident, a step-by-step description of the investigation, and the process used to recover from the incident.

It is best to start on the report as soon as possible after the incident. Even though the logbooks contain a great amount of useful information, it is surprising how much information does not make its way there. The original authors of the logbooks may need to be interviewed. In the process of taking notes, especially when actively involved in a security incident, an author may scribble or abbreviate words. Sometimes handwriting is unclear or open to interpretation. Debriefing sessions with all those involved are useful for filling in the details and clarifying the entries in the logbooks.

Format

Time is relative. Incidents are likely to span time zones. It is imperative to indicate the time zone. In the case where there is information from many time zones, it may be useful to report the time in Universal Time Coordinates (Greenwich Mean Time).

The incident timeline should include both a narrative of the incident and a graphical time-line representation of major events in the incident. The narrative should give extensive details and references to the original source material from which the timeline is drawn.

With today's multimedia documentation tools, it may be beneficial to create an interlinked document which includes graphical timeline and reference material. Packaging the complete record may assist in managing evidence needed to facilitate prosecution.

- **Narrative Timeline** – The timeline narrative gives a chronological description of the events that took place during the incident. It can start as a consolidation and sanitization of the response team's logs. It will need to include more detail from original material created by the logs of the information system.

  The following example shows an entry for the narrative timeline indicating a "disk full" issue.

1999 Dec 31 - 11:59 PST   The network management system re-ported that three network servers failed with "disk full" conditions.

- **Graphical Timeline** – A graphical timeline can be used to simplify the narrative timeline into a single graphic that contains references to key points in the incident. It can be a handy reference for discussions about the incident. There are a number of products that can be used to create timelines and associate events on the timeline. Hypertext tools can be used to interconnect the graphical and narrative timeline, the footnotes and the original material.

- **Footnote References** – It is imperative that the summarized information can be sup-ported by the original documentation. The information in the timeline should be extensively footnoted, referencing the original logbook entries or system logs. It is crucial, therefore, that a footnoting scheme is put in place so that documentation can easily reference the original material. An appendix with excerpts of relevant sections of these original materials will make a complete package. The original material will include personal logbooks, system logs, audit trails, information from tapes, timestamps, and contents of files.

  The sources being referenced with the footnotes are not typical literary sources, so standard forms may not adequately define the source material. The footnote should contain the creator of the information and must specify the source location of the information and the media that contains the source files, as well as the date of the information.

Network Error Log, systemA:/var/netcenter/logs/network.errors,
1999 Dec 31, 11:59-0800 UTC, backup tape NSA991231.

This footnote indicates that the network error log from "systemA" which is in the file "/var/netcenter/logs/network.errors" has an entry that can be found at the time index "1999 Dec 31, 11:59-0800 UTC" and the file is archived on backup "NSA991231." This is all the information necessary to locate the backup tape, retrieve the file, and examine the record to verify the information that references the footnote.

Content

Be as specific and detailed as possible. Most of the data for the postmortem report has already been collected. This is a chance to organize and clarify the information. Keep to the facts and identify assumptions and speculations as such. Understanding why decisions are made can be as valuable as the decision itself. Do not worry about too much detail; there will be both a technical and a managerial summary.

- **Discovery** – The major part of the incident timeline starts when the incident is discovered and details the steps taken until the problem is resolved. However, the timeline actually begins when the incident first started, and by this point you should have a good idea of when that was. Identify the earliest time that evidence indicates that the system had been compromised.

   Discovery is the time when official channels become aware of the issues that are suspected of being a security incident. Detail the events that took place that caused the incident to become detected. A detailed description of how the incident was discovered and by whom, as well as the process that the person who discovered the incident went through to report it, should be included.

   Understanding how an incident was discovered will assist in improving the intrusion detection systems; seeing the process that was used to report the incident will be helpful in evaluating the quality of the security awareness program and the incident reporting procedures.

   Once an official notification has been reported and recorded, the logbooks and other official documentation should detail the communications and processes that took place between when the incident was first reported and when it was determined to be a security incident.

- **Determination** – Incident determination is that point in time when there has been enough investigation to differentiate a false alarm and a security incident. It is also the point in time when the incident response plan is officially invoked. It requires that the appropriate level of management (level required to officially institute the incident response plan) be given enough information to warrant invoking the plan.

Invoking an information response plan will require additional or special funding of overtime, tools, consultants, and other unexpected expenses. Security incidents are not budgeted, so they require special consideration. Indicate what logical steps were taken to determine that this was a computer security incident, by whom, and when. Indicate the reasoning that went into the decisions.

By the time it is determined that an incident is underway, the investigation phase is already started.

- **Investigation** – The investigation details the step-by-step process that was taken to determine the cause of the incident, who was responsible, how the incident was perpetrated and when it took place.

Investigations generally involve numerous activities by many people. Their individual logbooks must be integrated to build the complete picture. The logbook of the incident coordinator is the best place to start since it should contain references to the individuals and the activities assigned. It should serve as a framework for all the activities.

A graphical timeline is very useful, especially with long and involved incidents. The use of project management software can help track the activities of all the individuals involved in the incident and can be easily correlated to the information in the report and to a graphic timeline.

Activities that lead to dead ends are just as important as those which prove fruitful. These details allow for a complete understanding of the incident and will help improve the process in the future.

Finally, a description of what caused the incident, what vulnerabilities were exploited, and a preliminary cost estimate should be included.

The investigation is often the longest part of a security incident. Although its logical conclusion is to determine a direction for repairing the damage from the incident and defining the steps required to prevent it from happening again, these steps are often started while the investigation continues.

- **Recovery** – The recovery process should detail the processes taken to recover from the security incident. It is a consolidation of the actions of all of those involved, describing the decisions made in selecting the recovery process, and should include both successful and unsuccessful actions. The recovery process includes incident containment, the point in time when the attackers access is severed, regaining control, the point in time where the malicious software has been disabled, and the restoration of information and systems. Each of these phases of recovery should be highlighted in the timeline.

A significant aspect of this part of the report is the analysis of how well the current security philosophy, procedures, and policies helped or hindered the organization during the incident. Expanding on what worked well and what did not work will help in the preparation for the next incident.

Finally, the timeline should indicate when the incident is considered over – that point in time when there is enough confidence that the attacker will not be able to return and the information and systems have had their integrity restored.

The details of the recovery process will rely heavily on logbook entries. These logs are written chronologically by the people who are attempting to stop the attack and bring the system back under control.

• **Attacker's Activities** – Even though detailing the attacker's activities is rarely complete or completely accurate, there is enough evidence from the compromised systems and logs to reconstruct a viable description of the attacker's activities. Systems and security logs give a point in time when specific activities occurred. Timestamps on compromised systems, although suspect, can give insight to the activities of the attacker.

In most instances one should be able to determine when the attacker first left evidence of his presence – the appearance of covert software, changes in data, or modification of logs. You will be able to determine which systems were compromised and when. You should be able to determine where he was able to gain access and how he was able to gain authorizations. You will know what damage was caused and when, as well as the types of attack tools used.

All of these observations draw a fairly complete picture of the attacker's activities. If the attacker is identified and apprehended, he may be willing to relate his exploits to you along with why he did what he did.

Detail every session in the timeline – start time, stop time, activities – as best as can be determined.

The timeline, once developed, can then be used as a basis for writing the technical and executive summaries of the incident.

Technical Summary

The technical summary is a report that is prepared so that the incident can be reviewed by other systems and security management to determine the applicability of the security issues and the recovery procedures to their environments. Technical summaries are generally maintained within the corporation. However, they may also be used to communicate the incident with an external emergency response team.

The technical summary should be easily understandable by anyone with a technical background in information systems. In long incidents the timeline may become large; this is why there is a need for a technical summary.

The technical summary can be shared with other technical groups within the organization to help them be prepared for security incidents and to help them structure their response teams.

The summary is derived from the timeline. The technical summary needs to highlight the major events and when they occurred. This will illustrate the amount of time that the system was compromised before it was discovered and the time that was required to mobilize a response.

Cause

The technical description of the cause of the incident should focus on the details of the process – what, when, and how vulnerabilities were exploited. It should include a description of the technical ability of the attacker and a description of the tools that were used.

- **Who** – For the technical summary it is not necessary to identify the specific individual or individuals who caused the security incident. It is more important to be able to profile the technical ability of the attacker or attackers.

  Describe any patterns in the attack. Patterns of attack can indicate quite a bit about the attacker. The time of day of the attack can indicate the location or schedule of the attacker.

  Summarize the tools that were used in the attack. The number, type, and age of the tools used in the attack can indicate the skill level of the attacker as well as where he might have gotten the tools and how recently. Tools which are unidentifiable or have been handcrafted may indicate that the attacker has the skills necessary to build his own tools.

  Indicate the attacker success rate of compromising systems. The success rate of compromising systems indicates the ability of the attacker to select targets and use appropriate tools. A large percentage of unsuccessful attacks and the utilization of tools on inappropriate target indicates someone who is not well versed in attacking information systems.

- **What** – The technical report should summarize what type of systems were attacked, both successfully and unsuccessfully and what vulnerabilities were exploited and attempted. Highlight any common threads.

  Categorize the attacked systems by system hardware, operating system, applications running, and type of data contained. The evaluation of common threads can indicate the target of the attack, the knowledge and skill of the attacker, or the vulnerability exploited.

- **How** – You should include an explanation of the technical details of how the incident occurred. This includes a description of the vulnerabilities that were exploited, how they were exploited, and how the safeguards that were in place to prevent this type of exploit were bypassed. Describe what access and authorizations had to be acquired to be able to exploit the vulnerability. How and when were these privileges acquired?

  The description of the attack should be specific enough so that the exploits can be understood by other system managers (so they can test for the same vulnerability), yet not so specific as to be able to reproduce the exploit. If it was a known vulnerability that was exploited, there should be a reference to the advisory that describes it.

  Describe the process used to gain access to the information system. Detail the intermediary systems that were used. Gaining access electronically is a network or perimeter issue that is usually under the control of the network security or firewall group. Physical access issues are the domain of the organization's physical or building security group. These groups have probably been involved with the incident and certainly need to be involved with incident follow-up discussions.

  List the authorizations that were achieved by the attacker and the process by which each one was compromised. Gaining authorizations is generally a system security issue which has to be addressed by systems or application support organizations.

- **When** – Generally, a security incident is composed of a number of attacks that allow the attacker to gain access and authorizations to achieve his goal. Depending on the duration of the incident, the timing of the individual attacks can be enlightening.

  The time of day the attacks take place can indicate the schedule and location of the attacker. Indicate the length of each attack. The duration of the attacks can indicate the attacker's determination and focus. It will also indicate where monitoring systems might be effective and what type of traps would be most likely to attract the attacker so that more information can be gathered about the attacker.

  Determine if the attacks were manual or automated. Manual attacks require the presence of the attacker, while automated attacks can be scheduled to occur at any time.

- **Where** – Identify where the attack was coming from and be as specific as possible. Internal attacks are generally the actions of disgruntled employees while external attacks can be acts of industrial espionage or just acts of vandalism.

  Map out the path the attacker used to access the system. Understanding where the attacks originated from can illustrate where security measures can be placed to prevent the incident from reoccurring.

  Enumerate all the systems that were utilized and explain how they were compromised. Describe the process used to move from each system to the next.

Impact

The impact of the security incident includes the hardware and software systems, and the information that was compromised, as well as the people and equipment required to contain the incident.

- **Systems** – From a technical point of view, the impact of an incident is closely related to the number of systems compromised. The effort to correct the exploited vulnerability, clean the compromised systems, and recover damaged data is dependent on the number of systems compromised.

  Give a specific description of the systems that were compromised. Include the hardware vendor, operating system revision, software services, and the patch level of each. This will indicate the type of expertise needed to recover from the attack and what might be able to prevent it next time.

  Summarize the number of systems of each type that were compromised. They can be grouped by operating system and by software services. This may highlight attacks against specific software vulnerabilities. This can also indicate the ability of the attacker to compromise a specific type of system, which may be the result of the tools and talents of the attacker or the vulnerabilities of the system and software.

  Describe any relationship between the compromised systems. This should include network topology and the information or the type of processing done on the system, as well as the operating systems and software services on the system.

- **Data** – Data is the usual goal of the attack. Determining the scope of impact on the data can indicate the reason for the attack as well as the possible financial impact.

  Indicate what type of data was contaminated. This can indicate the motive for the disturbance of the information. Log data is altered to cover up the activities of the attacker.

  Describe how was the data contaminated. Was the information made unavailable, was it destroyed, or was the information disclosed or corrupted?

  Detail the volume of data that was contaminated. Describe how the information was contaminated. Indicate whether it was altered or deleted.

  Describe the format of the contaminated data. Describe the storage environment of the contaminated data as file system, database, etc. The format that the information was in can indicate the level of knowledge that attacker has of the system. To understand the data in a database one must know the schema; understanding binary data requires understanding the format data and type, while text data can be read directly.

Determine if the backup media was compromised. Destruction of offline storage usually indicates a greater knowledge of the internal workings of the information system procedures.

- **Downtime** – Detail the amount of downtime suffered by computer systems, data, networks, processes, and other information systems resources. Include and differentiate both downtime caused by the incident and the downtime that is a result of the resolution of the incident. Include downstream effects – those processes that do not directly utilize the resources that are unavailable but are dependent on the results of the resource being available.

List what resources were made unavailable and for how long. Denial of service is a visible and aggravating attack that can have significant immediate consequences. However, denial of service attacks only block access to the resources and thereby have only limited long-term effects. Denial of service attacks are on the increase.

Describe which resources were unavailable due to the resources being consumed by the attacker. Consumption of resources is in some cases the target of the attacker, while in other cases it is only a by-product of the attacker's activities. Consumption of resources may have collateral damage – the consumption of one resource may impact the availability of other resources.

Determine which resources were disabled or destroyed. The destruction of information does not necessarily imply that the information was compromised. It is often possible to remove information from a system without being able to read the information.

Describe which resources were unstable or unusable. Resources which have become unstable are more aggravating to users than those destroyed. Unstable resources have intermittent access or appear to be operating when they are not.

- **Recovery** – The recovery process is often a large technical endeavor. It takes a number of people with specific technical knowledge and skills to successfully recover a system. There is also an amount of time required to restore and verify systems before they can be put back online. All of these things are part of recovery.

Summarize the effort involved in recovering from the incident. The focus of the summary should be on the time and the number of people required to perform the recovery.

Include the time used to restore the systems and data and the time needed to process the business activities while the information system was unavailable.

Describe the number of people required with specific skills. Describe any resource shortages or conflicts.

- **People** – The impact on people is the most visible, or at least the most vocal, part of a security incident.

Determine how many people were affected by the incident. Indicate the number of individuals and the total man-hours lost to the incident. Differentiate between lost productivity and the people involved in the restoration of the system.

Describe the type of work that the people who were affected by the incident were involved in. Determine how many were end-users and what part was involved in finding the attacker and resolving the problem. Indicate if they were administrators, operators, consultants, etc.

Resolution

Resolution includes the diagnosis and containment of the incident, repairing the damage caused by it, and securing the systems to prevent reoccurrence.

- **Diagnosis** – Diagnosis of the incident is key to being able to bring about a rapid resolution to the security incident.

  Include information about the individual who discovered the attack and the process used to determine that it was an actual attack. Compare this with the process defined by policy, highlighting any tools that were used and their effectiveness.

  Describe the process that was taken to identify the specifics of the incident and determine the appropriate response.

- **Containment** – Bringing the incident under control is required before the incident can be resolved. Containing the incident requires stopping the ability of the attacker to gain access to the systems and keeping the incident from spreading to other systems. Elimination of reoccurrence is necessary to provide a stable environment.

  Describe the vulnerabilities that were exploited during the incident. Give references to the advisories that describe them or other sources of detailed information.

  Describe the modifications made to the system to halt the attack.

  Describe how the incident was contained. Include both successful and unsuccessful attempts to stop the incident. Evaluate the effectiveness of each attempt.

  Detail the steps taken to secure the affected system. Include specific details so that other systems can gain from the experience.

- **Restoration** – Restoration of information and systems is the goal of the problem resolution phase of a security incident. Restoration includes making the systems and data available and assuring the accuracy and privacy of the information.

  Describe how the systems and information were repaired. Explain why each different process was selected for restoration.

Explain the process used to identify the affected information and systems.

Describe the process used to restore the affected systems.

Improvement

List what things should be done to improve the security of the information system. Include both what can be done technically to keep this from happening again, as well as what modifications to policy, procedures, and processes that could have prevented or lessened the impact of the incident

There are basically four areas of concern that can be addressed to improve the level of security:

- **Remove Vulnerabilities** – Vulnerabilities must be removed to keep them from being exploited again. Even vulnerabilities that were not exploited during the incident must be addressed.

  Describe the process used to remove each vulnerability. Give details on the patches that were applied, and describe what will be done about those vulnerabilities that do not have patches.

  Explain the process to be implemented to monitor for new vulnerabilities and facilitate their repair.

- **Increase Safeguards** – Additional safeguards can reduce the likelihood of security incidents.

  Describe the safeguards that can be added that would reduce the likelihood of a security incident reoccurring.

  Determine if the safeguards need to be specific to this incident or if they can be generalized to address a class of problems.

- **Improve Detection** – Improved detection can reduce the response time to a security incident and significantly reduce the impact of that incident.

  Determine if any detection process could have prevented the incident or reduced its impact. Determine if the detection needs to be specific to this incident or if it can be generalized to address a class of problems.

- **Automate Response** – Automated responses can improve the speed and consistency in the response to a security incident.

  Describe the responses that could be automated and how the automation of these processes would improve the responsiveness to an incident. Detail other automated responses that would be beneficial.

Executive Summary

The executive summary is a report for upper management so that they can understand the issues that pertain to the security incident and its impact on business.

The executive summary differs from the technical summary in that it should be brief, direct, and focused on the business and financial impact of the incident. The report should be coached in business terms addressing managerial concerns. It is a complete, concise management level analysis to the incident detailing what happened so that decisions can be made about how the incident follow-up should be performed.

The executive summary also differs from the technical summary in that it focuses less on detail and more on process. The majority of the information will be derived from the timeline and the financial data supplied by business function managers. These are the people who are responsible for the financial impact of the incident and can best define the direct and indirect costs.

The executive summary should be able to be presented in 20 minutes including a minimum number of slides highlighting major points.

Cause

The executive summary contains less technical detail than the technical summary, and focuses more on information that could be used for financial analysis and budgeting. It should describe, in layman's terms, what caused the incident, including how the incident occurred, who was responsible, and what their motive was. The executive summary should also focus on the information needed to address public relations and possible legal action.

- **Why** – Explain why the incident happened. If it was caused by accident, explain how the accident occurred and how it was allowed to cause the incident. If the cause was malicious, explain the motives for the attack. Without the identification of the attacker or attackers, specific motives might not be able to be determined. However, there is a lot of information that will indicate probable motives for the attack.

  Detail the importance of the information that was compromised. Determine if the information compromised was of a business or personal nature. This can indicate if the attack was to gain a business advantage or to cause damage to the business, or if the attacker was after information about a specific individual.

  Describe the relationship between the attacker and the organization; this can go a long way to understanding his motives. Insider attacks are usually either a personal issue or theft of information for profit. In both cases, the attacker is generally a disgruntled employee. Employees with personal motives usually believe that they have been victimized by the company. They are motivated by revenge and are likely to destroy information or damage systems as well as steal information. Those employees who are determined to gain financially from the organization may try reselling the stolen information or blackmailing the organization.

Describe the targets of the attack. Correlation of a pattern of the systems attacked may yield a motive. Sometimes systems are targeted because of the type of system that they are – the attacker has tools for that type of system — while other times the attack is focused on specific information, so the systems that are attacked are likely to have access to that information or are involved with or related to the information.

Understanding the type of attack can indicate the motives of the attacker. Denial of service attacks and destruction of information are attempts to disrupt normal operations of the organization. Theft of resource attacks are attacks against specific, usually unique, resources that the attacker wants to utilize. Common targets include supercomputers and modem servers. The theft of information is usually focused on financial reward by selling the information or blackmailing the organization or embarrassing the organization if it is made public. Corruption of information can be an attack to damage the organization's ability to conduct business. With enough knowledge of the information, a hacker can make changes to it in the hope that the changes will go unnoticed, so that bad data will be utilized by the organization and in some fashion benefit the attacker.

What was the goal of the attack? Attacks that attempt to create a denial of service are usually more malicious as compared to attacks that attempt to steal corporate information.

- **Who** – Describe the attacker. In the technical summary you are more concerned with the technical skills of the attacker; in the executive summary you are more interested in the relationship the attacker has with the company.

If the attacker was identified, relate relevant information – relationship to organization, age, history of misconduct, etc.

Determine if the attack was caused by a single individual or a group. Most attacks are the work of a singe attacker. Group attacks require more planning and coordination as well as a reward for all of those involved. Individual attackers are more likely to have personal motives.

Determine if the attack was manual or automated. The number and type of tools used in an attack can indicate the level of experience and expertise that attacker has. It may also indicate an association with other hackers or hacker sites to get the tools.

Describe the origin of the attack. Internal attacks require some level of legitimate access; therefore, the attacker may have some relationship with the organization.

- **When**– List the key times of the security incident. Include the time the incident began, when it was discovered, when the attack was stopped, and when the recovery was complete. This will illustrate the speed of detection and response to the intrusion. The time of the attack is important on operations. There are many cyclical processes that have critical availability needs at specific times.

- **Where** – Understanding the origin of the attack can help to determine the reason for the attack. Identify where the attack was coming from. A graphical map of the attack can be very useful in explaining how the attacker progresses from systems over the life of the incident.

  With internal attacks, the department or even the system that the attacks originated from can be identified.

  In the case of external attacks, identify both the network origin and physical origin if possible. Describe any problems with resolving the incident because of the location of the attacker.

- **How** – Describe how the perpetrator caused the problem. Unlike in the technical summary, it is not necessary to give a technical discussion of the exact vulnerability. Rather, examine whether he exploited a vulnerability in hardware, software, or infrastructure, or whether he used social engineering.

  Was the vulnerability a design flaw, innovative misuse, or an incorrect implementation? Describe the level of inside information necessary to have performed the intrusion, the level of technical knowledge that was required to have performed the intrusion, and the function of the systems that were exploited.

- **What** – While the technical summary focused on the type of systems attacked and the vulnerabilities exploited, the executive summary is more interested in the impact on the organization.

Impact

The executive summary should explore the bottom line financial impact of the incident on the organization. This includes losses of revenue and productivity as well as tangible and intangible costs. It must consider both the immediate and long-term impact.

- **Actual Losses** – Actual losses reflect the real assets that are actually stolen by the attacker. This could be stolen computer equipment, a transfer of funds, or other convertible assets. If equipment is stolen, you must consider both the book value of the asset and the current market value. You must also consider the value of the information on the system that was stolen.

Not all stolen property may be taken at the time of the incident. There have been incidents where falsified purchase orders are inserted into the system to have products shipped to the attacker and for which there will be no payment.

- **Direct Losses** – Direct losses are a direct result of the incident. Losses include intellectual property and loss from fraudulent use of the system. They also may include downtime if a machine is taken down or damaged. This includes losses from denial of service.

- **Lost Revenue** – Lost revenue is the loss of sales or orders because the information systems were unavailable to process those transactions. There is also a cost of delayed sales. There may also be losses caused as a result of unauthorized changes that manifest themselves later (e.g., billing information is changed that is later billed incorrectly).

  There are other lost revenues that may not be apparent. The loss of customer confidence may result in lost business.

- **Lost Productivity** – Lost productivity is the cost of time that is wasted because the information is unavailable. This affects users throughout the organization and even partners that are dependent on your information, as well as developers and administrators whose activities are dependent on the information systems. Some of these individuals may have recovered some of their time by working on other activities while the information was unavailable. However, there is still an impact to all of those whose work is related to the organization's information.

  Loss of productivity must be considered for both those who would have been utilizing the system if it were not compromised and those who were involved in its restoration who would otherwise have other duties to perform.

  Downtime and personnel costs involved in a restoration, or an investigation may also be involved.

  How long was the organization unable to perform because of the outage?

- **Recovery Costs** – Information recovery costs includes restoring deleted information and verifying the accuracy of the information.

  The cost of recovery is measured primarily in man-hours, the time that it takes to clean the affected systems and to recover the compromised data. It includes both the cost of the time spent by those directly involved with detecting, locating and repairing the incident and the time of the support personnel. Much of this time is off-hours, and therefore overtime pay. It should also include the time it takes to determine that there is an incident, diagnose the problem, formulate the response, test the changes, and monitor the system for reinfection as well as the costs of managing the public relations.

  There are also the additional costs of materials consumed in the recovery process. This is the actual cost for products and supplies that were required to facilitate the repair process – logbooks, software tools, media for additional backups, any external consult-ants. There are often additional costs in facilitating sufficient secure communications.

Additional unrelated expenses to support the long hours that the recovery team put in are also included. This can include such things as food and lodging if recovery person-nel had to be brought in from remote locations.

- **Intangible Costs** – Intangible costs are more difficult to measure. They include the loss of confidence in the organization because of the security incident, the impact on the organization due to information disclosure, and other forms of lost future revenue.

Measuring the impact of an incident is an involved process. Use the information inventory to justify the value of the information and help support the calculated numbers. In some cases the costs of implementing new security measures is included. However, the new security mea-sures that are deployed as a result of a security incident are usually measures that should have been taken anyway.

Resolution

Describe how the problem was resolved. Include the amount of time required to deter-mine and evaluate the attack. Explain the successful strategy that stopped the attack, how it was able to correct the incident, and how it will prevent it from happening again.

Take this opportunity to recognize those individuals and groups who went beyond what was required to help resolve the incident. Describe any issues with organizations who were requested to assist with the incident.

Supply enough information about the perpetrator, if he was identified, so that management can make an informed decision on what type of punishment should being sought. If the attacker came from inside the organization, they will need to decide whether to pursue legal action or to use internal options for punishment, such as demotion or firing.

Improvement

This is the opportunity to present to management what should be done to prevent this from happening again. It should address issues that pertain to policy, procedures, and systems that can better enable a more secure enterprise. Describe the costs of the improvements to systems and processes that can eliminate or minimize the impact of future security incidents. Recom-mend changes to systems and processes that would have limited the exposure of the incident. Detail financial information on the losses that these changes would have reduced and the ex-pected costs of the changes.

Each part of the incident documentation serves a specific function. Documentation is not complete unless the timeline (based on logs), the technical summary, and the executive summary are all produced.

Checklist

— Assemble the information from all involved, including incident log books. Also gather help desk, network, system, administration, access, accounting, audit, and security logs.

— Conduct post-incident briefings to gather information that was not recorded.

— Develop an incident timeline on which the other reports are based.

— Produce a technical summary that can be evaluated for applicability to other systems.

— Write an executive summary for upper management to understand the incident's issues and impact.

— Create the incident documentation for specific audiences.

CHAPTER 29

Incident Evaluation

Only 19 percent of IT professionals surveyed have a complete, descriptive policy to monitor their security practices and solutions.[112]

The process review examines the current incident response plan and evaluates how well the defined process was able to help with the current situation. It is understood that every incident is unique and will offer challenges that were not planned for in the incident response plan. The incident response plan needs to have guidelines that are general enough to be applied to unexpected events. Generally, a great deal of effort goes into the creation of an incident response plan. That effort needs to be evaluated and capitalized on for its ability to cope with an actual incident.

As in all things, it is important that you learn and improve. You should strive to learn how the incident happened and how to prevent another similar incident from occurring again. You must analyze your processes and decide what worked and what did not, where and how it can be improved, where there were gaps in your policies and procedures and whether all contingencies were covered in this case.

Most businesses will want a financial analysis which details how much the incident cost the company in physical losses, the cost to restore data, and the losses of revenue due to downtime. In some cases this will be a complete business impact analysis.

An analysis of the incident must be performed. This analysis should investigate the incident with the intention of improving the process. The following questions should be answered:

- Exactly what happened at what times?
- How well did the staff perform?
- What information was required by the staff and how could they have gotten it sooner?
- What should be done differently in the next incident?

---

[112] PricewaterhouseCooper, " Global Security Survey," *Information Week*, 1998.

The analysis should also provide a chronology of events and all information gathered during the incident. A monetary estimate of the damage should be determined for all information resources affected by the incident. These may be required for any prosecution that takes place as a result of the incident.

Identify Processes for Improvement

The first step is to identify the process in the plan that failed or could have worked better. Processes should be clearly defined in the procedure and practices, as well as the policy it supports. Identify the flaw or what can be done to improve it and its impact on policy.

Processes do not have to be a security process to impact the quality of information security. They can be anywhere in the organization. Human resource policies can have a significant impact and may need to be evaluated to determine if their changes can improve security.

Any process that has the ability to prevent a future incident, to increase the speed or accuracy of detecting an incident, or to increase the speed or quality of the response to the incident should be reviewed.

Process

The processes defined in the response plan are the core components of the quality of the response. These processes must be reviewed and evaluated.

Rate the quality and availability of the plan. The plan must be easily accessible to everyone involved in the operation. It will be used to guide the direction of the response and referenced when new developments arise. Therefore, it is critical that the plan is readily available and easily understandable by all. Good indexing and cross-referencing is a tremendous help to quickly locate the specific details when they are needed. The language needs to be clear and concise to avoid confusion and misunderstanding.

How soon was the plan evoked? Utilize the plan early in an incident to help eliminate false starts and to assure that everyone involved is "on the same page."

How closely was the plan followed? The plan is an accumulation of the knowledge and experience of those who developed the plan and those who have used it since its inception. Describe the deviations from the plan and the reasons for those deviations. How effective were the changes?

Where did the plan work well? To continue to capitalize on your successes, you must be able to expand those things that work well. Evaluating the sections of the response plan that work well can help with a more beneficial design of the plan. Sharing the successful sections of the response plan with other departments can improve security response throughout the organization.

Where did the plan fail? Describe the events that took place that were not covered by the plan or where the planned response was not adequate. Detail how the situation was handled and if the results should be integrated into the plan. Describe the stumbling blocks that caused the plan to fail. Give suggestions on how to fix the plan.

What happened that was not covered in the plan? Every incident brings along some new twists. It is likely that there was some part of the incident that was not covered by the response plan. Detail these events and describe how they were handled. Describe if the response was appropriate and adequate. Describe how it should have been responded to and how well the plan applied to these areas.

People

People are the all-important resource. You will need to review how well the people involved in the incident performed.

Had all the appropriate people been identified? Getting the right people involved is important to a rapid resolution. Individuals with all of the necessary talents, experience, and skills are needed to resolve the problem. The rapid change of information systems technology can change the skills that are required to resolve the situation. Without constant updating, an individual's skills rapidly become out of date.

Was the contact list up-to-date? In today's information systems environment, people change job responsibilities rapidly. Having out-of-date information can greatly slow the response to an incident.

Were they available? There needs to be enough depth of resources defined in the plan to be able to manage scheduling conflicts. One person being unavailable cannot be allowed to compromise the response plan.

Were all the people available to participate? During a disaster there are situations that can keep individuals from participating in the response. Understanding the personal impact from a disaster and utilizing flexible scheduling can help make more people available.

Were the participants familiar with the response plan? Being familiar with the plan and knowing what is expected saves time when it is most valuable. It simplifies instructions, reduces communications, and gets the process off to a faster start.

Were they appropriately prepared? Preparedness is key to the rapid resolution of security incidents. During a security incident participants have to hit the ground running. Without preparation, critical time is lost.

Was there the right number of people? Adequate resource planning is important to an appropriate response. Having an insufficient number of participants will lengthen the incident as it takes time for the individuals to get to all the tasks at hand. Having too many individuals will cause an overlap of duties which will lead to repetitive work and interpersonal friction.

Communications

Communication is always a critical resource during a security incident. The ability to coordinate efforts and allocate resources is dependent on good communications.

Were those involved able to contact the right people in a timely fashion? If the primary people weren't available, were their backups?

Were secured communications used so that the attacker was unable to intercept discussions of the incident, or even know that such discussions took place? Sometimes even the knowledge that he or she is being discussed can cause an attacker to try to better cover his or her tracks.

Where were the problems in communications? Are there alternatives for those areas in which communications broke down?

Tools

The right tool for the job simplifies and expedites the task. The available tools need to be evaluated for the applicability to the situation at hand.

Were the correct tools available? Incident response usually requires unique tools necessary to locate and track an attacker. These tools are often unused except during an incident. However, they must be available at the time of the incident.

Were the tools current? The information systems environment is constantly changing so tools that are specific for a system or attack scenario can rapidly become out of date. Keeping them current requires a certain amount of monitoring and administration.

Was there the expertise needed to use the tools? Being able to use the tools and understand the results requires an understanding of the specific tool. This knowledge becomes obsolete quickly and requires time to be familiar with the tools.

Was there appropriate documentation? Tools will have variations between revisions and implementations. In a crisis situation, such as during the response to a security incident, even the most experienced person will forget options or specific details of a specific tool and need reference. Correct, complete documentation is necessary to facilitate rapid response to a security incident.

Process Improvement

Once the successes and failures of the processes, people, communications, and tools have been determined, the changes to each that must be made to improve response in future incidents must be decided on.

Determine Resources Required

Determine what resources are required to make the changes. This includes man hours, new equipment, and software. Creating a complete cost picture is necessary to adequately compare and prioritize options. However, the cost estimates only need to be budgetary numbers.

- **Equipment** – Determine what equipment will need to be acquired or utilized to create, implement, and support the changes. This includes not only computer equipment, but also support equipment, such as network equipment, communication equipment, office equipment, and test and diagnostic equipment. Determine the amount of time each system will be needed and if there are systems that can be of multiuse.

- **People** – Determine the number of people required to design, implement, support, and administer the process. Evaluate the workload requirements to implement and the long-term costs to maintain and support the improvements. Categorize the people into appropriate job descriptions – operators, programmers, etc.

- **Expertise** – Define the specific knowledge and skills required to complete the project. Determine if they are available from within the organization or if there is a need for outside expertise. If there is a need for external expertise, give suggestions on where to locate the expertise and how to determine the individual's applicability.

- **Time** – Build the schedule for implementation. Requirements for specific equipment, people, or expertise can affect the timeline. Evaluate implications of multiple projects on the timeline. Where specific requirements significantly effect the timeline, alternate options should be considered.

Prioritize

Prioritizing which of the processes that have been identified as needing improvement is most important. Priority should be based on what is the most beneficial to the organization – what makes the most business sense. However, given the political landscape inside organizations, this is not always the actual selection criteria. Many things go into the equation of priority. Some elements that will need to be evaluated to determine priority are:

- **Return on Investment** – Return on investment is a financial evaluation of the cost savings and increased revenue as compared to the costs of implementing the changes. Common sense says that return on investment would be the primary concern in prioritizing processes, and it often is. However, there are other factors that influence this decision.

- **Most Visibility** – Completing a widely visible project can be used to show the commitment to improvement or as an awareness piece. A highly visible project can be used as a marketing springboard. The visibility creates a large audience to whom you can address the issues of security, the organization's commitment to security, and its ability to solve security issues. It allows you to maintain visibility to management which is needed to facilitate commitment and budget. .

- **Management's Biggest Concerns** – Addressing management's concerns creates visibility with management. This is sometimes the selection criteria because of direct management intervention. Other times it is a political decision to improve perception and increase budgeting.

- **Quickest to Implement** – Implementing projects that are quick to be put into place first can give an organization experience and confidence. Rapidly completing a project illustrates commitment. It creates the impression that progress is being made.

- **Least Expensive** – An organization with a limited budget can complete some projects and use these successes to leverage additional budgets.

Develop a Project Plan

Develop a plan to implement the changes. The plan should be based on the prioritized list of projects. Determine the specific resources required and the availability of those resources; from this information develop a project schedule. These costs need to be accurate enough to allocate funds.

Determine the impact on other processes. Changes to security impacts other processes, especially those that the security measures protect. Evaluate the impact of implementing the security on those systems. Be particularly aware of the impact on production systems. Fixing one problem should not cause another.

Look for synergies between projects. Scheduling external resources at the same time for multiple projects can reduce costs and system outages. This can reduce the total outage time.

Gain Management Commitment

When it comes to issues that concern security, commitment from the highest level of management is required. Management has the most to lose from poor security practices and thereby the most to gain from implementing improvements to the information security system.

Allocate Resources

The allocation of resources is a major step in project planning. The resources required are dependent on the decisions of what is to be implemented. Resources include equipment, time, people, and expertise. Once the needed resources are identified, there are a number of decisions on how to acquire the resources. An evaluation of the costs in the form of time and money is required. This involves determining if the needed resources are available internally or if external resources are needed to implement the changes in a timely manner. The choice of internal or external resources will impact the schedule, cost, and quality of the implementation.

There are often specialized skills or knowledge that are required and not widely available. Organizations often find themselves without the people who have these specialized skills. The management of these critical resources is key to an efficient implementation. These skills are often in short supply internally and relatively expensive externally. One may be able to schedule the resources to optimize the use of these specialized skills.

The selection of resources can impact other processes. The effect on these other projects need to be evaluated to determine the best allocation of resources.

Implement Changes

Start putting into place the changes that have been determined to be implemented. The monitoring and management of changes to security systems must be closely controlled to ensure the integrity of the entire system.

Change management is a requirement to be able to control and audit the security related activities.

Continue to monitor and evaluate the implication the new changes will have on other systems. These other systems include hardware, software, infrastructure, procedures, and practices. Make sure that the implications are well documented so that follow-up is done on the associated systems.

Regular progress reports will ensure that progress is being made and that management is aware of the value of their information security investment. Management support is needed in all security endeavors. However, the response to one incident is an opportunity to show the value of security with wide visibility. You should make the most of it.

Checklist

— Utilize post-incident review sessions to assist in evaluating the incident response.

— Determine what worked well and why.

— Determine what did not work well.
  • Where did it fail?
  • How could it be improved?

— Evaluate:
  • Communication
  • Tools
  • Processes
  • Personnel

Public Relations

Eighty-three percent of businesses report that the main reason they do not report security incidents is the possibility of bad publicity. [113]

Public relations, perception management, rumor control: whatever you call it, it may be more important than any other aspect of response. Even if everything was done perfectly, if the perception is that things were out of control, the truth doesn't matter. Customer perception –or misconception – can ruin a company.

The same incident might be reported as "Hacker Cracks Corporate Computers" or "Local Company Aids Police in Tracking Down Hackers." The only difference is perception.

The organization's public relations officer, the incident response team, the appropriate level of management and the organization's legal department must work closely together to determine what, when, and how much information should be made public.

The Right People

Public relations is best left to the professionals who can put the incident in the best light for the company and who can weigh the issues of bad press from the incident versus bad press if the incident is discovered from outside sources.

Companies should limit the number of people who talk to the press, preferably to individuals who are experienced in communicating with the media.

Identify the correct individuals in the public relations department to be responsible for communications to the public. The public relations department usually has good contacts with upper management and can help with internal, as well as external, communications.

The press may contact individuals who are involved with the incident, but who are not empowered to speak for the organization. It is important that everyone understand their role in communications about the incident and that any comments made can end up in print.

---

[113]   "1998 CSI/FBI Computer Crime and Security Survey," *Computer Security Issues & Trends*, Spring 1998.

All contact with the media should be approved in advance by management, as should the "spin" that is put on the incident for the press. Management, the public relations department, and the incident response team must work closely together to ensure that the information given to the press is both accurate and cast in the appropriate light.

The legal department must be involved early on and should clear any statements that may affect the potential for liability.

The Right Time

Letting people know at the right time will limit the rumors that may otherwise be created. All those involved with the security incident should be given the same story. Policy should state how, when, and by whom information about a security incident is disseminated to management, to employees, and to the public.

If possible, it is best not to make any public comments about the incident until it is over. At this time you can present it as an incident which your company's expertise enabled to be detected and put an end to quickly. In some cases the media might get tips about the incident – occasionally from the hacker himself – and will contact your organization before the incident has been quelled. Here, it may be best to give minimal information with the comment that you don't want to compromise an ongoing investigation. Then, when the incident is over, you can release further information with a positive spin on how it was handled.

It is key not to give out any information during the incident that allows the hacker any knowledge of your activities and investigation. It is also important not to lie to the media because such untruths, if discovered, can lead to the loss of confidence which you were trying to deter in the first place.

Decisions about external reporting should be postponed until the internal investigation reveals the nature and extent of the incident. Decisions regarding the public release of information must be made by top level management. Management must have enough information to be able to make an informed decision about publicly reporting the incident.

Most organizations will not report incidents publicly unless absolutely necessary. If it is necessary to have legal involvement to assist in the investigation or to pursue a legal remedy, this will require a certain amount of public reporting.

The Right Message

It is imperative that the right message be conveyed to the media. It must be clear – without the possibility of misconception. It needs to be delivered as a complete story with the correct level of detail so the recipient of the message is satisfied. It must contain the correct spin so that your organization is presented in a positive, competent light.

The media contact person will need to provide simple explanations of technical points that describe the problem without giving unnecessary or damaging details. It is likely that someone in the technical staff will be requested to supply the public relations department with background information and nontechnical explanations of technical issues. This person may need to be available at the press meeting to handle any specific technical questions. He should consult with the public relations department ahead of time regarding what is and is not appropriately discussed in response to questions from the press. He should review with the actual presenter to be assured that the presenter understands the material supplied.

The Right Forum

The media attention with an incident that has become public can consume as much or more time as any other aspect of handling the incident. A flood of media requests can overwhelm a switchboard. Some members of the press may ask to speak directly to someone in the information systems department or even call them at home. To control the impact on the recovery operations and to allow the people responding to the incident to focus on the incident, media issues should be consolidated through the public affairs department and in a forum that can efficiently disseminate the appropriate information. There are a number of methods of communicating with the press, each of which affords different levels of interaction and control.

Press Release

Written press releases are the most common form of communication with the media. Someone in the public relations department of the organization should write the press release, verifying the details with a member of the incident response staff. This process gives the most control over the exact message that is communicated. The press release can be reviewed, edited, and rewritten before it is made public.

Press Conference

A press conference allows you to meet with many journalists at one time. You have less control over the information presented than in a press release because there is generally a question and answer period after a prepared statement is read. Your prepared statement should cover the topics and set the scope and limits of the communication. This part of the conference is a one-way communication that can address exactly what you want to cover. When you open the floor to questions, anticipate a wide range of difficult questions and prepare answers in advance.

Timing of the press conference is important – keep the deadlines for the various media in mind. Something as simple as a couple of hours difference in the timing of the conference can affect which media outlet breaks the story. If your organization has an adversarial relationship with one media outlet but a friendly relationship with others, keep the various deadlines in mind so that the story is broken by one that is most likely to put a positive spin on it. Let the public's first exposure to the news come from a friend.

Everyone who may be called on to speak should dress appropriately and be aware of nonverbal communication.

Set an ending time so that you can limit the number of questions. Be equitable in fielding questions from both different types of media and from different journalists. Keep to the subject – try to avoid off-topic questions.

Interview

A one-on-one interview gives you the greatest interaction with an individual journalist but is the most likely to stray from the set topic. The interviewer will lead the conversation. Allow the interviewer to lead, but control the direction and content of the interview. The interviewer may have his or her own agenda, so it is important to learn about the reporter, the outlet, and the audience in advance.

If you have a friendly reporter at your local paper or broadcast outlet, it is sometimes wise to contact them and offer them an interview before a more antagonistic reporter is assigned your story.

Learn as much as possible about the interview in which you are going to participate in and prepare accordingly. Try to determine the general attitude and approach of the reporter in the past, both with your company and others, to get a feel for what direction he may try to take the interview and what his approach will be.

Understand time limits and how the interview will be used – interviews may be trimmed down to a sound bite. Generally, a print journalist will use more of what is said than a broadcast journalist.

Outline major points you wish to communicate. Make sure that these points are covered and that the correct message is communicated.

There are a variety of styles of interviews. They can be information gathering that will be edited, creating a study for later publication, or they can be a live or recorded interview for a later broadcast.

With audio interviews, well organized notes can be very useful to address the questions that were anticipated and to have statistics and details at hand.

Video interviews give way to greater concerns of physical presence, such as how you come across to the camera. You will want to thumb through notes less, so be very well prepared with a few clearly laid out easy to read notes for a television interview.

Telephone interviews are utilized for minor stories and when the media outlet is not nearby. Choose a familiar, comfortable location with all necessary resources close at hand. Use a good hard-wired telephone to minimize the background noise and interference.

Occasionally a television journalist may ask for shots of the computer system or some other visual to cut in with your interview to provide more visual interest than just a talking head. Think carefully before allowing this – is the information in the shot, such as what type of hardware you have, something that might be useful to a hacker?

The Right Attitude

It is important to have the right attitude when dealing with the press. It is your information. You need to maintain control and stay focused. Take the initiative. Control the presentation so that you get the message you want delivered. Allow the interviewer to lead the conversation, but steer it to the points you wish to make.

Try not to get intimidated and avoid becoming defensive. Take a breath and regain control. Do not take any comment personally. Be diplomatic and turn the interview in the direction you wish. Use positive terms expressing that everything is under control and proceeding as expected.

If you are asked a question that you do not know the answer to, admit it. Explain that you do not at this time have those details. Follow up, if appropriate, and leave follow-up contact information so that questions that arise after the presentation can be asked and answered.

Checklist

— Enlist the communication professionals in the organization.

— Brief communication professionals on technical details.

— Put a positive spin on the incident.

— Ensure that no information is released that might be useful to the attacker.

— Even if you are not ready to release information on the incident, be prepared for the media to hear about it from other sources, including the attacker himself.

CHAPTER 31

Legal Prosecution

Even though 72% of companies reported that they have suffered financial losses from computer security breaches, only 17% reported these to law enforcement.[114]

A security incident has many legal considerations. The organization's legal department should be notified early on in the process so that they can provide input to the legal ramifications of steps taken to protect information resources. The legal department can also provide input into the types of documentation that may be required for future legal action.

Legal recourse can be either criminal or civil. In a criminal prosecution, the value of the time and effort that it takes to restore the system to its initial condition may be a consideration as part of the penalty phase to determine restitution. In a civil case, you will have to itemize damages to be able to recover those damages.

Prosecution of a particular abuse may serve as a deterrent to future abuse. Deterrence may be particularly warranted if the method being used is already generally known by the public. The true value of deterrence is questionable. Many perpetrators act with irrational motives. Few are actually concerned with the chances of being caught, prosecuted and incarcerated.

Prosecution is very important in deterring hacking. Not only will the hacker be aware that other hackers have been prosecuted for the same activities in which he was planning to participate, but each case helps define the scope of the laws and makes subsequent cases that much easier to prosecute.

Many companies are wary of legal prosecution. They fear the costs in time and personnel that will be involved and the public perception. These fears are not unfounded, but they may be overstated. To help understand the real scope of these fears, the MIS managers and computer security management should contact their company's legal office, if they have one, the local

---

[114]   "1998 CSI/FBI Computer Crime and Security Survey," *Computer Security Issues & Trends*, Spring 1998.

prosecutor's office, or the local law enforcement investigation bureau. Be sure to ask if there is a computer or hi-tech unit.

Getting to know these people before you need them is very useful. You will better understand their processes and procedures and when and how to get them involved. This will help you understand what the impact of prosecution will be on your company.

Computer Crime Laws

Computer crime is any illegal act which involves a computer system, whether the computer is an object of crime, an instrument used to commit a crime, or a repository of evidence related to a crime. In the United States, the earliest law specifically addressing crimes committed through computers was the Computer Fraud and Abuse Act of 1984.

Computer crime laws are relatively new and untested. The usefulness of a law is determined by its ability to be applied and effectively enforced. This is only discovered after the law is challenged in the court system.

Writing the Laws

Writing laws is a difficult task to begin with. The language of the law is open to interpretation. It is difficult to adequately define the scope of the law so that it covers the behavior that it intends to control, but not so broadly as to be applied to unrelated activities. In addition to this lawmakers are not computer experts, yet they are tasked with creating laws that address technologies that they do not fully understand and which require the use of a technical language which is not understood. This often creates laws that are not well constructed.

Laws are often passed in response to a specific event. These laws are written quickly and address only the specifics of the recent event. They are commands written with a view of today, without addressing larger issues or seeing where technology is going. This leads to laws that rapidly become obsolete as technology changes.

Today in the U. S. few federal laws apply to computer crime, and the state computer crime laws are widely varied. Some are very narrowly drafted, while others are quite broad. Many states claim jurisdiction on any electronic transaction that crosses its border.

Interpreting the Laws

Courts in a common-law system base their decisions in a large part on precedent – decisions that have previously been made. With new technologies there is no direct precedent to refer to, so they try to apply existing precedent to the new situations – often trying to apply laws that govern the physical world to a technology that is quite different from the physical world. When something is stolen in the physical world, the victim no longer has the item – with information, the theft does not deprive the victim of the information.

Technology is poorly understood by many legal practitioners. This makes it difficult to apply an understanding of the law in the physical world to the computer crime.

The lawyers who bring the cases to court are often not very computer savvy. The judges who evaluate the merits of the cases that are brought before them are not particularly computer literate. If a case is decided by a jury, it is likely that the members of the jury are going to be even less computer literate.

Unless the attacker is found with the stolen information in his possession, most computer crimes lack a preponderance of physical evidence. The evidence tends to be electronic logs from electronic systems. This type of evidence is intangible and difficult to explain and generally lacks the credibility of physical evidence.

> The Texas Computer Crimes Act, which is not substantially different than that of any other state, defines that "a person commits an offense if the person knowingly accesses a computer system without the effective consent of the owner." The offense is a felony if the person's intent is to obtain a benefit from the action. A computer systems is defined by statute as a "data processing device that functions by the manipulation of electronic or magnetic impulses" and access is "make use of." By this definition looking a someone's digital watch without permission could be a felony.[115]

Enforcing the Laws

If you are the victim of an incident, you won't have much control over which law or laws the criminal will be prosecuted under or even if he will be prosecuted. Criminal cases are brought to trial by the prosecuting attorney's office. They evaluate the crime not only on the merits of the case, but also on the ability to get a conviction.

The victim can pursue civil remedies by bringing a civil suit against the perpetrator. However, the purpose of a civil suit is to get remuneration for damages caused. This requires that the victim be able to adequately show financial losses or damages caused by the attacker. Even when the claim can be proven, a hacker may have little or no income or assets and would be unable to pay any judgment.

Jurisdiction

Information travels over networks which cross geopolitical boundaries, each of which may have their own regulations on information security. A single incident may cross many jurisdictions and require the involvement of different law enforcement agencies. These agencies may all have different requirements and procedures for getting involved with a security incident and may lead to issues of positioning on who is in charge of the investigation.

---

[115]   *$USR/News,* May 1994.

A computer crime may violate a number of laws at both the federal and local levels that could have either civil or criminal remedies. This will create a variety of options when it comes to prosecuting the attacker. However, it may also cause a great deal of confusion in the direction to take during the investigation. This issue is compounded by the international nature of the Internet.

Even the simplest of jurisdiction issues – when there are multiple computers involved in a transaction, where the transaction took place – is still debated, case by case.

With the explosive growth of the Internet worldwide, computer crimes are increasingly prone to have international dimensions. Some of the challenges faced by law enforcement on the international front include: harmonization of countries' criminal laws, locating and identifying perpetrators across borders, and securing electronic evidence of their crimes so that they may be brought to justice. Complex jurisdictional issues arise at each step.

Extradition

The ability to bring a computer criminal to justice is often as difficult as finding the hacker in the first place. Many jurisdictions are involved and extradition from one jurisdiction to another can be difficult, especially across national boundaries, since extradition is based on treaties between countries. This requires a certain level of cooperation between countries and their law enforcement organizations. In addition the computer crime laws vary dramatically between countries; what is criminal in one country may not be elsewhere.

> Authorities in Argentina arrested Julio Cesar Ardita, better known as "El Griton," in the computer underground. He was accused of systematic and major unauthorized intrusions into systems at a number of major U.S. universities, the U.S. Navy, NASA, and also computer systems in Brazil, Chile, Korea, Mexico, and Taiwan. Government officials in Argentina seized his computer and modem in January. Despite close cooperation between authorities in Argentina and the U.S., the man was released without charge because Argentina has no law criminalizing unauthorized intrusion in computer systems. In addition, because of the requirement for "dual criminality" in international law, it was not possible for Argentinian authorities to extradite Ardita to the United States (the requirement states that an action must be defined as criminal in both countries before a person can be extradited).[116]

---

[116]   Penebery, Adam, "The Hacker Threat," *Forbes.com,* 26 December 1997.

Collection of Evidence

Any information that is collected under normal operations or in accordance with written policy and procedures can be used as evidence. Evidence is often contained on backups and on system and security logs. It is important that a written log detailing when and by whom backups are taken is kept. You may be able to collect information that the police cannot. You may, in compliance with policy, capture keystroke information which is admissible as evidence, but a law officer may not be able to tell you to collect this information due to issues of entrapment and other investigative restrictions. This is why it is important to consult an attorney to determine when to bring law officers into a security incident.

When you are collecting evidence during and after an attack you need to date and sign all printouts and keep a detailed log describing where, when, and how the information was found. Generally, online evidence by itself will be insufficient to prosecute. However, it will be sufficient to get a search warrant which may uncover other evidence.

During a security incident, complete documentation must be kept of the events as they transpire, including the affected resources. Each person involved in the incident must start a log that is date/timestamped.

Documentation

You are probably going to collect a significant amount of evidence before you contact law enforcement. Evidence collection must be done on a system that is secure from tampering. The use of removable media or write-once media is useful.

A complete system snapshot, including unused portions of the disk, should be made of all of the disks attached to the compromised system. This allows you to freely examine a copy of the information on the disks without the possibility of contaminating the original media. Hackers often hide tools and information in unallocated areas of the disks.

System backups offer a series of snapshots in time. They can illustrate before and after views of the incident. They can contain the progress of the attack over time. System logs contain transactions that take place on the system. They have a more detailed view of the activities on the system.

Document everything that you do related to the investigation. Keep a notebook. If the case goes to court, you may have to testify about it many years down the road.

Audit trails and similar evidence should be collected and secured as appropriate for internal problem analysis: use as evidence in relation to potential breaches of contract or breach of regulatory requirement; negotiating for compensation from software and service suppliers; and evidence in the event of proceedings under computer misuse or data protection legislation.

Every piece of evidence needs to be uniquely identified, dated, signed, and sealed in a tamper-proof container. This information should be cross-referenced in the incident logbook and must be appropriately stored to protect the chain of custody.

Chain of Custody

No matter what the quality of evidence collected, if it is not maintained properly in the time between collection and when it is needed in court it will be of little value. This is the one item that pertains to all evidence: chain of possession. This means that for evidence to be admitted in court, the prosecution has to be able to show who obtained the evidence, who secured it, and who has had control of it.

You should make it a practice to sufficiently identify and secure your backups. This will not only help in the prosecution, but it will increase your confidence when you recover and ensure that your backup is the correct one and has not been tampered with. Some states have passed laws providing for the protection of proprietary information from being revealed in open court.

Data Reduction

The amount of information collected by information systems, especially during an attack, is often overwhelming. Information is logged by computer systems, applications, network device, and security systems. Most of these systems log information at a very detailed level. A simple connection to a system may generate dozens of log entries in a number of different logs. Some of these details may be needed to illustrate exactly how a vulnerability was compromised, but the log information will have to be reduced to be able to show the larger picture of what happened during the attack.

To create a complete picture it is usually necessary to compare and correlate information from a number of sources. It is likely that the information from these sources may have discrepancies in the way that they identify an individual or system – inconsistent naming, inconsistent time, etc.

It is likely that someone will have to prepare reports summarizing information extracted from logs and other resources of online information into a form that is understandable to a layman. Many law enforcement offices, lawyers, judges, and jurors are not necessarily going to be very computer-literate, so the evidence will have to be presented in a way that it is understandable and explainable. The procedures used to reduce the data will also have to be well-documented to show that the report is accurate and complete.

Impact on Operations

All responses to a security incident will have impact on the operation of the system. Additional backups may have to be made, and personnel will have to assist in the prosecution. Minimally, some personnel will be called as witnesses. It is likely that the prosecution will require the involvement of personnel, who will assist in identifying the property and as technical advisors. It is best to assign a specific person to be a liaison between the company and the police during the investigation. This will help limit the impact of the investigation on the day-to-day operation of the company. This person can help manage the scheduling of people.

Successful Prosecution

Successful prosecution of an attacker depends upon the strength of the evidence. Since most intrusions are remote, the perpetrator is virtually invisible and there is limited physical evidence. The electronic evidence will indicate when accounts are used maliciously, but will not be able to prove beyond a reasonable doubt that the specific individual was the attacker. It is imperative that this connection be firmly established. It must also be shown that the evidence was collected appropriately and handled correctly. The amount of detailed records concerning the intrusion incident that must be presented is overwhelming. Judges and juries do not normally have a technical background, so the evidence must be presented in such a way as to be understood by the jury. The evidence will need to be summarized in a clear and concise manner.

Connecting the attacker to the activities requires that once the hacker is identified a search warrant be obtained and his computer equipment (magnetic and other data media) and documents be seized and examined for evidence. A forensic consultant must analyze the seized materials to establish the connection between them and the evidence collected from your computer system. The prosecution will present its findings from the computer materials seized during the search. Expert testimony is necessary to prove that the alleged hacker is the one who perpetrated the intrusion. An expert's findings, conclusions, and opinions are the underpinning of the entire case.

Sympathetic

Computer crime, like other white-collar crime, is not violent. It generally does not cause bodily injury. It is often difficult to explain the crime to a jury. The theft of information does not deny the victim the information; it is a copy which is stolen. Some people have sympathy for hackers who have been caught.

Many people are enamored of hackers. Much like Robin Hood, who committed crimes against the rich and became a hero of the poor, the victims of computer crimes are generally big businesses. Some people believe that it is acceptable to steal information from companies if their systems are not secure enough to keep them out. This makes it difficult to enlist a sympathetic jury. In computer crime cases, the defense will capitalize on the David and Goliath syndrome. They will paint the hacker as the little guy and the company as evil. This is true throughout the world.

> Israeli Prime Minister Benjamin Netanyahu praised a teenage hacker, known as the "Analyzer," who intruded upon hundreds of government computers in the U.S. and Israel. After the incident, the hacker was drafted into the Israeli army to serve in an information warfare division, an assignment which will utilize his computer talents.

> Before his induction, he celebrated with friends at a disco near his hometown of Hod Hasharon, north of Tel Aviv, where the disc jockey told the crowd "The Analyzer"' had done their town proud.[117]

Age

Many hackers are minors and not held to the same level of responsibility as adults. The criminal justice system in the U. S. and other countries makes a clear distinction between adults and minors. There are separate courts, separate detention centers, and separate views of how the laws should be applied and the punishment implemented. Punishment for juveniles, even if convicted, is often little more than a slap on the wrist.

> A 15-year-old hacker chose to launch an attack on the Television Corporation of Singapore's (TCS) Internet site after seeing an advertisement for it on television. He replaced all the pages on the new channel's site with a variety of obscene and abusive messages for about 10 hours for no discernible reason.
>
> The judge passing sentence requested that the boy be home before 6 p.m. every night for a year, and demanded that he write a formal apology, to be posted on the news channel's web site.[118]

Appropriate Punishment

Getting convictions and sentencing on computer crimes is also hampered by a perceived inequity between the crime and the punishment. Often the crimes are presented as little more than pranks that got out of hand. Many of the crimes are felonies. Juries are concerned over ruining a young person's life over a "prank." Punishment can range from a slap on the wrist in some countries to a sentence that seems way out of proportion to the crime in others.

> A court in the southern city of Yangzhou sentenced one man to death and his elder brother to life imprisonment for hacking into a bank's computer system to steal $31,500, according to the state-run newspaper Beijing Morning Post. An appeal by the two brothers was rejected after a higher court upheld the recent decision by the Yangzhou Intermediate Court.

[117]   "Israeli Teen Hacker Details Prowess," *Associated Press*, April 1998.
[118]   Knight, Will, "Hacker Grounded for Worlds Easiest Crack," *ZD Net UK*, 30 September 1999.

> The brothers used a homemade computer to hack into the Industrial and Commercial Bank of China's system, where they set up fake bank accounts. By the time they were caught, they had withdrawn $30,266 in embezzled funds. Police recovered all but $1,200 of it, the report said.[119]

Many cases are never prosecuted because the business has evaluated that the cost of prosecution, including legal costs, operational disruption, and publicity is not worth it, especially if the hacker is an employee that they can discipline. However, you may not be able to recover the stolen information if you decide not to prosecute.

It has become a legal imperative to post warning banners on all information systems. These banners should state that the system is the property of the organization, is subject to monitoring, that there is no expectation of privacy, and that unauthorized use is prohibited. The exact wording should be determined by your legal department.

---

[119] "Chinese Bank Hacker Gets Death," *AP*, 3 December 1999.

Checklist

— Meet with law enforcement before there is an incident.
  • Determine what assistance they can provide.
  • How do you enlist their assistance?

— Meet with legal counsel before there is an incident.
  • Explore legal options and issues.
  • Understand the process of prosecuting an intruder.
  • Understand the issues of defending yourself in a lawsuit.

— Evaluate investigative options
  • In-house abilities
  • Consultants
  • Private Investigators
  • Law Enforcement

The Future of Information Security

Information has become critical to the success of business. Many businesses are built on information including software companies, brokerages, and advertising and marketing companies. Companies are discovering that their data warehouse contains more valuable assets than their product warehouse.

Since information is critical to the success of an organization, it requires the same standards of care as any company asset. Without the appropriate level of care, the organization and its officers are subject to issues of liability. There are actually different standards that apply to different situations. The standard of *due care* is the standard of care that applies to the president, the board of directors, and other executives which demands that they exercise reasonable care to protect the corporate assets, both tangible and intangible. Neglecting to adequately protect these assets would make the corporation and its officers liable to the shareholders, investors, and lenders. The standard of *duty of trust* dictates that reasonable care be used in protecting the information about individuals that has been entrusted to the organization. These individuals usually include your clients, customers, employees, and anyone that the organization has privileged information about. The organization and, in turn, its executives have a duty to the individual to maintain the confidentiality of that information they hold. *Due diligence* defines the appropriate level of protection and the timeliness of response based on what a reasonable person would do in that situation.

Information may be more fragile than physical assets – it is more easily lost, destroyed, and stolen. Hence, the security measures required to protect the organization from the devastating losses associated with compromised information must be more stringent – more comprehensive – than those used for physical assets. With today's rapid rate of change these security measures must be more flexible – more responsive – than ever before.

A World Without Borders

Classical boundaries that restrict the flow of information are disappearing. New business relationships and access methods are making it extremely difficult to differentiate between "us" and "them." Instead, the more flexible security domain will become the definition of how information is managed and controlled. These security domains will cross physical boundaries, share networks and systems, and require that every system be secure to support the security domains that utilize it.

Compartmentalization will be accomplished through cryptographic methods instead of physical isolation.

It is no longer sufficient to define inside and outside and keep the bad people out. Information is everywhere. Valid users are everywhere. Today, the issue is how to allow valid users access to the information resources.

Information should be made available to any authenticated user, in accordance with his or her authorizations, whenever and wherever it is needed, while guaranteeing the information's integrity and privacy and with full accountability of every transaction. Is this a lofty goal or a minimum requirement, or both?

As information systems continue to evolve, the manner in which information is protected will change. However, the fundamental phases of information security will remain the same. That is, you have to understand what it is you are protecting and its value. You must be able to assign levels of importance for the attributes of availability, confidentiality, and integrity. You must realize that there are threats to these attributes and be able to decide the level of protection to be afforded them. This is the inspection phase.

The processes involved in the protection phase will change as information systems evolve, but the basic attributes of protection will be the same. Access to information resources requires users to provide identification, which will be authenticated to determine what activities are authorized. All of the activities will be audited. These are the fundamental business practices required to maintain the integrity of the business system.

Service-based Architecture

The architecture of information services is changing to support the explosive growth of the Internet. Information systems are becoming more service-oriented. Monolithic systems are being replaced with systems that are distributed, object-oriented, and often outsourced. Security systems will also have to become more modular and service-oriented. Security will no longer be able to be contained within the application; rather, applications will have to utilize distributed security services. Independent services will arise to address the fundamental aspects of security.

Access Server

As computing continues to evolve, the variety of access methods will expand. These access methods in large part influence the type of identification and authentication that is required and what authorizations will be granted. Access servers are systems which manage the process by which systems are accessed.

Access servers will take a wide variety of forms, some designed to solve the issues of the access media itself (e.g. wireless access servers), others to facilitate the greatest amount of connectivity and throughput to more efficiently utilize communication resources, and others will be gatekeepers, limiting access and controlling the flow of information.

Identification Server

Identification is the foundation of all security. Identification services are information systems that facilitate global, unique identification of all information resources and consumers of information resources.

They will be the repository of a great deal of information. They will contain a number of verification tokens for each identity and for the different methods of authentication which may be required. They will contain the associations in which the identity belongs and other information that is specific to the individual entity.

Identification servers will have to be highly available, with strong integrity and privacy in both the storage of the information and its communication with requesting services.

Authentication Server

Authentication servers will request that an entity prove its identity based on the rules for that entity, the access methods, the privileges requested, and the security classification of the information resources. It will determine if the entity has adequately authenticated itself and will grant credentials to the entity which will be used to gain privileges. If an entity has authorization for privileges requested but its credentials are insufficient, it may be required to reauthenticate with a more secure authentication method.

Authorization Server

The authorization server is responsible for applying business rules to decide what information resources are made available to which users. It will utilize the authenticated identity that is supplied or request stronger authentication if the request warrants it. Authorizations will be global to the enterprise defined as business rules. Applications will have to use the authorization server so that a single change to a business rule is realized immediately throughout the enterprise.

Application Server

The application server ensures the accuracy or integrity of the business transaction. Integrity issues have been viewed as a data issue. Two-phase commit, a form of enforcing business logic, is delegated to being a database issue. Business transactions continue to become more involved, including services from many sources. Online transactions incorporate many services like electronic funds transfers, credit card processing, shipping manifest management, inventory control and enabling customer access to new e-services. Each of these services can be supplied by a different online company. Now the issues of controlling the transaction and being assured that the transaction is completed and committed at one time become very complex. Transaction integrity will be required in a much more distributed method than ever before.

Information Storage Server

Storage servers are primarily responsible for availability, but they must also provide privacy and integrity. Information storage is creating an entire new area of computing devices – network storage and storage area networks (SANS). These systems are specialized hardware built as repositories for huge amounts of storage that is highly available through the use of redundancy. Many offer off-line backup systems to increase availability. Today, these systems supply storage space to general purpose computers. In the future, SANS will grow into areas with higher level interfaces. This could be SQL or DAP or other protocols. In this manner, the information server will supply organized information, not just storage space.

Accountability Server

Accountability servers will create a centralized and standardized environment for logging transactions for auditing. Systems, applications, and services will all send their audit logs to a central accountability server. This server will facilitate appropriate storage for the logs so that they will be usable as evidence. It will enable the consolidation of logs to monitor for inappropriate behavior. They will enable better intrusion detection through the centralization of logs from systems, applications, and business processes throughout the enterprise. The accountability server will enable enterprise-wide utilization reporting and billing which will simplify the organization's billing and budgeting issues.

Administration Server

Administration servers are commonplace today. System and network administration is often consolidated into a central location which monitors all the activities in the information systems and reports issues. These servers will expand their realm by administering applications, services, and security. Their monitoring facilities will be improved by the services provided by the accountability server.

Many levels of administration which are required today will become more integrated with the administration of the services that they support. Changes to hardware and operating system parameters will be controlled by the setting of application tuning parameters. Hardware and software platforms will become information appliances.

Basic Business Principles

No matter how much technology changes the way business is transacted, the basic business practices will remain unchanged. Transactions will have to be recorded, they will have to be verifiable, and someone will be fiduciarily responsible.

Checks and Balances

Checks and balances are processes that provide the ability to verify the integrity of transactions. Every transaction is recorded at least twice, usually by different people. The location of these entries are often in dispersed locations, such as accounting ledgers, check registers, or shipping logs. Each of these are totaled and checked against the others. Discrepancies have to be accounted for and repaired.

Separation of Duties

A separation of duties ensures that no single individual has the ability to falsify all parts of a transaction. It implies that the transaction entries are reviewed by a different party than the one who created them. Critical transactions may require multiple entries to be performed by different people; for example the addition of a new user to a system would require one person to add the new user identifier and another to enable the identifier, thereby keeping a single party from creating a usable account.

Audit Trail

An audit trail must be created and maintained so that a transaction can be re-created after the fact. Audit logs are the primary source of information in the investigation of improper business transactions. They create a trail that allows investigators to follow the flow of funds and products. Auditing ties original source documents, such as invoices or checks, to transactions.

Pervasive Security

As we move into this new environment where business decisions are automated, where computers think and act on our behalf, and where they become ubiquitous (in your car, in your wallet, in your toaster), these security fundamentals must be in place to form a solid foundation to secure the future.

In this environment it becomes obvious that security controls are a requirement. Without them, every aspect of everyone's life, personal and professional, would be exposed to monitoring or tampering.

Information security will need to become easily understood and implemented. It will need to be as commonplace as locking a door or sealing a letter into an envelope (a form of information security itself): an everyday activity that is just part of life.

Glossary

acceptable use policy

A policy that describes the appropriate and inappropriate behavior of users on a system, spelling out the rights and responsibilities of all parties involved.

access

The method by which a user is able to utilize an information resource.

access control

The physical or logical safeguards that prevent unauthorized access to information resources

access control list (ACL)

A method of defining access that utilizes a list of users and permissions to determine access rights to a resource.

accountability

The ability to associate users with their actions and actions with the users that caused them.

accuracy

The quality of information which is dependent on the quality of the source of the information and the quality of the handling of the information.

administration

The process of managing and maintaining the information systems.

attacker

A person who attempts to penetrate a computer system's security controls.

authentication

The process of verifying the identity of a user.

authorization

A capability assigned to a user account by administrators that allows the user certain privileges. A privilege allows you to perform an action; an authorization gives you privileges.

availability

The state of being able to utilize an information resource.

awareness

The process of educating users on the use of information security features, their importance, and how to spot and report misuse.

backdoor

An undocumented software feature that allows a user to gain access or privileges through its use. These features may be a software bug or something that was added by a programmer during development that was not removed when it was put into production. More likely back doors are put into the system by hackers to help facilitate their hacking.

business impact analysis

An evaluation of the ramifications to the organization caused by a security incident.

business resumption program

A plan designed to minimize the unavailability of business processes.

change management

The process of controlling and tracking the modifications made to a system.

confidentiality

The requirement to preserve the secrecy or privacy of information, such that only those authorized to have knowledge of it actually do so.

denial of service

An attack that renders part of the information system unusable.

digital signature

A cryptographic means of uniquely identifying the sender of a message that can be used by the recipient to confirm the authenticity of the message. It is often implemented as a variation of public key cryptography.

discretionary access control

An access control in which an "owner" of a resource can define who else can access the resource. Usually, there are no restrictions on to whom the owner can grant access or the kind of access granted. The traditional UNIX mode bits and the access control lists are examples of discretionary access control.

due care

The assurance that all reasonable and prudent precautions have been taken in the handling of a company's resources.

dumpster diving

The process of looking through the trash in order to find information.

encryption

The process of mathematically converting information into a form such that the original information can not be restored without use of a specific unique key.

fail over system

A secondary system which will assume the roles of the primary system in the event of a failure.

firewall

A firewall is used on some networks to provide added security by blocking access to certain services in the private network from the rest of the internet. In the same way that a firewall in a building keeps fire from spreading, an internet firewall keeps hackers from spreading.

identification

The process of presenting an identifier to an information system.

identifier

That which is used to uniquely represent a specific user.

in-band communication

The use of the same connection to manage a device as the connection that the device controls.

information resource

Any of the processes or systems that contain, process, or utilize information and the information itself.

infoterrorism

An act of terrorism that is carried out through the use of computer systems.

integrity

The assurance of accuracy, completeness and performance according to specifications.

Internet time

An expression that reflects that time moves faster on the Internet. Due to the limited costs of entry, business can rapidly appear on the internet and can rapidly change their tactics, so survival depends on the ability to react and change.

least privilege

The security philosophy of granting the minimum privileges for the minimum amount of time to allow the user to complete the required task.

logic bomb

Code hidden in an application that causes it to perform some destructive activity when specific criteria are met.

mandatory access control

An access control in which access is based on criteria defined by system administrators, and not definable by the owner of an information resource.

out-of-band configuration

The use of a communication path to configure a network device which is not the communication path that the network device controls.

parasite

Software that attaches itself to a program to utilize the resources of the host program.

permissions

Authorization attributes assigned to a resource that indicate what privileges are granted to which users.

PIN—Personal Identification Number

A password that is used with a physical card, together producing stronger authentication.

policy

A written definition of a security standard.

practice

A specific performed activity that supports a security procedure.

privileges

The rights granted to a user that define what the user can do with the resource.

procedure

A specific activity that supports a security policy.

public key encryption

An cryptographic method that uses two keys such that whatever is encrypted with one key can only be decrypted with the other. It can be used for both security and digital signatures.

redundancy

The use of multiple systems to minimize unavailability.

security by obscurity

The theory that if no one knows about a security flaw then no one will abuse it, and if no one is told about the flaw, they will not find it on their own.

security perimeter

A border that defines what is, and what is not, controlled by a specific security policy.

self healing system

A system that is able to detect a failure and repair it without outside intervention.

smart card

A physical authentication device used in conjunction with a password to give greater assurance of authentication.

social engineering

The process of gathering information from people by use of deception and obfuscation.

spoof

A program that impersonates another program to gather information.

superhacker

The possibly mythical hacker whose skill allows him to move freely from system to system and network to network without detection.

threat

That which if unchecked will cause a loss to the organization.

Trojan horse

A program that appears to be a useful program, but in reality performs malicious acts.

trusted advisor

A hacker who used his position and knowledge to his advantage by appearing to be trustworthy.

trusted hosts

A process by which a group of hosts can share a single authentication, such that once a user is authenticated onto one host in the trusted group he can access all the hosts without having to authenticate himself again.

user

Any entity that utilizes information resources. A user can be an individual, a software program, a computer system, a network, etc.

virus

A program that replicates itself by embedding a copy of itself in other programs.

vulnerability

A facet that can be utilized to gain an inappropriate level of access or privileges with an information resource.

worm

A program that makes its way across a network, copying itself as it goes.

wrapper program

A program used to augment another program without requiring reconstruction of the original program.

Index

A

B

C